The End of Money

Also by David Wolman

A Left-Hand Turn Around the World

Righting the Mother Tongue

The End of Money

Counterfeiters, Preachers, Techies, Dreamers—
and the Coming Cashless Society

DAVID WOLMAN

DA CAPO PRESS
A Member of the Perseus Books Group

Published by Da Capo Press
A Member of the Perseus Books Group
www.dacapopress.com

Da Capo Press books are available at special discounts for bulk purchases in the U.S. by corporations, institutions, and other organizations. For more information, please contact the Special Markets Department at the Perseus Books Group, 2300 Chestnut Street, Suite 200, Philadelphia, PA 19103, or call (800) 810-4145, ext. 5000, or e-mail special.markets@perseusbooks.com.

Set in Minion Pro by The Perseus Books Group

First Da Capo Press edition 2012

Library of Congress Cataloging-in-Publication Data
Wolman, David.
    The end of money : counterfeiters, preachers, techies, dreamers—and the coming cashless society / David Wolman.
        p. cm.
    Includes bibliographical references and index.
    ISBN 978-0-306-81883-7 (hardcover)—ISBN 978-0-306-81946-9 (e-book) 1. Money—History. 2. Paper money. 3. Coins. I. Title.

HG231.W75 2012
332.4—dc23

2011038991

10 9 8 7 6 5 4 3 2

CONTENTS

INTRODUCTION

On Christmas Eve 2009, Umar Farouk Abdulmutallab began the journey he thought would take him from this world into the next, and into the awaiting embrace of six dozen virgins. He carried nothing more than a small duffle bag and, in his underwear, the ingredients for plastic explosives. If not for some fumbling on the part of the aspiring bomber and the reflexes of a few passengers and the crew, Northwest Airlines Flight 253 would have exploded somewhere over Watford, Ontario.

Eight days earlier, Farouk Abdulmutallab stood at an airport ticket counter in West Africa. With $2,381 in cash he purchased a one-way ticket from Lagos, Nigeria, to Detroit, connecting through Amsterdam.[1] Pardon me for my ignorance about the inner workings of the global war on terror and airline ticketing procedures, and for a line of reasoning that promises to infuriate the ACLU, tax-evading militiamen, the U.S. Treasury, and the Russian mob, but I have to ask: in the post-9/11 age, who uses $2,381 in cash to buy a one-way ticket to the other side of the world besides crooks and terrorists? Think of all the mileage points lost!

Money is no object. Maybe so for a lucky few. Except, of course, money *is* an object—tearable, flammable, even wearable. It's also an object of obsession, inquiry, aspiration, remorse, delight, disdain, curiosity, and just about every other sentiment imaginable. Money takes different forms, too: credit and debit cards, checks, money orders, lottery tickets, gift cards, Disney Dollars, ones and zeroes on distant servers, and, for the time being at least, rectangular slips of paper and round coins that economists call physical representations of sovereign currency, and that the rest of us call cash.

A few years ago, I started bumping into stories about the cost of manufacturing coins and maintaining them in the economy, and suggestions by some pundits that the United States go cold turkey on pennies. A scientist at MIT founded Citizens for Retiring the Penny, and for a few years the guy was everywhere: *60 Minutes, NPR,* the *New York Times, ABC World News Tonight,* the *Boston Globe, The Colbert Report.* He had his talking points down pat, about time and materials wasted, potential benefits to the economy, and research showing that rounding prices up wouldn't hurt consumers.

The debate made me realize that I have a bit of a soft spot for pennies, probably because of Bazooka chewing gum and a Bostonian named Bob. When my older brother and I would take the train home from school back in the early 1980s, we would often stop at a corner store called Bob's Waban News. While Bob griped about the Red Sox and served coffee to his regulars at the bar, kids filtered in and out to order Slush Puppies or purchase Charleston Chew candy bars. And if we had any pennies, we'd take our shot at the box.

Above the register, just below where the wall met the ceiling, Bob had affixed a cardboard box, perhaps sixteen inches across. It had no top, and inside was a bell. If you lobbed a penny up and missed the box or—more demoralizing—your penny landed inside but failed to hit the hidden bell, you got nothing. If you hit the bell, you earned a piece of Bazooka bubble gum, not to mention glory. *Ding!* If we close the book on pennies, what would happen to this kind of game? What would people throw into wishing wells?

Yet nowadays, nobody seems to like coins except collectors, which may explain why those Coinstar machines standing post outside supermarkets process more coins than the U.S. Mint manufactures in a year. In the words of one anonymity-requesting economist I spoke with at the

U.S. Treasury: "I hate coins. Why do we even have them?" One answer is that pennies honor Abraham Lincoln. But maybe the national holiday, a gigantic memorial, and his face on a banknote (purple fives!) are sufficient. Some might even say it's an insult to the sixteenth president to put his image on unwanted coins that can't buy anything.

Despite my nostalgia for Bob's Waban News and those brick-like pieces of Bazooka gum, the logic expressed by retire-the-penny types resonated with me. I didn't care that they had once been mocked on an episode of *The West Wing*, but I did think that to avoid sounding petty, they needed to amp up the bluster. I wrote an essay for *Wired* advocating not merely for the end of small change, but an end to physical money, period. And I didn't hold back. "In an era when books, movies, music, and newsprint are transmuting from atoms to bits, money remains irritatingly analog," I declared. "Physical currency is a bulky, germ-smeared, carbon-intensive, expensive medium of exchange. Let's dump it."

Reader responses were . . . passionate. "Wolman is a fascist. . . . Taking away cash would be like taking away our guns: One needs it most only after it's gone." Another read: "My cash is my business." I was accused of shilling for secret lobbying groups, and of sacrificing "the last vestiges of privacy" so that "those bastions of clarity and honesty called banks and credit card companies can mine our every transaction."

I had smacked a nerve. People are willing to kill for cash—we know that. But what I was hearing made me think that people might kill to keep it. That got me wondering: what is cash, anyway? The simple answer is little metal discs and strips of paper bedecked with dead white guys and cryptic messages that make Nicholas Cage go even more bug-eyed. But what is its place in our economy, our culture, and our minds? Could we ever do without it? Should we?

Although predictions about the end of cash are as old as credit cards, a number of developments are ganging up on paper and metal money like never before: mistrust of national currencies, novel payment tools, anxiety about government debt, the triumph of mobile phones, the rise of virtual and alternative currencies, environmental concerns, and a wave of evidence showing that physical money is most harmful to the billions of people who have so little of it.

This book is about the twilight of money in its most commonly understood form, and a search for the places, people, and ideas that provide a glimpse of what comes next. The individuals you'll meet within these pages inhabit a vast spectrum of thinking about cash, its machinations, and its role in our lives. They are oracles to some, eccentrics to others. But all of them are visionaries merely for contemplating, and at times reimagining, something so fundamental, so uncontested. They just might convince you that a monetary revolution is afoot.

CHAPTER 1

The Missionary

Money doesn't talk, it swears.

—BOB DYLAN

Marco Polo thought the Chinese were out of their minds. Paper money was born in China, perhaps as far back as AD 800. But it was during the Yuan Dynasty, beginning in the thirteenth century, when the sovereign first replaced coins with paper.[1] When Marco Polo cast his eyes upon this monetary system some 100 years later, he was flabbergasted. The emperor's mint "hath the secret of alchemy in perfection," he wrote. Instead of circulating coins, the ruling authority passed out slips of paper stamped with a number—an amount corresponding to an equivalent handful of coins safeguarded in storage. It wasn't real money in the way anyone had ever understood it. Yet somehow, it worked.

Adorned with marks and seals of officialdom, this special paper made from mulberry trees circulated freely, enriching the kingdom and turbo-boosting commerce. When people far and wide readily accept the same medium of exchange, opportunities for trade expand exponentially. The emperor had mandated the notes' pass-ability, while making them redeemable for coinage. Anytime you wanted to, you could turn in the paper for coins.

In the uneconomically titled chapter of Polo's travelogue, "How the Great Kaan [Kublai Khan] causeth the bark of trees, made into something like paper, to pass for money over all his country," he described the bizarre arrangement, this sleight of hand that somehow wasn't. Yet the explorer knew full well that for his readers back in Europe, the explanation would likely fall short. "For, tell it how I might, you never would be satisfied that I was keeping within truth and reason!" I kid you not, Polo was saying. This paper money thing is out of this world.

The ingredients of strict enforcement—anyone refusing to accept the paper currency was given the death sentence—and redeem-ability were what made the system viable. To further reinforce faith in the banknotes and in the *issuing authority*, the text on the notes declared that they would be valid for all eternity. In a recent interview with the BBC, the governor of the Bank of England, Mervyn King, took a stab at explaining the meaning of "forever value." Paper money, he said, is "an implicit contract between people and the decisions they believe will be made in the years and decades to come, about preserving the value of that money. It's just a piece of paper. There's nothing intrinsic in value to it." Its value, he said, is determined by the perceived stability of the institutions behind it. If the public remains confident in those issuing institutions, people will regularly accept and use paper money. If that confidence breaks down, the currency, and economy, will collapse.

Nowadays, paper money printed with lofty language isn't surprising. If anything, it would be odd to see material money lacking in patriotic rah-rah. But for people living under the Yuan Dynasty, banknotes were wildly new technology. The fact that people believed this promise (and, yes, were executed if they didn't) enabled the emperor's novel form of money to be used "universally over all his kingdoms and provinces and territories."

◆

WE THINK ABOUT MONEY always and never. Always: employment, retirement, state of the economy, college tuition, terrorism funding, trade balance with China, Goldman Sachs, and quick runs to the ATM. Never: how it actually works. In the age of zeroes-happy bank bailouts and even larger amounts of new money created by the Federal Reserve (abracadabra!), the workings of money have become so abstract that they have all but gotten away from those of us who aren't specialists in monetary policy.

But cash we think we know. It's real, at least real enough that you can hold it, smell it, and want to wash your hands after handling it. Paper notes and metal coins are the treasures of our childhoods, tucked under pillows by tooth fairies, delivered in secret by doting grannies, and stashed safely in colorful lock boxes as we saved up for a new toy. Despite money's dull textbook definition—*medium of exchange, unit of account, store of value, and method of deferred payment*—it is by way of cash that we first come to have any understanding of or relationship to this civilization-powering invention. When the word *money* reaches the ears, even Wall Streeters who hawk collateralized debt obligations will, at some level, picture a pile of Benjamins.

(The language of money, by the way, is easily garbled. You may stop at the ATM to get some *cash*, but when you read in the *Wall Street Journal* that Intel or Boeing has a lot of cash, that obviously doesn't mean physical notes and coins. It means liquid assets: money that can readily be spent. In this book, when I use the word *cash*, I'm talking about physical objects. I will also sometimes use *hard currency*, *physical money*, or *material money*, just to mix it up a little. When I use *money* or *currency*, I'm talking in general terms, which means both material and electronic forms, unless otherwise specified.)

Our adult brains may get hung up on money's poor distribution, tendency to inflate, and penchant for catalyzing strife, but that childhood longing for cash in hand still lingers in corners of the mind reserved for simpler thoughts. This may explain why spotting a penny on the ground can spark a tiny subconscious rush, one that is then, just as quickly, extinguished by our more rational selves, which know full well that a penny—let alone a dime—is essentially, and increasingly, worthless.

Economists will tell you that it's not even worth the time and financial hazard involved in stooping down to pick it up, possibly resulting in a back injury.

Complain as we may about reckless bankers or the federal budget, we are believers in cash. We even worship it. You may not have a god or buddha in your life, but you very much have this faith. I don't mean you covet money like some jerk, unless you do, in which case you are. No, you have faith in money's value. You believe in it because everyone else does, which means our faith in it is also a trust in each other—a belief in a shared purpose, or at least a shared hallucination. By the mere act of using the national currency, we all participate in this peculiar religion.

This notion is pedestrian to economists, who are busy calculating the Herfindahl-Hirschman index and the Kakutani fixed-point theorem, or struggling to figure out how to reduce unemployment while keeping inflation in check. Slide money under the microscope, though, and it reveals a simultaneously petrifying and marvelous secret: its value lives and dies in our heads. As the writer and satirist Kurt Tucholsky once put it: "Money has value because it's universally accepted, and it's universally accepted because it has value." That is, until something breaks the spell.

Ironically, Kublai Khan's success with paper money is precisely what led to economic catastrophe. The Yuan Dynasty rulers gave in to a temptation that has plagued currency issuers and grade-schoolers throughout history: if no one ever bothers to redeem his banknotes for coinage, why not just print more? You can almost imagine the conversations among Khan's advisory team: *Sire, your subjects have such confidence in the redeem-ability of the paper that they never bother to. The perceived value of the paper means you no longer need a one-to-one correspondence between your stockpile of coinage and the amount of paper produced. Heck, boss, you don't even need a one-to-ten correspondence.*

But faith is a fragile thing. Doubt can be sowed by all kinds of events: war, natural disaster, counterfeiting, and bank failures being some of the most common culprits. For the Great Khan, the poison was an inundation of new money into the economy. When you can enrich yourself merely by printing more paper promises that never get challenged, it's hard not to do so. Monetary systems, however, require that there be a certain scarcity, or perceived scarcity, of the stuff. When Khan's currency lost that, the value—the purchasing power—of the peoples' money suddenly plummeted, and the paper money system collapsed. It would be centuries before it would resurface, this time in Europe.

◆

ON A FIERCELY COLD AND windy December morning, Glenn Guest walks into an unmarked diner in the northeastern Georgia hamlet of Bowman, orders a bacon-egg-and-cheese biscuit, helps himself to a cup of coffee, and sits down to discuss the Antichrist. Jim's Grill used to be "a proper diner" just up the road, but after a fire the owners relocated here, to a small brown barn with green trim. Locals dressed in coveralls and camouflage, on their way to work at poultry farms or one of the nearby granite foundries, stop in to discuss Georgia Bulldogs football and vacuum up scrambled eggs, sausage, grits, and biscuits served on Styrofoam plates.

Guest is the pastor at Shiloh Baptist Church in the neighboring town of Danielsville. He eats at Jim's Grill at least once a week, and often finds himself in conversations about scripture. He isn't a pushy proselytizer.

"I'm not saying I'm smarter than the average bear. Not by a long shot," says the fifty-nine-year-old Georgia native, speaking in a slow cadence, and frequently affixing the phrase "Lord willing" to the start or finish of his sentences. He wears blue jeans, a navy blue flannel shirt, and a black parka. His gray mustache is closely cropped, and his dark gray hair holds the wake lines of his comb for much of the day.

Guest doesn't believe people who claim to know exactly the date and time Jesus will make his encore. "But of course it *is* coming," he says. "These things must come to pass." Then: "If you don't eat grits very much, you'll like them more, I think, with some extra salt. I like to use more salt."

I follow his advice but still find the grits to be inferior to the sloppy peach cobbler. Certain information in the Bible and the Book of Revelation, Guest says, is there for all to see. Jesus will come back; the events will be ugly for nonbelievers; signs of the impending showdown—or hoedown—are hiding in plain sight. Many signs are already evident, and one of them is what's happening to money.

Guest carries a leather case with two zipped pouches, inside of which he tucks his marked-up copy of the King James Bible, as well as a mess of papers, and a small maroon electronic device that looks like a foreign language dictionary. It's a Bible passage locator, searchable by keyword.

When I ask about cash and how it relates to the end of the world, Guest doesn't need to look anything up. With clasped hands resting on the edge of the diner's fold-up table, he recites Scripture's most forceful and instructive passage connecting the money in our pockets to Satan's grand plan:

> And he causeth all, both small and great, rich and poor, free and bond, to receive a mark on their right hand, or on their foreheads; And that no man might buy or sell, save he that had the mark, or the name of the beast, or the number of his name. (Revelation 13: 16–17)

A few years ago, Guest wrote a book called *Steps Toward the Mark of the Beast*. When I found Guest's book online, I figured that he might be able to help me understand why so many people loathe the prospect of a cashless society. "I didn't want to write the book," he says. "I really didn't. But the Lord wanted me to, and so I prayed that he help me write it in a way that would be easy for people to understand." In the book, Guest explains that one of the ways the devil will try to supplant God in the days before judgment will be to control commerce. Cash transactions are anonymous and untraceable, which means putting an end to them will help the Beast seize the reigns of the economy.

"Once Satan has control, we will have a completely closed economic system," says Guest. Only those who accept the Mark of the Beast—if not in the form of a literal mark on the forehead, then perhaps a microchip under the skin—will be able to participate in commerce. All transactions will be knowable to Satan. From his hyper-wired Orwellian lair, the devil will know that you were unwilling to accept the mark. He will then turn you and all other refuseniks into "economic nonentities," unable to buy or sell, thereby excluding you from society and blocking your access to food or shelter. On the upside, those who resist the mark and maintain their faith in the Lord will receive the ultimate hardship pay: eternal bliss.

Guest told me about a Spanish resort where patrons can have a microchip implanted under the skin to make transactions simpler and, presumably, to coax them into spending more at the bar. (It's not easy to carry a wallet in a thong bikini.) It sounds like something right out of *Blade Runner*. Yet evidence supporting Guest's fear about controlled commerce isn't confined to such oddities. In the winter of 2010 the *New York Times* echoed this prophecy in an editorial about the decision by MasterCard, VISA, PayPal, and others to stop processing payments for Wikileaks: "A handful of big banks could potentially bar any organization they disliked from the payments system, essentially cutting them off from the world economy."

I tell Guest that I recently met with electronics experts at Hitachi in Tokyo, who are developing biometric devices for seamless transactions. One of these technologies uses the unique three-dimensional pattern of veins within every person's fingertip. Touch your finger to a register, vending machine, or subway turnstile and you can instantly settle up without having to break your stride. I resist sharing that I'm eager to see these innovations put to use. Provided they have adequate privacy controls, and supposing for a moment that they will not bring about the end of the world, I have a hard time seeing this kind of technology as negative.

I'm also a little reluctant to share my pro-digital sensibilities with Guest because many people see cash's anonymity as an almost sacred virtue, as if *cash* and *liberty* are synonyms. When you buy something with cash, it's hard for anyone to know that you did so. You may still have your receipt, but that connection between you and the purchase is yours to control—or tear up. When using cash, versus credit, to score some cocaine, buy a secret Valentine's Day gift for your mistress, or pay a field crew of undocumented workers, you can be confident that your transaction can't be traced, or at least can't be traced by the method of payment itself. (In-store surveillance is a different story.)

In the movie *Minority Report*, Tom Cruise's character sees personalized ads as he walks through a public space, thanks to specialized cameras that use the pattern of his irises to confirm his whereabouts. (The cameras actually mistake him for someone else because he's using a pair of stolen eyes, but bear with me.) The ads speak to his personal tastes, or an estimated version of them, based, the audience infers, on his extensively recorded and analyzed consumer history. Most of us don't like this idea; it crosses what Google executive chairman Eric Schmidt, of all people, once called "the creepy line."[2] We also worry about our digital footprints because data from transactions with credit cards, for example, can be exploited by identity thieves. Stick with cash and you're that much more off the radar.

Guest knows a thing or two about these and other relevant electronic money technologies. While serving in the U.S. Navy in the early 1970s, he helped maintain machines in Key West, Florida, that coded and decoded radio messages sent between the mainland and the fleet at sea. Since then, he has kept close tabs on advances in wireless communications, especially ones at the core of cashless transactions. These are the very tools, he says, that are setting the stage for the beginning of the end.

It was one evening in Key West when Guest came to believe in the Lord. There were no fireworks or sudden speaking in tongues. "I was just sitting there in our living room. It was a very nice mobile home park there on Stock Island, just across from Key West. We were maybe 200 yards from the water, there was a pool, and they cut your grass for you and everything. Anyway, I came to see that God was in a position to deal with me, and that he always had been." For Guest, a sense of guilt had been lifted, although not because he had lived an especially sinister life. "We are all sinners. With revelation, I could see that Jesus was the propitiation—the payment—for the sins of the world."

With newfound faith, he and his wife returned to rural Georgia, where they had both been raised. Guest joined the ministry and has since been doing his best to warn anyone who will listen about what to expect when the end is finally here. What most people fail to notice, he explains, is that the slow lead-up to the tribulation can be disguised to look like progress. Much like the move from coins to banknotes, checks to credit cards, and now credit cards to payment technologies that live inside our cellphones, the Mark of the Beast may seem like just another positive innovation.

This illusion, says Guest, is to be expected, considering the serpent's cunning. "Imagine that all of your personal information is embedded in a chip beneath the skin—let's say on the back of your right hand. If you were to get sick and go to the hospital someplace far from your home, doctors could use the chip to learn who you are and what your medical condition is. That information could save your life." Guest speculates that people may end up dying because they *don't* have the chip, which will compel the rest of us to conclude that some kind of biometric identification system at the national or international level is both prudent and moral. From there, the move to completely digitized commerce is almost a given.

But eliminating cash is only the latest step toward the mark. Guest explains that prior ones include the elimination of the gold standard, the establishment of the United Nations, the growing power of Wall Street banks, the advent of barcodes, and the more recent use of radio-frequency-emitting microchips used to track merchandise.

If Guest had his way, we would return to the gold standard, or something like it; a system of "real value" for currency. "People think a paper dollar is worth such and such. Because people believe that, you can still exchange it for goods and services. But I could print '1 basketball' on a dollar—that doesn't make it a basketball." Money has no intrinsic value anymore, but at least with cash, says Guest, flawed as it may be, we can preserve the freedom that Satan aspires to eliminate.

"Hey, what will the Rapture be like?" I ask.

"I can't imagine what the wrath of God will be like," says Guest. "No one can." He finishes his biscuit and stands to refill his coffee at the beverage bar. "But those who are reconciled with the Lord and pray that he open heaven's treasury of wisdom to them have nothing to fear."

Another customer opens the front door, and the sparkly paper snowflakes hanging from the ceiling are sent swinging in a rush of wind.

◆

FOR MOST OF HUMAN HISTORY, money didn't exist. Tribe or village chieftains told their minions who would do what, who would eat what, and who would have what. If the people desired or needed more spears, women, or real estate, they just did battle with some other village, hoping to come out of the fray with a greater net worth, or they just had to make more spears and have more children.

These no-commerce communities did pretty well, communism's recent flops notwithstanding. Indigenous peoples from the Arctic Circle to the Australian outback successfully distributed goods and divvied up labor and wealth. Not that this life was easy. For these societies to function, they often depended on iron-fisted rulers, slavery, and the all-around hassle of having to gather one's own firewood, hunt food, build shelter, and defend against marauding invaders who were after your limited supply of everything.

The technology known as money came about because we are driven to trade. Some scientists speculate that the motivation to trade is even part of our evolutionary programming.[3] If you're sitting on a pile of vegetables but you're freezing cold, while I'm hungry and carrying more animal furs than I could ever use, wouldn't we, almost instinctively, see a mutually beneficial accord in the making? Let's make a deal!

Swapping your food for my furs will suit us well, but this form of trade hinges on what British economist William Stanley Jevons famously dubbed the "double coincidence of wants." Should you not want to trade your potatoes for my furs because it's summertime, we're out of luck.

That is, unless we could come up with something else for me to give you—something that you know some third party will also willingly accept in an exchange conducted four hours or four months from now. What we need is money.

No dolphin or chimpanzee will ever paint a Picasso, compose a symphony, or pen a sonnet. Music and art are often the go-to examples of what sets humans apart from other animals. Yet so does money. It's usually excluded, though, from discussions about human ingenuity, treated more like a slovenly step-cousin. We should keep it at arm's length, deal with it only when we have to, and get back to reflecting upon more spiritually enriching endeavors.

Such a narrow view of money belies its inner magic and civilizing power. In this we could learn a thing or two from economists. They see just how ingenious and perplexing money is, and how creative, foolish, and passionate we are in our handling of it. Perhaps more than anyone, economists understand that money is a fiction, and that the entire financial system rests on the head of this socially constructed pin. Scary as that may be, it also means money can be anything we want it to be. Print "1 basketball" on a dollar, and it actually can be a basketball, as long as we all play along.

For millennia, money took the form of various objects: things you could hold in your hand or hitch to a post. Feathers, shells, coconuts, butter, salt, whale teeth, logs, cacao seeds, tobacco, dried fish, livestock, and slabs of rock as big as a car.[4] Stone monuments that look like table-size sand dollars were, and to a limited extent still are, used for money on the Micronesian island of Yap, but their primary use today seems to be as economists' favorite example of the zany, and ultimately arbitrary, forms that money can take, and to illustrate the point that items themselves don't have to move for them to function as money.

Only the understanding of ownership has to move. Value can transfer without the object doing any travel because the people involved in the exchange are cool with it. If something can perform this function, it can be money. "Money represents pure interaction," wrote the celebrated

German philosopher Georg Simmel in *The Philosophy of Money*. "It is an individual thing whose essential significance is to reach beyond individualities."[5] Money is what money does.

Part of its genius is that it allows us to specialize. If you think you're busy now, imagine having to also grow and prepare all of your own food, heat your house, sew all of your own clothes, educate your children, perform your own surgeries, build your own computers, make your own movies, and write your own books. Money saves you from all that by enabling trade. As capitalism godfather Adam Smith once put it: "Man continually standing in the need of the assistance of others, must fall upon some means to procure their help."[6] Thanks to money, whatever we earn plying our individual trades will, or should be, exchangeable for the goods we need and—for those of us fortunate enough to afford more—the goods we want.

But even with the early forms of money, before the arrival of coins a few thousand years ago, a schism was brewing between media of exchange that were useful items versus purely representative stuff. You can count cows easily enough, and you can also drink their milk or eat them. Red feathers, however, have no intrinsic value, unless you're a red bird. In currencies like feathers or stone monuments, we see the precursors to modern cash: without collective belief in their value, they're worthless.

The inadequacies of early currencies became more and more acute as economies grew. For one thing, not all feathers, shells, or whale teeth are alike. Even if you try to limit trading to similar ones, you run into the problem of nonstandardized units. These objects also weren't limited in supply. A sudden glut could undermine the value of all of the existing ones, while a shortchanged supply of money could compel people to find new and more violent means of procuring goods and services.

Another hiccup with these rudimentary exchange systems was decay. What if those feathers start to fall apart, or the dowry payment of five cows just keeled over? Money needs to be a dependable store of value through time. As trade expanded—not just to the next village, but to the next kingdom, country, or continent—the need for consistent value only intensified. The invention of coins some 2,600 years ago in the ancient Greek kingdom of Lydia helped circumvent many of the limitations of prior currencies. The ruling power would deem coins of a standard shape, weight, and size to be worth *x* amount of labor, crops, livestock, or belly-dancing lessons, so that you didn't need a wallet full of livestock to conduct business, and you didn't have the problem of decay like you did with tobacco leaves or sacks full of fish heads.

With metal coins, trade could extend however far the belief in the coins' value could travel. Although a chest full of silver sounds inconvenient, transactions had never known such clarity and compactness. With few exceptions, money in the form of coinage became almost universally accepted throughout the world, a characteristic of cash that was essential to its success. Today, your notes and coins are perfectly populist. Your ability to possess this form of wealth has nothing to do with your citizenship, education, age, credit score, hunting skill, or political or religious persuasions. Your cash is indeed your business.

Coinage also scored high marks for *fungibility*. This is one of those annoying econ words, but all it means is that cash is interchangeable across uses. Say I give you $500 to support your family, and I stipulate that you *not* buy junk food with that money. How meaningful is that? Even if you follow my instructions, you may still, indirectly, use it to acquire junk food, because using my money to buy milk or soccer cleats now frees up other money you've obtained from other sources, which you can spend on Doritos. That is fungibility, and it helps explain why cash has persisted through the ages and is almost universally acceptable: it can be used across nearly *all* uses.

But fungibility was only one of coinage's great triumphs. It also formally married the mega-abstractions of the state and money. By splashing the face of a sovereign or other political symbols onto the coins and forcing people to accept them as payment when conducting commerce, rulers literally stamped their authority into existence. The word *coin*, after all, also means to invent. One of the fundamental ways kingdoms and states establish power is by making the money, controlling its form and supply within their territories, and using it to collect revenue.[7]

By the seventeenth and eighteenth centuries, government mints of Europe and parts of Asia were cranking out huge volumes of coins. Iron, bronze, copper, and lead enjoyed sporadic time in the currency limelight, but they paled in comparison to silver and, of course, gold.

You could say that the story of the monetary system that came to be known as the gold standard begins with our fondness for bling. No one will ever be able to pinpoint when it happened, or who led this reformation in thinking, but one day ages ago, a well-fed and influential someone, somewhere, decided that this shiny material is special—that it's *worth* something. Its resemblance to the sun probably gave it an edge. Once our ancestors started convincing each other that their respective deities preferred this material, they went bananas for it: painting it on their faces, entombing it alongside dead pharaohs, wearing chunks of it as jewelry, and using it to jazz up ceremonies and rituals. Its scarcity only added to its allure.

Our love of gold (and silver, but let's stick with gold for the moment) injected it with value, fusing the idea of money to a substance like never before. It turns out that those ancestors chose wisely. If you're going to have physical money, gold is hard to beat: it's durable and malleable, not poisonous to handle, easy to test for authenticity, and nonreactive, meaning it won't decay or catch fire. It's also just scarce enough. All the gold ever mined totals a little over 165,000 tons, which is roughly the same weight as one-and-a-half U.S. Navy aircraft carriers.[8]

The psychological sorcery that makes us value something we can't eat or heat our homes with, and probably don't want to snuggle up to, is immeasurably powerful. People tend to think, for instance, that gold, silver, diamonds, and even dollars have inherent worth, as if that value emanated from the atoms within these objects, or from the U.S. Treasury imprimatur. Diamonds are the most stellar example of this phenomenon, because the industry, which is to say one monopolistic company, De Beers, has had such success convincing us that diamonds are rare and therefore expensive. They're worthless, though, unless you want to cut something extremely hard, or plan to use them for some high-tech electronics. But try telling that to a bride-to-be who has her heart set on a certain engagement ring.

By the nineteenth century, gold had become the foundation of the world's monetary system, with national currencies stamped out in set weights of it, as well as corresponding coins of silver. Economies chugged along impressively under this new regime, except when they didn't, which was often, because of revolutions and depressions. Gradually, many governments and economists would come to see gold as precariously inflexible. How can you boost an economy's money supply when it's in need of one if the money itself depends on Mother Earth's willingness to cough it up from some faraway mine?

Another problem with gold coins was that economic conditions sometimes led people to believe their interests were better served if they didn't spend or invest. This hoarding only further limited the availability of money. Silver created similar problems but was also subject to oversupply. The Spanish Empire learned this lesson the hard way. After it became unfathomably rich plundering the silver mines of South America in the sixteenth century, a glut of silver eventually led to steep price hikes and steeper drops in the purchasing power of the peoples' money, similar to the crash in value of those Yuan Dynasty banknotes. When money grows on trees, it becomes no more sought after than leaves.

As world-changing of an invention as coinage was, it was proving to be a less than ideal form of money.

◆

BACK AT JIM'S GRILL IN BOWMAN, Pastor Guest admits without hesitation that he and his wife benefit from modern electronic conveniences. "We have a savings account, and we have a credit card, yes we do. But we try not to use it because we don't want to go into debt," he says. People want cash, though, because it has a measure of freedom. "If you have something I want, and if I have cash, we can transact right now."

Like many people and institutions, Guest believes the writing is on the wall as far as cash is concerned, in light of the sweep of technological advances over the past half century. "Money's destiny is to become digital" was how a 2002 study from the Organization for Economic Cooperation and Development put it.[9] Guest thinks it will happen sooner than most people realize. Indeed, if you follow a script of end-time events that includes the Beast's takeover of buying and selling, an end to cash *has* to happen.

Guest isn't frightened, though. "God knows what he's doing. Those who have the Lord in their hearts have nothing to fear." But he does worry for others. He doesn't say so, but considering the Bible and the cinderblock-size reference book he gave me yesterday, I'm pretty sure this includes me.

We finish our coffee and head toward the register to settle up. On the beam next to the counter is an antique sign that reads: "Beware of pickpockets and loose women."

"Thank you, Chris. That was real nice," says Guest, handing a $10 bill to owner Chris White. "Now here," Guest says to me, gesturing to the register, "they only take cash. No credit cards."

Guest is the kind of gracious host who would never have let me pay, which is good because I can't. When I first set out to explore physical money's role in our lives, I decided to give this inquiry a personal twist by attempting to avoid cash for an entire year. In so doing, I hoped to glimpse just how feasible or unrealistic it would be to completely do away with it.

I ask White why he refuses to accept plastic. He looks me straight in the eye for an awkwardly extended moment, perhaps wondering if I'm a covert operative with the IRS.

"It's just easy," he finally says. "Simple. We like to keep things simple 'round here." White proceeds to make change as if on autopilot.

"Chris also took the course a while back," Guest says. "The one on the Revelation that I teach at Elberton Christian School, about the Mark of the Beast and the steps."

"Oh." I look back over to White. "Well then, there's that reason too . . . " I say, trailing off so as to indicate that I've been briefed about electronic money's role as precursor to the coming carnage.

White gives a single nod. "Yes, there is."

"And those credit card companies want to pinch the pot, too," says Guest. "Taking a percentage of your business."

"That there's another reason," says White. "Now we are up to three."

We thank him for breakfast, and as we head out the door, Guest tells me White sometimes gives out copies of *Steps Toward the Mark of the Beast*. "I meant to bring him a few more today. I don't charge nothing for it."

◆

PAPER MONEY WAS REBORN in Europe in the seventeenth century. Coins and precious metals of specific weight were still the "it" form of money, but some goldsmiths were about to change that. People would head down to the local goldsmith to have their gold or silver fashioned into jewelry or, if they were down on their luck, have their jewelry fashioned into gold coins or bars—a centuries-old foreshadowing of today's depressing "We Buy Gold!" ads on late-night cable, and the popular History Channel reality show *Pawn Stars*.

When you give a goldsmith your gold or silver goods, he gives you a receipt as evidence that he's got your money and you'll soon get it back. That slip of paper represents an amount of gold. Provided you have ample trust in the goldsmith, and the butcher does too, there's no reason you can't exchange "goldsmith notes" for lamb chops.[10] Goldsmiths soon realized that as long as people weren't checking up daily on their deposited gold, they could hand out—issue—more paper than what numerically corresponded to the stock of gold in their charge. Voila: modern banking was born.

The next leap in the evolution of cash came in colonial-era America, when paper money went from being backed by coins or bullion to being backed by a government's promise to eventually pay out in coins, or pay out in something. In a way, this development marked the second coming of the Yuan banknotes, but with a crucial difference: in China the ruling authority, the issuer, concealed the fact that the paper no longer represented a corresponding stash of coins or bullion. With modern money, no one pretends.

Before independence, America's disparate colonial economies struggled with a very material financial hang-up: there just wasn't enough money to go around. The colonists were importing many of their needed goods from Europe, so the pennies and shillings that made it into their purses were soon traveling back across the Atlantic. Colonial governments attempted to solve this problem by using tobacco, nails, and animal pelts for currency, assigning them a set amount of shillings or pennies so that they could intermix with the existing system.

The most successful ad hoc currency was wampum, a particular kind of bead made from the shells of ocean critters. But eventually the value of this currency, like that of other alternative currencies of the day, was undermined by oversupply and counterfeiting.[11] (That's right: counterfeit wampum. They were produced by dyeing like-shaped shells with berry juice, mimicking the purple color of the real thing.)

It was a crew of Puritans from Boston who first put their faith in paper. Initially, the Massachusetts Bay Colony tried to issue colonial coinage. The pieces themselves, struck in 1652, were made from a mash-up of poor-quality silver and were soon outlawed by the Brits. Less than a decade later the colonists tried again. They were forced to, really, because they owed money to the crown to help fund Britain's war against France, yet lacked any currency with which to pay up. They called the paper "bills of credit." The local government essentially said to the people: *Here, just use this. It's real money. We'll sort out redeem-ability later.* Due to a combination of faith in government and, probably more so, no better option, the people began using the new currency.

Cash similar to what we have today had finally arrived. Country to country, it still varied: some issuances were from private banks, some were from state-chartered banks; some were certificates of deposit, others were bills of credit or promissory notes from the government—as in, *We promise that this will be valuable someday, as long as you never ask if today is that day.* There were endless debates, from prairie farmlands to the floor of Congress, about whether this paper was real money or just a smoke-and-mirrors scheme destined to end badly. In the United States that dispute, between the fear of paper and the advantages of national currency, would rage for more than a century, and it is even front and center in the Constitution.

During the Continental Congress, the founding fathers deliberately forbid the nascent federal government from issuing "bills of credit." Paper money, one delegate noted, was "as alarming as the Mark of the Beast." The federal government was, however, granted authority "to coin money, regulate the value thereof . . . and fit the standard of weights and measure."[12]

But paper issued by the federal government would get its chance, thanks to the Civil War and its economic fallout. To foot the bill of the Union Army's campaign, the government had to issue $450 million in greenbacks (about $8.1 billion in 2011 dollars). They may have been un-constitutional, but they worked, making it possible to buy equipment and pay soldiers. War has a habit of quieting concerns about the cur-rency's backing.

The end of the war, however, brought with it inflation and renewed attention to the constitutionality of paper money. It was Salmon P. Chase (*P* for Portland, not paper), who, first as the secretary of the Treasury Department, made the greenbacks possible. Then, as a Supreme Court justice less than a decade later, he made one of history's most famous flip-flops, ruling that currency notes were illegal. He made this deter-mination despite the fact that the face printed on them was none other than his own.

A reshuffled Supreme Court—two new justices were appointed by President Ulysses Grant the same day of that initial verdict against paper money—would quickly reverse the ruling. Two subsequent de-cisions in what became known as the Legal Tender Cases sealed the deal: the Constitution may not *explicitly* grant the federal government power to issue bills of credit, but it had the implicit right to do so because governing over a country, or at least this one, would be flat-out impossible without it.[13]

Before the advent of a single circulating national currency, though, thousands of private banks issued their own notes, sometimes backed by bullion or coinage in a safe, but just as often backed by nothing at all. This was a monetary free-for-all, and—considering the greenback's universal acceptability now—it's strange to imagine how, less than 150 years ago, money in America was a smorgasbord. Countless varieties of paper money circulated throughout the land, most issued by unchartered "Wildcat" banks, and much of it of questionable authenticity and unstable value.

Even during that chaotic time, however, the paper's value always depended, at least in theory, on the idea that you could exchange it for a weight of gold or silver. The conviction that precious metals are value incarnate was still as strong as it had been 2,000 years prior. It was inconceivable that currency could have value without this link to metals— that currency value might be fluid. That too would soon change, during what was the final stage in this metamorphosis from ancient money to the cash in your wallet.

The first step was in 1933, when President Franklin Roosevelt called in the public's gold supply as part of a radical effort to rebuild the economy during the Great Depression. Then in 1944, representatives of the major economies of the free world anointed the U.S. dollar to become the de facto currency of the globe—to replace gold, sort of. The dollar would still be locked at an exchange value to gold of $35 an ounce. Bizarre as it may sound, a small group of men sitting around a table determined that a 1-ounce nugget of gold would be worth, not $34 or $36.75, but $35. Other world currencies, instead of having their own correspondence to gold, would fix their value to the dollar, and wouldn't be allowed to change their exchange rates without special permission from the newly minted International Monetary Fund.

The rub was that this postwar agreement gave other countries the right to exchange their stashes of dollars for gold. By the early 1970s this policy, even if rarely acted upon, was becoming an increasingly obvious absurdity, as foreign banks held an amount of dollars equal to three times the amount of gold the U.S. owned.[14] The situation aggravated foreign governments because a war- and deficit-weakened U.S. economy also hurt the dollar, and that in turn dragged down other countries' currencies and economies. Most prominent among the ticked off was France, which converted billions of dollars into gold, hoping other countries would follow suit and force the U.S. to get its financial house in order.

But others didn't follow suit. Instead, on August 15, 1971, President Richard Nixon severed the last remaining connective tissue between a material substance and national currencies. Nobody could exchange greenbacks for gold anymore. The number of dollars required to buy an ounce of gold would from here on out be determined by the markets, just like it is for oil, sod, dental equipment, and tulips. Currencies would be measured against each other, like untethered balloons carried on a breeze.

The dollar, meanwhile, remained the anchor currency of the world: the one ring that kinda rules them all. Other governments hold on to dollars and use them for paying debts, and in the aisles of the global supermarket of goods, most items are priced in U.S. dollars.

This is what's so weird about commentators in the U.S. proudly declaring that the dollar is the most stable currency in the world, as if this were because of American economic policy today, when it's really just the result of negotiations a few generations ago that made it the backbone of the whole system. The greenback is stable because the U.S. economy is huge and the United States is a terrific republic—OK. But it's also stable because everyone else's well-being depends on it, and on belief in its stability. That may be changing, though.

As for paper money itself, the end of the gold standard meant that cash had become a total abstraction. Its value now comes from *fiat*, government mandate. It's a Latin word meaning *let there be*. In God we better trust.

◆

HEADING EAST on rural Highway 172, Guest and I discuss failed currencies of old. The currency of the Confederate States of America is one of history's most potent examples, certainly in this part of the country. Those promises to "pay the bearer" were first issued by the Confederacy in 1861 to fund the South's Civil War effort. As the war dragged on and the conflict began tipping in the North's favor, people understandably began to lose confidence in the Confederacy's ability to pay its debts. The rapidly increasing amount of paper added into circulation didn't help—all told, the banknote runs had a face value of $1.7 billion—and the currency eventually lost nearly all of its value, compounding the economic hardship of the defeated South. "They just printed all that money, but there was no backing, so it collapsed," says Guest. "It's now worth more as a collectible."

Guest's account reminds me of a story I once saw online. A routine presentation by Federal Reserve Chairman Ben Bernanke to the Senate Finance Committee ended with a Tourette's-like outburst of existentialism, undermining in one fell swoop the entire economic system as we know it. Pausing midway through a sentence about the prospect of raising a key interest rate, the chairman was seized by an unearthly force.

"You know what? It doesn't matter," Bernanke said. "None of this—this so-called 'money'—really matters at all. It's just an illusion." Brandishing a handful of greenbacks, he set them on the table between him and the microphone. "Just look at it: Meaningless pieces of paper with numbers printed on them. Worthless." Then he pulled out a lighter and lit them on fire.[15]

Thank God for *The Onion*. Bernanke, of course, would never say such things, and he probably doesn't carry a lighter, let alone big wads of cash. Still, you don't have to be Ron Paul to hear whispers of truth in this tale. "The money we use now is a lie," says Guest, as we drive past chicken farms and the river where he used to swim as a boy. "When the dollar collapses, a lot of people will be holding useless paper because they exchanged things of value—food, land, shelter—for nothing." I'm less pessimistic than Guest about the fate of the dollar, humanity, and, for that matter, non-Christians. But I am curious about paper's long-term place in all of this.

To further contemplate the biblical implications of cash's last stand, Guest and I decided to drive to a spot on the edge of the bucolic community of Dewey Rose. This part of Georgia is blessed with massive granite deposits, and chances are, most of the more expensive kitchen countertops in Atlanta, if not much of the region, came from here. That same gray stone was also used to make the weirdest monument in America: the Georgia Guidestones.

We turn right onto Guidestones Road and park in the small gravel lot. No one else is here. Thirty years ago an enigmatic religious group decided that a set of post-apocalyptic commandments, etched into huge granite slabs and arranged with astronomically significant exactitude, belonged right here, by the side of Highway 77.

The Guidestones have been nicknamed "American Stonehenge," although my first impression upon arriving at this hedgerow-enclosed square of desolate hilltop is less awe and more disorientation. It could be a gaudy mausoleum for local hero Ty Cobb, or possibly a misplaced war memorial—not ground zero for a freaky Ten Commandments redux. Yet here it is.*

Four light-gray slabs, each almost 20 feet tall and a foot-and-a-half wide, stand symmetrically around a central, narrower stone, making the shape of an "X" if you were looking down from your spaceship. The stones are positioned to track the sun's migration across the sky, and at noon every day the sun shines down through a tiny hole drilled through a capstone, 9 feet 8 inches by 6 feet 6 inches, with a message in Egyptian hieroglyphics, Sanskrit, Babylonian cuneiform, and classical Greek etched into each of its sides.

---

*One hypothesis about the Guidestones is that they were commissioned by a group of Rosicrucians, a mysterious cult-cum-religion with medieval roots and links to Protestantism.

The text is a sometimes innocuous, sometimes cryptic, sometimes eugenicist collection of ten instructions, elegantly engraved into the eight long walls of granite. The same message is repeated in the world's most widely spoken languages. Dewey Rose hasn't been flooded with Indian tourists over the past few decades, but the Hindi is here for them when they get here.

Hands jammed in his pockets and wool hat pulled over his ears to defend against the frigid wind, Guest reads aloud:

"'Maintain humanity under 500,000,000 in perpetual balance with nature.' Well gee," he says. "How are you going to do that? It sort of makes you think about Hitler. Let's see. 'Guide reproduction wisely—improving fitness and diversity.'" Pretty much the same deal. "And this one here," continues Guest. "'Unite humanity with a living new language.' Maybe that is a return to Babel, which God ended, remember?" Another commandment calls for an international court, a concept suggestive of the one-world government that believers who share Guest's faith say is part of the Antichrist's grand scheme.

Guest has visited this spot maybe a dozen times. He even held a church service here once. "I wanted to show everyone what others believe. It gets you thinking about the radical ways that people want to change the world, ways that are foretold by the Scripture. A lot of folks are going to fall for that," he says, pointing up at the strange directives for shaping a New World Order.

Profound change to the monetary system is part of that deception. Even though the U.S. dollar is one of the most valued currencies in the world, its apparent worthlessness, combined with our ever-more-digitized financial lives, is only paving the way for the end of days. "After there is no more cash, it will be very clear that we are on our way," Guest says, meaning on our way to Armageddon.

The Guidestone instruction that most speaks to the puzzle of money, he continues, is this one: "Balance personal rights with social duties." The "closed economic system" will mean a socialized economy—there will be no personal rights to balance. "Like I said, there are advantages to electronic money, no doubt. But it *will* be used by the Beast for total control."

"If you trust in the Lord, there is no need to be afraid. If you aren't going to believe," he says, staring up at the capstone, "as it says in the Gospel of Luke, 'Men's hearts will fail them for fear.'"

"Jeee-zus," I mutter, because this is just a thing I sometimes say—almost like an automatic exhale—when I hear a disturbing idea. This time I'm regretting it before the second syllable has escaped my lips. Guest doesn't hear me, though, or politely pretends not to.

A few minutes later, we hop back in the car to drive back to Bowman.

So many people think the end of cash is a foregone conclusion. Yet if you suggest that maybe we should hurry up and get on with it, that it might even be a good thing, you will be accused of kowtowing to Bank of America, lacking patriotism, trampling on some kind of sacrosanct institution, and rolling out the red carpet for Satan. Why?

Perhaps it starts with the misperception that cash is holier than thou.

CHAPTER 2

The Messenger

Money, so diabolically simple.
—FRANK HERBERT, *THE WHITE PLAGUE*

An hour into my flight to London for the annual Digital Money Forum, the flight attendants wheel their carts full of duty-free items down the aisles. The Saudi Arabian man sitting next to me uses his American Express card to buy his wife a silver necklace with a heart-shaped pendent. Should anyone else wish to make a purchase, they too will need plastic.

The cashless cabin policy emerged after reports that flight attendants were skimming off the top—"leakage," the industry reps called it. But the practice also took effect around the same time swine flu mania was sweeping the globe. Residents of Asia donned face shields, while everyone in Europe and North America practiced sneezing into their elbows and scowling at anyone in public who let loose an unguarded cough.

Yet even before H1N1 became part of the vernacular, cash transactions on planes caused me considerable dismay. It wasn't that the flight crew had to keep multilinear equations in their heads to track who in which row was owed what. No, what bugged me about cash in the cabin was its proximity to my food and drink. I would watch flight attendants' hands extend over seats to take a few bucks, sort them, and then add them to the wad of bills in their apron pockets. With those same green-backed fingers, they would hold cups by the rim, deposit lemon slices, and relay coffee stirrers. Then it was back to the cash again, this time received from the grubby hands of a passenger, like the guy on my flight in 24B who's wearing a tank-top and sitting with his arms folded behind his head for maximum armpit exposure.

Cash is filthy. Money may be a marvelous technology enabling life as we know it, but no amount of grandiose talk will change its microbe-infested reality. Aside from handshakes, commonly breathed air, and mutually held handrails on busses and subways, transacting in cash is one of the top ways in which we go about touching one another, or touching one another's more communicable goodies.

In the science-fiction novel *The White Plague* by *Dune* author Frank Herbert, a molecular biologist decides to exact revenge for his family's murder by poisoning paper money and distributing it in countries where the bad guys in the story live. The contamination spreads out of control and becomes a global plague. At one point, the U.S. president declares: "We've decontaminated and replaced the money to the point where we can start lifting the quarantine on the banks." Unfortunately, the plan falters.[1]

Banknotes and coins harbor all kinds of bugs.[2] Traces of the bacteria *staphylococcus* have been detected on 94 percent of all U.S. dollar bills.[3] In 2003, hysteria in China that banknotes could spread the SARS virus proved to be unfounded, but the Bank of China still decided that any bills it received would be held for twenty-four hours—the estimated lifespan of the virus—before being released back into the ocean of circulation. And Swiss researchers have found that moderate concentrations of flu virus could survive on banknotes for up to three days. When they tested the same bugs "in the presence of respiratory mucus," which sounds like a really fun experiment, they determined that the virus lived for up to seventeen days. "The unexpected stability of influenza virus in this nonbiological environment," wrote the scientists, "suggests that unusual environmental contamination should be considered in the setting of pandemic preparedness."[4] Could circulating banknotes help spread a future plague?

When I forwarded that study to a friend at the Centers for Disease Control, she was unimpressed. "Are the researchers sucking on banknotes or inserting them in their noses?" she asked. Without a perfect storm of transmission conditions—someone sneezes on a banknote, doesn't allow it to dry, stores it someplace dark and humid, doesn't rub it on other material like a leather wallet or pants pocket—maybe, and only maybe, enough viral particles could survive to infect the next person handling those bills. Unless people start using greenbacks as handkerchiefs, she told me, whatever germs do reside on cash or coins should die a quick death.*[5] That was reassuring, yet a friend who recently returned from Africa was kind enough to inform me that people in some of the more dangerous parts of the continent store cash in their underwear. As smart as my contact at the CDC might be, I suspect that when assuring me of cash's harmlessness, not even she was thinking of banknotes stored in skivvies.

Germs aren't the only stowaways on your cash. A chemical study from a couple of years ago found that most banknotes sampled from eighteen different U.S. cities tested positive for cocaine residue. Is cash so turbo liquid in its movement within the economy that most of it eventually makes it into the nostrils of cokeheads? No. When a bill-counting machine at a bank or casino gets contaminated by even a single note, that cocaine residue can then show up on a huge number of bills subsequently run through the same machine.[6] (Interestingly, the most cokeified bills in the country were found in Washington, D.C., while the fewest were found in Salt Lake City.) Another recent study found that 99 percent of England's paper money was contaminated with cocaine, an indicator to the good people of Britain that the Bank of England must

---

*Using a banknote as a tissue: an inflation hawk's publicity stunt, perhaps?

have bought its bill counters from none other than the late Pablo Escobar.

My distaste for cash has intensified of late because of my efforts to avoid it. I've been clean for almost four months now, with few noticeable hassles. Cash has already been bumped so far to the periphery of our daily lives that it wasn't proving difficult to steer clear of cash-only restaurants and parking meters. At the donut shop near my house, where the owners have instituted a $2.50 minimum for credit card transactions, I have to perform a kind of price gouging in reverse, insisting on a $2.50 charge for a $0.80 glazed donut.

The one breakdown came when I had to board a New Jersey Transit train bound for the financial capital of the world. I didn't have enough lead time to buy a ticket online or plan ahead for some other mode of transportation. Suddenly I found myself facing an impatient conductor armed with a machine that could dispense tickets, but that clearly couldn't process plastic. Luckily, I had some bills still sitting untouched in my wallet. After buying the ticket, I briefly examined the handful of coins that the conductor placed in my open palm, and proceeded to deposit them on the open seat in front of me.

A few stops later, a bald man shuffled into that seat and promptly pocketed the change. Or tried to pocket it: an errant quarter fell to the floor and landed next to my shoe. The guy had headphones on, though, so he didn't hear the telltale clinking of fallen change. When the train finally arrived at Penn Station and we stood to make our way to the exit, I tapped the man on the elbow and informed him that he had dropped a quarter. He said thanks, but looked confused. Despite the coin's proximity to my shoe, it became apparent to the bald man that I wasn't going to pick it up for him. Instead, I stepped passed him and hurried out onto the platform. It was awkward.

Cash has also lately been drawing me into a kind of values house of mirrors, thanks in part to Lawrence Weschler's biography of the artist J.S.G. Boggs. In the late 1980s, Boggs became famous for drawing exquisite copies of banknotes—dollars, pounds, Swiss francs, and others.

They weren't counterfeits, although he was accused and later acquitted of counterfeiting by the Bank of England, and harassed for years by authorities in the United States.

Boggs would finish a meal at a fancy restaurant, or approach the checkout desk at a hotel, and offer to pay the tab with his artwork—a drawing, say, of a $100 bill for a $71 dinner. He would deliver a jovial disquisition about money, and the value of his drawings, based on the hours of work that went into them, and the value the waiter or hotel staffer may or may not choose to assign them. (As further evidence of his disinterest in passing forgeries, Boggs would also offer to pay with real banknotes.) What captivated Boggs was value—how people determine and exchange it.[7]

By eschewing cash, I was hoping to conduct a similar kind of experiment in monetary contemplation. But what I didn't anticipate when I resolved not to handle any U.S. Mint issued coins or Federal Reserve Notes was that my refusal to touch banknotes and coins would mutate into a genuine aversion. In the first month or two, friends would try to hand me a few bucks, I would flick them away like mosquitoes, we would chuckle—"Wolman's on the cash wagon!"—and then the conversation would move on. After a few months, though, the repulsion became real, as if I was the only person in the world looking at cash with the help of those special purple lights from *CSI*—the ones that illuminate fingerprints and other traces of human activity. To this day, every time I see someone pull money from a wallet or pocket and place it on the countertop at a café, I can't help but imagine the stepped on, sweat-drenched, and hyper-handled life cycle of that cash. After depositing the banknotes in the register, the barista reaches for a cup to make my drink, and I have to bite my tongue so as not to yell *Hey! Ever heard of antibacterial gel?*

If we look beyond the cash in our wallets to physical money as an industry, the picture gets even dirtier. A 2010 British government report entitled "The UK's Payment Revolution" put it this way: "With around a billion bank notes created, distributed, collected and destroyed every year, the production and secure transportation of notes is an expensive and environmentally costly business paid for by the tax payer. A progressive move away from cash could hold many benefits."[8] In the United States, between 2008 and 2010, the coining process alone used up more than 32,397 tons of zinc, 41,245 tons of copper, and 4,185 tons of nickel. And cash's carbon footprint doesn't stop there.

Metals like zinc, nickel, and copper have many other, arguably more important, uses, like in the wiring of homes or in electric-car batteries. According to the multinational mining giant BHP Billiton, world consumption of copper over the next twenty-five years will exceed that of all copper ever mined to date.[9] Pollution? Nickel smelters belch sulfur dioxide, which is the main cause of acid rain. One heavy nickel-producing area in Siberia provides a fifth of the world's supply and emits more sulfur dioxide in a year than all of France.[10] Think of that the next time you're feeling annoyed by an unwieldy jarful of coins on the kitchen counter, or the small-change compartment of a wallet that has become so overloaded that it won't snap shut.

Even banknotes, made from cotton and linen or, more recently, plastic, aren't innocent. It takes close to half a gallon of water to grow the cotton used in a $100 bill (and 100 gallons to make a T-shirt). That cotton and water consumption may not spell doom for the planet, but you would be hard pressed to make the case that the manufacturing process, complete with the chemical dyes and printing equipment to be disposed of in some unlucky Maryland and Texas landfills, is environmentally benign.*

From there, the eco-costs of cash grow like compound interest: fuel for transport, electricity to run manufacturing plants and cash depots, and the armada of trucks and vans ferrying cash between banks, stores, and warehouses in what amounts to a worldwide logistical morass and emissions orgy hiding in plain sight.

---

*U.S. paper money is made at two facilities, one in Washington, D.C., and the other in Fort Worth, Texas.

◆

IN THE VICTORIAN BALLROOM of the Charing Cross Hotel in London, the thirteenth annual Digital Money Forum is wrapping up with a session of free beer and wine. Beneath brass chandeliers, people from the worlds of banking, telecom, academia, and international development have absorbed an entire weekend's worth of talk about money in the form of bits and bytes, and tomorrow's technologies for handling it.

I came here with high hopes, thinking it would open up a world of dazzling ideas and *Star Trek*–like technologies that are poised to usurp cash. But the forum proved to be just too conferencey, with its drip, drip, drip of PowerPoint presentations, impenetrable corporate jargon, and technical speak. There were a few high points, but by the tea-and-cakes break on the first afternoon, I was already feeling fidgety and uneasy. I'd lost sight of why I was here—whether it even matters, really, what form of money we use.

To get back on the cashless society track, the next morning in nearby Covent Gardens I meet technologist, ubiquitous future-of-money commentator, and self-described "anti-cash maniac" Dave Birch. Birch is the spiritual guru, organizer, and emcee of the forum. I had invited him to accompany me to the Bank of England so that I could hear him make the case against cash on its home turf.

With a gray beard and round glasses, the fifty-year-old Birch looks more like a theology professor than an electronic money and digital security expert. As we walk to the Tube station, we pass a street performer with a guitar singing Michael Jackson's "The Way You Make Me Feel." Birch slows to deliver a £1 coin into the man's guitar case. "We are going to have to figure out how to do *that* in the digital money future," he says.

A huge portion of the workforce, especially in the United States, depends on tips. They are real people with real jobs, often the kind that require long hours on your feet and the ability to provide service with a smile to customers undeserving of one. They are waiters, doormen, baristas, cab drivers, bartenders, strippers, and more, and it goes without saying that shunning cash for a year would be severely costly, if not impossible, for many of them.

Yet as straightforward a transaction as tipping appears—it's just a reward for good service, right?—think about the confusion that sometimes arises when trying to figure out how much you should leave when all you had was a beer, while your friend had the ribs-and-pork combo platter. Then there's the condition you might call Non-natives' Tipping Anxiety. I've seen many friends visiting from overseas fret about whether or how much to tip, where, and when. There are even disagreements among those of us who grew up with this custom. Leave a tip for the hotel staff that tidies your room? Some say only upon checkout, others say not at all. My sister says absolutely yes, every morning of your stay. And, of course, there is the mystifying calculus for determining just how much to leave. As Benjamin Franklin is believed to have said while living in Paris: "To overtip is to appear an ass: to undertip is to appear an even greater ass."[11]

The countries of Europe where wealthy Americans originally picked up the custom of tipping have long since replaced it with a more equitable and economical service tax. Should you be tempted to think that we simply must keep cash around because the generous act of tipping would become endangered without it, consider the fact that people tip more, on average, when paying with plastic. As for the street performers of the future, Birch says this is in fact a nominal obstacle, technologically speaking, on the road to cashlessness. Soon enough, we'll be able to give someone a few dollars or pounds simply by aiming an electronic device—if not our iPhones, Androids, and Blackberries, then something similar—and pressing a few keys. "The barriers to going with digital money across the board are coming down," he says.

We step into a coffee shop, but the queue is a dozen people deep. Birch U-turns for the exit, catching the swinging door. "I wouldn't be a real capitalist actor if I stayed to wait," he says, heading for another café just a block away.

The second stop is a window facing out onto the street. No line this time. Birch orders a latte to go. While fishing change from his pants pocket, he spills a handful of coins onto the curb. He pauses, staring down at the shrapnel. "There. Now you have another reason to do away with cash," he says, before stooping his portly frame to retrieve scattered 1-pound, 50-pence, and 25-pence pieces. His expression is reminiscent of a homeowner removing someone else's dog's crap from the front lawn. (The metaphor has precedent: Freud ventured that there is a psychological connection between money and feces.)

"Today something like one out of every twenty £1 coins is counterfeit," Birch says as we continue our walk through the drizzle. Those forged coins are presumably manufactured in grungy machine shops in countries like Romania and Bulgaria—someplace so poor that the economics of counterfeiting £1 coins makes sense. In the United States, we don't have counterfeit coins. Let me rephrase that: the government's tacit assumption is that coin-counterfeiting operations don't exist, or don't exist on a scale sufficient to justify the expense of looking for fakes. "Not that people even want coins," says Birch. "Something like 40 percent of all the pennies ever issued in the UK are unaccounted for. Did you know that?" Pennies are unaccounted for because people don't use them. The ones we get stuck with at the checkout counter usually end up lost for years in desk and bureau drawers.[12]

The useless coinage picture is no better in the United States. The U.S. Mint has manufactured about half a trillion coins over the past generation, yet the mint itself estimates that 200 billion of them have fallen out of circulation.[13] According to one estimate, Americans forfeit $1 billion a year due to the time spent dealing with pennies at cash registers and in wallets, when we could be doing something else, like generating income or thinking up the next Facebook. These small-change realities have compelled countries like Israel, Brazil, Australia, Finland, Argentina, and New Zealand to euthanize 0.01, and sometimes 0.05, currency pieces, while also shrinking the dimensions of their larger-denomination coins to further bring down manufacturing costs. Over the past few decades, Norway, Denmark, and Sweden eliminated all coins of value less than fifty øre (like fifty cents), and last year, Sweden's fifty øre was the latest to get the axe. It's an odd thing: killing money to save money. But that's exactly what's happening.

Pennies, nickels, and dimes can barely be described as money anymore. Legally they are, sure, but they don't exactly circulate. A store of value? Practically nil. Medium of exchange? Only if you have a boatload of them, which won't exactly endear you to whomever you're transacting with. A unit of account? Technically, but I don't know anyone who uses the hundredths place in his mental accounting. Marketing types will be quick to tell you that consumers treat $2.99 differently from $3.00, but that's because of the hypnotic power of the *left* digit. No one cares about the right one anymore. It's no wonder then that people so willingly pay the usurious 8.9 percent fee to use one of Coinstar's 20,000 kiosks to convert unwieldy jarfuls of metal into paper money.[14]

In the United States, the question of killing at least the penny and nickel surfaces whenever the price of metals spikes. A few years ago, the cost of making a penny peaked at 1.8 cents per cent, and nine cents for a nickel.[15] The penny has since come down; nickels are still at about six cents apiece, while each of the new dollar coins costs an impressive thirty-four cents. "The current situation is unprecedented," the director of the U.S. Mint told Congress in the summer of 2010. "Compared to their face values, never before in our nation's history has the government spent as much money to mint and issue coins." Never before has the United States faced such "spiraling" costs to issued coinage—more, in fact, than the coins' legal tender value. "This problem is needlessly wasting hundreds of millions of dollars."[16]

"Absolutely anyone else would get right out of the penny and nickel business," says Birch. At this point, you'd think the only staunch defenders of the penny and the nickel are the companies that provide the base materials, Coinstar, and politicians with a metallic sense of nostalgia or a coin-enthusiast relative. Yet a USA *Today*/Gallup Poll from a few years ago found that 55 percent of Americans say the penny is "useful" and shouldn't be eliminated. Who *are* these people?

The $1 note has its own powerful supporters, not the least of which are employees of the money factory itself, the Bureau of Engraving and Printing (BEP). In the mid-1990s, BEP employees, under the banner "Save the Greenback," stymied congressional efforts to phase out the $1 bill. (Paper money is cheaper than coins to produce, but it doesn't last as long, so it's actually more expensive in the long run.) Greenback defenders had help from Mississippi Senator Trent Lott and Massachusetts Senator Ted Kennedy, who had in mind the interests of Crane Paper of Dalton, Massachusetts, sole provider of U.S. currency paper, which is made from Mississippi-grown genetically engineered cotton. The group even proposed legislation explicitly prohibiting the elimination of the greenback, but the bill—the legislative one—never passed.

Yet there are at least a few signs that U.S. officialdom is rethinking coins. "What's a Penny (or a Nickel) Really Worth?" was the title of a 2007 paper published by the Federal Reserve Bank of Chicago. Since medieval times, the traditional fix when minting costs surpassed the face value of the coinage was to "debase the threatened coin, that is, make it of a cheaper material." Noting that this isn't possible under current law, the author's advice to Congress is to either give the Treasury the green light to find some cheaper substance for future pennies, or "discontinue the one-cent denomination and rebase pennies to be worth five cents."[17]

Discontinue. That is unusually decisive, if not subversive, language for a Fed official. Why? Because eliminating the penny is an admission of inflation. "You just don't do that," a seasoned financial journalist once told me, as if I'd just suggested toppling the government. "What does a formal acknowledgement of the worthlessness of 1¢ say about the worth of $1?" In other words, it doesn't help the economy to remind people that prices are continually rising, while the purchasing power of their money is continually falling, even though both are true. Acknowledging inflation makes people doubt, and as any priest, rabbi, imam, or shaman will tell you, doubt and faith don't go well together. Even though research suggests that killing the penny would benefit the economy, how can we be sure? All of a sudden, the seemingly small idea of ending pennies isn't merely about inconvenient objects or the various uses for zinc. It's about the whole damn economy.

We're sensitive about inflation because higher prices are a drag, and because of concerns, rational or otherwise, that it might metastasize into something much worse: *hyperinflation*. This is when the purchasing power of a currency falls off a cliff, while prices rocket upward so fast that people must race to get money out of their pockets before it devalues further in the next few days or even hours. A lifetime's savings last week can't buy a loaf of bread this week.*

The most famous example of hyperinflation hit the Weimar Republic (Germany) in the early 1920s, caused in large part by Germany's inability to pay World War I reparations owed to its neighbors. At its nadir, the exchange rate was 4,200,000,000,000 marks to 1 U.S. dollar, and the government was printing 100,000,000,000,000-mark banknotes (yes, one-hundred trillion) in a failing attempt to keep up with rising prices. The situation was so traumatic that it helped the insane ideas of Nazism take root and fester.

Forty years since the steep inflation of the 1970s, the prices Americans interact with in daily life have remained remarkably stable relative to incomes. A cold Florida winter might bump up the cost of oranges, and the price of oil rose high enough a few years ago for President George W. Bush to acknowledge the U.S. addiction to oil, but that's not inflation. In-your-face inflation is when you have to run down supermarket aisles, as people had to do for more than a decade in Brazil, to get ahead of the person whose job every few days was to increase the price of all the items. Younger Americans today have been so lulled by economic stability that the notion of all prices surging upward is alien. A $100 hot dog or a $10,000 sheet of plywood only reads like a typo because of our good fortune.

---

*What we should be sweating instead is deflation. Economists generally regard inflation's fraternal twin as more damaging and much harder to remedy. When prices go down, money in pockets becomes more valuable, which means it stays put, like hoarded gold, leading the economy to a precarious standstill. Business owners, consumers, investors—no one lends, spends, or hires.

Still, those images from pathological instances of hyperinflation are plenty searing: banknotes used as wallpaper in Zimbabwe, swept into the gutter in postwar Budapest, or spilling out of wheelbarrows in Germany like so many leaves. One German artist during the Weimar hyperinflation covered a park bench with 100,000-mark notes. He titled the work "Deutsche Bank," a pun on the German word for bench, which is *bank*. We can only pray that the same never happens here. Fears about inflation and hyperinflation may not always be rational, but countermeasures against them sure as hell are. In a roundabout way, then, maybe the wise move really is to spend whatever's necessary to fund small coinage so as to prevent worries about inflation. What's riskier: producing and circulating annoying coins at a loss, or injuring morale about the economy so much as to undermine faith in more than just the value of those little metal discs?[18]

The elegant fix to all of this, of course, is to keep the *denomination* known as the penny—heck, even bring back the half-penny if you're so inclined—but keep it sequestered in the cheaper and more efficient digital realm. Yet the Federal Reserve, Bank of England, European Central Bank, and most other central banks on the planet are pressing ahead with their coin orders. The next big coinage spree in the United States will be the $1 presidential series. By 2016, the Fed should have about $2 billion worth of $1 coins available, even though many merchants and cash handling companies won't stock them because people don't use them. Aside from those that end up stashed in collectors' cases, the rest will gather dust in government vaults until you and I can be convinced of their utility.[19] If you're wondering what in God's name these money managers are thinking, you're not alone.

◆

EXITING THE UNDERGROUND, Birch and I spot the Gherkin in all its eggy rocket-ship glory. Now we are in the thick of it, The City, as in the City of London. This cluster of broad classical buildings is the economic center of the former empire that built a colossal financial system out of stocks, bonds, and credit. The Royal Exchange is on our right, and the limestone fortress itself, the Bank of England, on our left. "This is the enemy," says Birch, turning into the entrance of the Bank Museum.

Fiat money wasn't invented here, but the Bank of England gave the world one of the first globally recognized currencies, the pound sterling, and showed how effectively states, particularly cash-strapped states at war, could raise funds by having a private bank issue government-backed currency in the form of paper. As such, the Old Lady of Threadneedle Street, as the Bank is affectionately known, is in many ways the die cast from which modern central banks are struck. Although banknotes aren't manufactured at central banks, this is the point of conception, where the miracle of cash's life begins.[20]

Inside the dark foyer, the first thing we see is a public service notice: a large pink poster announcing the withdrawal from circulation of all £20 notes with a portrait of classical music composer Sir Edward Elgar. After June 2010, only the new £20 notes, featuring Adam Smith, will be considered legal tender in the UK. Reissues, as we'll learn more about soon, usually happen because of counterfeiting. If you still happen to have any £20s with Elgar on them, tough luck. iPhone in hand, Birch inspects the poster and shakes his head. "New versions of expensive paper," he says. "Is this *really* what we need?"

Unlike most countries, which periodically demonetize certain coins or banknotes, all notes and coins ever issued in the United States are legal tender. This policy is supposed to reinforce the aura of U.S. economic stability. It's also why redesigns of greenbacks preserve those "legacy features," as the Federal Reserve calls them, that people associate with U.S. paper money: pukey light-green color, founding fathers, a jumble of fonts.[21] Although you technically could, you probably don't want to spend super-rare coins or bills inherited from your great grandmother, because their collector's value is a hundred times greater than their face value.

The museum is quiet and mostly empty today, which seems to happen at money museums on days when there are no school field trips scheduled, and when numismatists (coin geeks) and notaphilists (bank-note nerds) are stuck at their day jobs. One kid-friendly display in the main hall is a hot-air balloon basket, inside of which is an explanation about how central banks target inflation rates to keep economic growth on track. The idea is that adding or removing money from the economy is like adding or reducing the amount of hot air in a balloon, thereby keeping the flight on track. (To where, the exhibit doesn't say.) Birch looks up from his phone, which he has been tapping at for much of the day. "I already know about inflation. It's their fault," he says, bobbing his head toward the ceiling to indicate the bank's higher-ups.

To Americans, Birch may seem like a prototypical libertarian who wants to shutter his country's central bank and let the chips fall where they may. He is suspicious of government-issued currency because governments—notorious deficit spenders—have a dismal track record as guardians of money's worth. He's also enthusiastic about a future full of all sorts of different currencies, which we'll get to later. But Birch takes umbrage with the monetary system deployed by governments for reasons that are more technological than ideological. "I don't hate money. I hate cash!" A major reason for that hatred is the question of who foots the bill.

A typical burst of anti-cash restiveness on Birch's blog goes like this: "The cost of cash isn't only the cost of the notes and coins, the ATMs and armored cars, the night safes and counting machines. It's the lack of efficiency in the economy that goes with it. And economies that are stuck with cash are the worst off." And then *he's* off, serving up a rapid-fire summary of research results unearthed, conference highlights shared, media articles skimmed, and factoids gathered about the annual cost of cash-handling in Indonesia (more than $800 million); counterfeit bills in Canada; thieves tunneling their way into a bank vault in Argentina (he called it "the Shawshank Redistribution"); and reports from Europe that most banknotes in the euro zone are used for hoarding, not spending. "The purpose of cash is no longer to support commerce," he concludes.[22]

Birch wasn't always so obsessed with money's forms, friction, and future—not until he had to digitize it. His background is in computers, where he got his start helping to link up networks in the days before the Internet. His specialty was making networks secure, which led to a corporate job traveling the world to help with secure systems at NATO, satellite communications in Southeast Asia, and reliable data communications for California's Bay Area Rapid Transit. He was one of the founders of a consultancy in the 1980s.

Secure computer networks and financial transactions have many points in common, and Birch began to build a reputation as an expert in payment technologies and electronic money systems, with clients including the likes of VISA, American Express, MasterCard, Barclay's, and the European Commission. It was in this role that he started to obsess over the costs, hassles, and hazards of different forms of money, and with the machinations of how value zips around the world. It didn't take him long to learn that the most lumbering and expensive form of money, by far, is cash. It's tough to see why, though, without first understanding who it benefits.

"This note-issuing business is the most profitable nationalized industry in British history," he says. We are now in the museum's banknote gallery, looking over original sketches for banknote art and more recent examples of "today's technologically sophisticated notes," which apparently are not too sophisticated, considering the imminent replacement of the Elgar £20. "So here's a fifty-pound note," he says, tapping the display case. "Now where is that fifty pounds, really? This is just a piece of paper, so it's not here. Where is it? On a computer, yes, but where is that value?" he asks. "No one ever thinks about this, but the answer is that the bank has bought government securities with it. That cash is really a stealth tax."

Come again? Birch is griping about the weirdest and most technical aspect of national currencies. Everyone wants to make a profit, and the institutions that manufacture and issue the money are no different. The key is something called *seigniorage*. The opaqueness of the term itself bespeaks the "secret incantation" of central banks and "transactions so powerful and frightening they seem[ed] to lie beyond common understanding," as William Greider put it in *Secrets of the Temple: How the Federal Reserve Runs the Country.*[23] All it is, though, is profit pocketed by central banks and their governments, earned for providing us with currency with which to go about our business.

Because the cost of making a coin or banknote is (usually) less than the face value of the object itself, the supplier of the money gets to keep the difference. The new state quarters series issued by the U.S. Mint, for example, has already earned the Federal Reserve an estimated $4.6 billion in seigniorage.[24] In total, the Fed will have earned about $70 billion in 2010 and 2011 by way of providing you, me, and the rest of the greenback-using world with physical money.[25] (The Fed also earns seigniorage when it issues electronic money, but that's a more convoluted form of earning over time, compared with straight-shot profit, which is like any business that sells its product for more than it costs to produce. Then again, having a legal monopoly makes this very much unlike other businesses.)

Conspiracy theorists in the United States tend to obsess over seigniorage and the Federal Reserve's semi-private nature, claiming that the Fed is a malevolent secret society—think Knights Templar meets the Council on Foreign Relations. These evildoers, say the theorists, use their power and wealth to manipulate world governments to their benefit. The more boring fate of seigniorage is that the Fed transfers this profit to the Treasury at year's end. Nevertheless, Birch's notion of the stealth tax isn't wrong. Currency issued by the central bank *is* an interest-free loan from the people to the bank. It depends on your politics, though, whether this profit constitutes the government ripping off the people, or the government of the people earning revenue to spend on its citizens.

Whether we really need national currency in physical form is an offshoot of that broader debate. The thing you must remember about money, says Birch, is that it's not one thing. "Economists will tell you about all these different functions of money—unit of account, method of deferred payment, store of value and all that." Looking at money in this way, he says, illuminates the disadvantages and waste from using cash. "Think about how people and society have already replaced cash with electronic money in so many ways." It would be absurd, for example, for anyone today with adequate savings to hide all his wealth at home or make big-ticket purchases using cash. Say what you will about the deficiencies of banks and credit card companies—and there is plenty to say—but the comparative safety and relative security their products afford is precisely why they have become so enormously profitable. Storing value and transacting in cash, in contrast, is a risky and friction-filled proposition.

Birch is right that to transport, store, secure, examine, reissue, shred, and print all the money in the world costs a fortune. Precise numbers are hard to come by, perhaps not surprisingly considering the franchises at stake, but one estimate from 1994 is that the United States spent $60 billion on cash management. By 2005 that figure was estimated at $110 billion.[26] Processing paper checks adds another $50 billion on to that bill.[27] In 2007, Europe's €360 billion in cash transactions cost around €50 billion ($70 billion). That expense is primarily borne by merchants, although it doesn't take an economist to know that merchants pass those costs on to you and me in the form of higher prices.

By some estimates, countries could save 1 percent of their annual GDP if they were to shift from a paper to a fully digital monetary system.[28] For the United States, that would put the annual costs of cash in the ballpark of $150 billion, or about three times the annual budget of the U.S. Department of Education. True, these savings would be reduced by the cost of implementing and maintaining a digital money paradise, but the logistics would be so dramatically reduced that the savings would still be enormous.

Cash is a financial burden for just about everyone in its life cycle who has to handle it, aside from employees of the U.S. Mint, the printing bureaus and their contractors, and multi-billion-dollar logistics firms like Brinks and Loomis. Banks in particular don't like having to babysit physical money. In 2009 and 2010 there were more than 10,000 bank robberies in the United States alone. "Banks don't like cash and don't want to invest in it," says Michael T. Dan, chairman, president, and CEO of Texas-based Brinks. Might the bankers' judgment on this be a hint to the rest of us?[29]

Birch steps back into the foyer for a moment to make a call. He looks a little distressed. He's been to this museum a number of times before— know thine enemy, I suppose—but I get the sense that this place makes him physically uncomfortable. Far from signifying stately grandeur and a rock-solid economy, the stone walls and stodgy traditions symbolize the kind of fuddy-duddy refusal to move forward that is anathema to someone who accepts the premise that technological innovation drives positive change.

Maybe he's overreacting, though. Now that ATMs are pretty much everywhere, cash isn't exactly hard to come by. Doesn't that nullify, or at least weaken, the argument that cash is really so inconvenient and expensive? When I ask about this, Birch looks at me like I'm nuts.

ATMs may have lessened the costs of using cash for people in wealthy countries, because restocking our wallets is fairly easy, but in other ways they've only served to conceal costs—and add new ones. Securing them is the most obvious one. In one London neighborhood, ATM users have been mugged so many times that there's now a police hotline that people can call to request an escort to the ATM. "Who pays for that? We do!" Birch says.

This kind of inanity is Birch's specialty: the Shanghai man who saved 37,000 coins over the period of a decade, only to learn that exchanging them for banknotes requires a fee, one yuan for every fifty coins, which would total more than the overall value of his two sacks full of coins.[30] "Or did you see the story about the £60,000 in cash found rotting in a basement?" Birch asks. I had not. "We all pay for that. There is even the cost of the reissued £20," he says, gesturing back toward the poster about the doomed Elgar £20 series. In Japan, tens of thousands of police are deployed to banks and ATMs around the country on pension day, when elderly citizens withdrawing cash are at risk of being robbed or conned into some on-the-spot scam. Like it or not, citizens foot the bill for this police presence, just as they do for all of the investigations and prosecutions of cash crimes throughout the world.[31] In (literally) cash-strapped Argentina, inflation and a scarcity of bills have recently forced some residents to line up at the bank the night before it opens, to be able to withdraw money the next morning.[32] In Ireland in 2010, a government minister floated the idea of taxing people for ATM withdrawals. If people use them less, maybe the incentive for robbery would also decrease. He got the idea after a gang kidnapped a bank manager's wife and ransomed her for €300,000.[33] The tax proposal was quickly shot down.

◆

IN THE FALL OF 2010, the U.S. Treasury announced that the new $100 bill's official release date would be postponed. The new C-note was originally slated to enter circulation in 2008, but it was bumped once to 2011, and now it was being bumped again. Some of the paper fed into the presses had a slight fold, so the ink wasn't perfectly applied over the notes, and the bills came off the presses with a tiny blank spot.[34]

Because cash provides numerous benefits to society, I had hoped, perhaps naively, Treasury or Bureau of Engraving and Printing officials might talk openly about the mistake. Without sharing how-to secrets with counterfeiters, they could use the episode as an opportunity to remind the public of the benefits of cash, and that providing an ample and secure supply of hard currency is no simple feat.

For the time being, however, no one is talking, and it's doubtful the costs of this snafu will ever be made public. It would be interesting math. The plagued bills, we've been told, cost $120 million to make, but at press time $1 billion worth of the notes were still quarantined and awaiting inspection by BEP and Treasury officials. The investigation and cleanup will prove costly: retrieving, examining, and destroying the old notes; repairing or replacing equipment; the expense borne by banks that need to resupply their cash supplies; and all those indirect costs, like fuel and CO_2 emissions from all those armored trucks that have had to fetch the bunk bills and then redeliver the good ones some-time in the near future.[35]

By and large, though, most people are disinclined to contemplate the costs of their cash. In the United States, it's as if we are so consumed with anger toward credit card companies and overpaid investment bankers that we just don't have energy left to fret, complain about, or even notice the liabilities of cash. If anything, the opposite is true: according to a recent Fed survey, almost 67 percent of people said cash is a "very low cost" form of payment—the least costly, *by far*, compared to credit and debit cards, checks, prepaid cards, and bank transfers.[36] How could we be so far off the mark?

Another recent Fed study took a closer look at rewards cards—the ones that provide airline miles, hotel points, shopping or restaurant discounts, and other "cashback" incentives. Not surprisingly, customers who use this type of credit card are generally more affluent. Low-income people, if they can afford credit cards at all, aren't going to sign up for ones requiring an annual fee.

Someone has to pay for those supposed freebies. The banks cough up part of the dough, but the Fed economists found that the rest of it comes from cash users, which is to say poorer households. To cover the fees levied by the card companies for the "privilege" of electronic payment, merchants charge higher prices across the board. The result is "an implicit monetary transfer to credit card users from no-card (or 'cash') users," wrote the Fed economists. While the average cardholder enrolled in a perks program receives about $750 worth of rewards every year, the average cash user pays about $20 a year so that someone he or she doesn't know can score a free night at the Marriott.

The report opened peoples' eyes, if only a little, to the fact that these rewards aren't gifts—someone always has to pay. I'm all for information that gets people thinking more critically about the workings and hidden costs of different forms of money, but when Birch read this study he saw something else: a continuation, really, of material money's Houdini-like ability to escape criticism. No one ever looks at, or even mentions, the negative impacts of cash on society as a whole. It's as if we just can't come to terms with the notion that cash has costs.

When viewed through this lens, says Birch, "credit card and non-cash users are subsidizing cash users," to the detriment of all. In other words, the steep costs of cash are absorbed by everyone, including people who choose to bypass using it.[37] And should you be tempted to think that the poor might be disenfranchised by all this pro-digital money talk, or that the needs of lower-income people aren't being addressed by the likes of Birch and his banking industry pals, don't. We'll get to how cash is hardest on the poor soon enough.

Retailers on the other end of your transactions have mixed feelings about cash. Some hate credit and debit cards because of the fees, so they take the cash-only route, thinking these are their only realistic options, which is often the case—for now. One study suggests that a sale by way of a credit card can cost a merchant as much as six times what the same sale might cost if the costumer paid in cash.[38] And cash is obviously effective for merchants who are of a mind to dodge the taxman.

Other merchants, however, are waking up to the high price of using cash in their operations. The risk of robbery has always been a big one for mom-and-pop shops, and accepting and dispensing cash costs businesses millions of dollars' worth of labor hours due to the time and manpower required for cashiers to hand out correct change down to the last penny.[39] That price only increases for businesses that maintain cash's availability for fewer and fewer customers who use it.[40] Kill cash, and you can have fewer cashiers, fewer security issues, no employees skimming off the top, and fewer germs to boot.

As a business owner, there's nothing stopping you from forsaking cash except convention. In the United States, no federal statute requires merchants to accept legal tender. You get to set the terms of payment—the money's form, price, pay schedule, currency—that you're to receive in exchange for your proffered goods and services. *Legal tender* only means that if I already have a debt, in dollars, owed to you or your bank, you can't suddenly refuse me when I try to pay up with greenbacks. Otherwise, as a business owner, you are well within your rights to stipulate that you only accept payment in the form of Japanese yen, tango lessons, uncut rubies, electronic transfer of airline miles, or gold coins in an on-line videogame.

The cashless cabin policy of many major airlines is case in point. Another example is an uppity Manhattan restaurant called Commerce. Explaining his decision to quit accepting cash payments, co-owner Tony Zazula told the *Wall Street Journal*: "If you don't have a credit card, you can use a debit card. If you don't have a debit card, you probably don't have a checking account. And if you don't have a checking account, you probably shouldn't be eating at Commerce to begin with." Think of it as the Zazula plan to reduce America's addiction to debt, one overpriced, classist meal at a time. Customers can, however, leave cash tips.[41]

◆

BIRCH IS PLEASED to report new allies lining up in support of the war on cash, even if their stance is less "militant" than his own. Recognizing the inefficiencies of checks, the government of the UK has set a target to abolish them by the fall of 2018.[42] True, checks aren't banknotes, but they're similarly inefficient and expensive. Paying for something with a check is like opening your wallet to a bunch of strangers on the street, and each of them—the check-printing firm, financial institution, transit company, clearing house, banks, and, if you get your voided checks back in the mail, the postal service—all get a cut or need some form of external compensation.[43]

Meanwhile, university and corporate campuses, hospitals, and military bases are already cashless mini-societies, where residents use payment systems like barcode badges linked to personal accounts, or stored-value cards. (This is basically the same technology that makes your payment as you glide through an EZ-pass toll booth.) And a quiet uprising against cash is underway in other settings, too. In the Netherlands, supermarkets are aiming to be cashless by 2014, and a Dutch consortium of retailers has established a commission (code name: Taskforce

Cashless) to educate the public that electronic money equals saving money.[44]

The countries of Scandinavia, especially Sweden, are taking an even harder line. Swedes have a cultural tradition of using cash, and, as a result, they also have a lot of robberies. One of them took place in the fall of 2009. With a stolen helicopter, thieves landed on the roof of a cash depot outside of Stockholm, rappelled through a blown-out hole in a skylight, and within minutes had filled duffle bags with seven million Swedish krona (about $5 million) before climbing back into the helicopter and taking off to the north.* Yet even before this Hollywood-style heist, crusaders like Birch had already been eyeing Sweden, where the governor of the central bank, Stefan Ingves, was earning a reputation for speaking up about the costs of physical money.[45]

"People don't think they should pay for getting cash," Ingves told me. "They think money is a free good, and that they should have access to cash and correct change anywhere and always. They take for granted that there are enough notes and coins available wherever they go to buy things, without thinking about how that works." The distribution and safeguarding of cash is a centuries-old challenge that many governments and banks have risen to quite impressively. Yet we forget that this isn't just a service of the commercial bank or the company that owns the ATM. It's also a service paid for by the government supplying the notes in the first place. Every day throughout the world, some 500 million new banknotes move between printers, central banks, and their customers.[46] And that's just the new stuff.

In one speech, Ingves argued that the cost of robberies, from security personnel and insurance payouts to investigations and prosecutions, should be factored into the overall accounting when a country considers what it spends, and what it ought to spend, on cash.[47] In the past few

---

*A few years earlier, another cash depot, this one in Britain, was hit for more than £53 million ($92.5 million) after the depot manager was abducted and his wife and son held hostage.

years, Swedish police, citizens, politicians, and bankers have intensified the anti-cash campaign. A union of thousands of bank employees is lobbying the government to eliminate material money, and their campaign has even received the odd but irresistibly noteworthy endorsement of former Abba band member Bjorn Ulvaeus.[48]

But if you hadn't already guessed, most governments still don't see cash in such a negative light. As with coins, orders for banknotes are up—way up—even though cash usage continues declining. For the U.S. dollar, the value of cash in circulation has gone from $51 billion in 1970 to $1 trillion in 2011.[49]

More physical money delivered into circulation yet declining reliance on it for doing business—how could that be? Where's it going? A cash-friendly interpretation of this trend is that people are turning to it as a more reliable place to park wealth in times of economic turmoil. If interest rates and inflation are both low, why not just hold on to your cash? If your confidence in, or enthusiasm for, financial institutions has been shaken of late—and unless you live under a rock, it has—then even more reason to cling to your paper.[50]

People have indeed retreated from using credit cards in recent years. Many consumers even turned away from debit cards, in a kind of backlash against any bank product (except the central bank's). In one study, 42 percent of people surveyed reported that they were using cash more in 2010 than they were in 2009.[51] Unfortunately, this shift in behavior only accounts for a small fraction of the physical money in the system, and it fails to thoroughly explain why there is so much cash circulating, how people use it, and why it's so coveted.

As if channeling the anti–Robin Hood, Birch lays it out plainly. "Cash is a black hole for tax revenue." We're lingering beside a museum display case crowded with centuries-old receipts, written in sweeping cursive, documenting loan amounts, payments made, and taxes collected. By supplying us with cash, he says, governments enable the very evasion they wish to curb. "Doesn't anyone else find this at all odd?"

Birch elaborated in a blog post: "No one uses 500-euro notes for day-to-day transactions, and if they were withdrawn from circulation it wouldn't make the slightest difference to the 99.97% of the European population that isn't trying to avoid Spanish property taxes."[52] Similar critiques have been leveled against $100 bills. Although Benjamins are "small denomination currency," according to the Bureau of Engraving and Printing's website, they account for about 60 percent of notes in circulation.[53] In 2010 alone, $268 billion worth of $100 bills were printed, the majority of which were or will soon be whisked overseas because that's where most of the banks and drug dealers demanding it are.[54] The Fed itself estimates that 90 percent of all C-notes have been sent to foreign banks, and most of those notes have no interest in repatriating.[55]

Although governments profit by providing cash, they're also swindled out of huge amounts because of it. It's part of what the IRS calls the tax gap: the difference between what taxpayers should cough up and what they actually pay.[56] In 2008, some 84 percent of Americans voluntarily reported and paid what they owed.[57] But there's still that gap: almost $350 *billion* a year.

On his blog, Birch recounts a conversation he had with a fellow consultant. The guy had just boasted that he was saving a lot of money by paying his contractors in cash—"£50 notes in bundles of £2,000." Birch responded that he should be reported to the police and prosecuted for conspiring to evade taxes, because that was obviously why the contractors wanted cash. "My objection," Birch continued, "is that by helping other people [and himself] to evade tax, the person in question was making me pay more tax: the use of cash facilitates the transfer of wealth from the law-abiding (e.g., me) to the law-breaking (e.g., his builders). This seems immoral to me."[58] It also helps illuminate why Birch defies the easy characterization often assigned to people who complain about fiat currencies. Part of the reason he favors electronic money is precisely because it would *help* government, insofar as making tax evasion harder.

In the United States overt evasion, or for that matter cash-enabled evasion, doesn't account for all uncollected taxes. Intentional evasion is only one piece of the noncompliance equation. Noncompliance, or taxes not paid, can result from underreporting (accidental or intentional), underpayment (accidental or intentional), and nonfiling (accidental or intentional, but let's not kid ourselves—this one is intentional, as jailed actor Wesley Snipes can attest). Every year the U.S. government loses nearly $260 billion due to individuals underreporting, underpaying, or not filing their taxes. The rest of the gap is from businesses.*

Yet dodging taxes has become such a regular part of life that the Dave Birches of the world end up sounding like spoilers, even though his is a decidedly unradical plea: pay your share, so everyone can have as low a tax rate as possible.

One peculiar aspect of tax evasion in the United States is that the demographic most likely to engage in it is often the same one that gripes about one of its more severe consequences: the deflating dollar. Think about what happens to countries in which people grossly underpay their taxes. (I'm looking at you, Greece.) The government, economy, and currency are weakened to the breaking point. Even if the government isn't about to capsize, a monstrous tax gap can compound budgetary problems—which hurts the economy, which hurts confidence in the currency, which can send the currency's value south. By worsening the government's budgetary woes, tax evaders contribute to the diminishment of everyone's money, including their own unreported cache.

It's almost amusing to hear people say the government should keep its hands off their money. Not that government should confiscate peoples' wealth, but this complaint reveals just how poorly we understand money's value. You may have seen the anti-Obama bumper stickers or placards at Tea Party events: "I'll keep my money, freedom, & guns. You keep the change." But as long as you're talking about the national currency, the government *is* your money or, more accurately, your money only has value because of confidence in the government's capacity to

---

*These are 2001 figures, which, unfortunately, is the last time the tax gap was measured.

govern and cover its debts. If the government truly kept its hands off your money, you'd definitely be left with none.

Practically speaking, though, there is a big difference between an impoverished housecleaner failing to report a few hundred dollars, and corporations and individuals hiding tens of billions of dollars overseas or behind convoluted legal schemes. The economy being as tight as it is for so many people, it's hard not to sympathize with the housecleaner, and millions of other people teetering on the financial edge, for underpaying taxes. How would I not do the same if it were a matter of putting food on the table?

But in principle, there are no gradations of deliberate evasion, and it's a curious thing that this $350 billion tax gap is of such little interest to the public. Despite that other ethic, the one that advises us to mind our own business, Birch is right. It is our business whether our fellow citizens pay their share. Functioning democracy depends on it, and, even if you don't buy that, let's at least be honest about the difference between legitimate arguments in favor of cash and objections that are really only about preserving the freedom to skip paying taxes.

Not that the criminality stops there.

◆

THE PREVIOUS DAY, during the Digital Money Forum, a presentation that did grab my attention was one that detailed cash's role as the currency of the underworld. In Italy, off-the-books transactions rob the government of about €100 billion annually, or about 20 percent of the country's GDP. For Greece, it's over 27 percent.[59] Not to pick on these two countries: the United States, Belgium, Spain, and even stereotypically square Germany are all near or in the double digits when it comes to the magnitude of their shadow economies.

Much of this is made possible by the existence of high-denomination banknotes. Everyday citizens increasingly avoid carrying them, yet 500-, 200- and 100-euro notes make up 60 percent of the nearly half a trillion euros of cash circulating on the continent, although "circulating," as we've seen, is a relative term. A recent Bank of Italy study concluded that the €500 bill is the beloved tool of smugglers, money launderers, and drug dealers. In Spain, the €500 note is nicknamed the "Bin Laden": no one has ever seen one, but everyone knows what they look like.

It's just that much easier to store, manage, and move large amounts of money when each banknote has more value. In 2003, U.S. soldiers in Iraq discovered $650 million in crisp new Benjamins in one of Saddam Hussein's palaces. One million dollars in C-notes weighs twenty-two pounds, whereas the equivalent value in euros only weighs between 3.5 and four pounds. When an Afghan official was accused in 2010 of taking $52 million out of Afghanistan, he proclaimed his innocence by saying: "It's not true. $52 million is a pile of money as big as this room!" (He hasn't been charged with anything.)[60] Meanwhile, U.S. military officials working in Iraq and Afghanistan are trying to replace physical money with debit cards and other electronic systems. The goal is to reduce the "insidious military consequences of this large-scale reliance on cash," writes one senior army official, because when you want to buy weapons on the black market, cash is the bomb.[61]

Birch seems to relish illustrations of cash's role in crime—validations, really, that cash is a "menace" that often undermines the efforts of the very governments that supply it. While cotton-industry lobbyists wield trite nationalism-tinged defenses for banknotes, and thieves and tax evaders rob the rest of us blind, they do so, says Birch, with cash provided to them by us. "We make their business possible, or at least much, much easier. Cash lets criminals maintain anonymity, store value, make payments—everything," which means we provide them with "a cross subsidy," he says. "When you kick down a Mexican drug dealers' door to find $205 million in cash, which happened a few years ago, you have to wonder whose side the Treasury is on."[62]

This is not a fringe opinion. The Wall Street Journal reported in July 2010: "Gangsters, drug dealers and money launderers appear to be playing their part in helping shore up the financial stability of the euro zone. That is thanks to their demand, according to European authorities, for high-denomination euro bank notes, in particular the €200 and €500 bills. The European Central Bank issues these notes for a hefty profit that is welcome at a time when its response to the financial crisis has called its financial strength into question." Banking executives as mainstream as Citigroup's chief economist have taken note of the euro's role as "currency of choice for underground and black economies."*[63]

Responding to cash's role as evasion enabler and currency of crime, some countries are trying to limit how much cash you can get, or how big a transaction you can make with paper. In Italy, any transaction involving more than €5,000 has to be paid by other means. In Greece, the government now prohibits citizens from using cash in transactions larger than €1,500.[64] A viable way to capture lost tax revenue? Probably not. How do you enforce this kind of thing? But I wouldn't call these measures ridiculous, either. If using cash for expensive one-way airline tickets were illegal, the twenty-three-year-old kid who tried to blow up that flight to Detroit may not have so easily boarded the plane. Hijacking, piracy, armed robbery—perhaps the head of the Stockholm Police Department said it best: "Cash is the blood in the veins of crime."[65]

Other governments have decided to eliminate high-value notes or push them to the periphery. Canada withdrew its CA$1,000 bill in 2000 "as part of the fight against money laundering and organized crime," according to the central bank. Money exchanges in the UK have stopped offering €500 notes after British investigators concluded that 90 percent of these notes within the country were being used domestically by—you guessed it—gangs, drug dealers, and money launderers.[66] This was the rationale of none other than the U.S. Treasury when it decided in 1969 to stop issuing $500, $1,000, $5,000, and $10,000 notes. Not that they're necessarily making much headway against the dealers and launderers. A 2010 study by U.S. Immigration and Customs Enforcement found that Mexican drug cartels launder much of their profits by shipping cash

---

*For the record, Singapore's rarely used 10,000-dollar bill, worth about $7,700 in 2011, is the world's highest value note, followed by Switzerland's 1,000-franc, which is worth about $1,100.

south across the border—between $19 billion and $29 billion a year—and then using it to buy cars, land, hotels, and other goods.[67]

The most direct link between cash and crime, of course, is robbery. Every year, 800 or so Americans are killed in cash robberies.[68] More than 10,000 bank robberies in 2009 and 2010 in the United States alone wouldn't have happened if crooks knew there was no cash to be had. Yet never have I heard someone imagine a world without cash robberies. It's as if our affection for Bonnie and Clyde, Jesse James, Butch Cassidy and the Sundance Kid, and so many other venerated villains makes us want to keep bank heists around like some kind of treasured pastime.

In 2009 a quiet French citizen named Toni Musulin, who worked as an armored car driver for ten years, finally gave in to the temptation to drive away with his cargo, which on that particular autumn day was worth an estimated €11.6 million (about $17 million). He was in over his head, though, and a few days later, Musulin walked into a police station in Monaco and surrendered.

Online, Musulin was an instant folk hero. Facebook fan pages with thousands of viewers and cascades of posts declared their support for Musulin. "Allez Toni!" one man wrote. "Viva La Revolución!" wrote another. In what feels like perilously uncertain economic times, here was this unknown man, standing up in the only way he could, to corrupt politicians and greedy bankers. That's the sweetheart version, anyway. Unfortunately for Musulin, there's no correlation between legions of Facebook admirers and the laws of France. He's currently serving five years.

As for the costs of all those bank robberies, we're stuck speculating, again. The FBI tracks information such as the "modus operandi used" (in 2010, guns were used less than 1,500 times, while vault or safe theft occurred only seventeen times) and occurrences by day of the week and time (Tuesday and Friday mornings are popular). It also tracks the number of injuries (106, mostly to bank employees), the number of deaths (sixteen, mostly perpetrators), and the amount of loot taken that year (almost $43 million in 2010). But what about the cost of physical therapy and counseling for the injured, repairs from explosions, installation of new security systems, investigations, trials, and beds in already maxed-out prisons?[69] By some estimates, eliminating cash robberies—at banks and garden-variety stickups—could save the United States almost $150 billion a year.

Graft is yet another fun use for cash. In 2009 former New Orleans Democratic representative William Jefferson was convicted of taking bribes of over $400,000—not a headliner sum in the history of payoffs by any stretch, but the $90,000 stashed in his freezer was something you don't hear about every day.[70] In 2010 investigators found that a major money-transfer business in Afghanistan was laundering billions of dollars in drug-trafficking earnings on behalf of the Taliban—made possible by sending cash overseas.[71] If that wasn't serious enough, a few months later we learned that the government of Iran regularly delivers bags of cash to one of the Afghan president's top lieutenants. Adding irony to this insult is the fact that the payments are denominated in euros. Apparently not even Iranian or Afghan officials perceive their own currencies as trustworthy stores of value.

To borrow a line from Birch: doesn't anyone else find this at all odd? In a world without cash, financial crime wouldn't disappear. But the fact that we have, and always will have, electronic theft isn't exactly a stellar reason for keeping cash around.

Birch and I finish our museum tour with a pass through the gift shop. There's no one here except an old lady stationed behind the cash register. On a whim, I decide to buy two chocolate bars. They're packaged to look like gold bars, with *Bank of England* emblazoned in a regal font. They could be fodder for a disquieting meditation about gold, money, commodities, central banking, and value itself, but the truth is that I just want some chocolate.

There's a problem at the register, though. The charge won't go through. The credit-card reader or the cashier herself isn't working properly. Either that or my cards have been canceled—I suppose the Bank of England is as good a place as any to hide from creditors. In fact, this kind of hang-up is common for Americans visiting Europe. Whereas credit cards in the United States use magnetic strip technology, cards in Europe are embedded with a little computer chip and validated when the payer enters a password. Many terminals and kiosks in Europe can't read magnetic strip-type cards. Birch probably knows more about the intricacies of this technology and the communication networks underlying it than anyone, and in this instance it looks like the equipment is capable of processing my payment. But because Birch doesn't want to embarrass the old lady by showing her what she's doing wrong, he charitably chooses to pay for my chocolate souvenirs with his British Airways American Express card.

Leaving the bank, we walk to the Underground station at Canterbury Lane. "Maybe the problem is that they're not doing the sums properly *across* government agencies," says Birch. While national treasuries receive revenue from seigniorage, other branches of government—from the IRS and FBI, to the Department of Justice and Drug Enforcement Agency—are paying up big for cash's mélange of downstream consequences. Birch asks a fair question: don't those respective budgets eventually impact how things are looking over at the Treasury?

One shorter-term proposal floated by Birch and others for taking a bite out of cash-related crime—not to mention national debts—is to demonetize higher-value banknotes, namely the $100, €500, €200, and €100. Preposterous? Probably. The United States is now rolling out its latest redo of the $100 bill. Besides, there's that whole forever-value myth to safeguard. Still, the savings from ending the C-Note would be substantial, and there's something undeniably seductive about the idea of making criminals pay for the next stimulus package.[72] "We are all getting poorer while the people who don't pay tax are getting better and better off," says Birch.[73]

He is surprisingly optimistic, though, about the direction of the war on cash, although he has no illusions about the power of opposition like the Bank of England and the Federal Reserve. Nevertheless, Birch is emboldened by an expanding legion of supporters, and the fact that those who are growing discontent with physical money's costs, and taking steps to eliminate it, are a diverse and expanding army. It's the collection of governments trying to limit cash payments; it's the money exchanges no longer selling high-value bills; it's retailers; it's bank employees; it's even military officials.

On the other hand, governments and banknote manufacturers are fighting back, hard. One way they hope to prevail is by rolling out high-tech strategies to thwart still another species of criminal, one that owes its existence to cash: counterfeiters.

CHAPTER 3

The Counterfeiters

I took out my money and unfolded it, took one glimpse and nearly fainted.
Five millions of dollars! Why, it made my head swim.

—MARK TWAIN, "THE £1,000,000 BANK NOTE"

While visiting California in the summer of 2008, a Taiwanese woman named Mei Ling Chen anxiously awaited the arrival of a parcel of dehydrated seafood she had mailed to herself from Taipei. On that July afternoon, customs officers at San Francisco International Airport Air Mail Center hit a jackpot of sorts. Inside Chen's box of would-be seafood were stacks of counterfeit U.S. $100 bills, with a face value of $380,000.[1]

The discovery was kept under wraps so that the U.S. Secret Service, the federal agency charged with thwarting currency counterfeiters, could hide a tracking device inside the package. After she was caught in the act of spending the fakes, Chen pled guilty to charges of bringing counterfeit U.S. currency into the country and passing counterfeit currency.[2] She was sentenced to almost three years in federal prison and had to forfeit goods "purchased" at Louis Vuitton, Coach, and Foot Locker.

Sounds brazen, but in the annals of counterfeiting lore, Chen is a small fish compared with, say, the $7 million worth of fake notes a Los

Angeles man produced in the early 2000s on an inkjet printer that he bought at Staples, or the millions of forged $100 notes printed by Art Williams in the 1990s, or the $16.5 million in fake bills printed by the German graphic artist Hans-Jürgen Kuhl between 2003 and 2005. Certainly Chen wasn't as daring as counterfeiters who forged coin of the realm back when the crime was punishable by death.[3] One such forger was William Chaloner, an enterprising seventeenth-century British charlatan and sex-toy salesman. After his capture and conviction by Sir Isaac Newton, then head of the Royal Mint, Chaloner was hanged, drawn, and quartered.

Yet the story of Chen's parcel is ominous because of its link to more end-of-days-style threats: nukes and terrorism.[4] The counterfeits she tried to smuggle into the United States are part of a sprawling investigation that has spanned twenty years, led U.S. authorities to 130 countries, and resulted in more than 200 arrests. Those bogus $100s are part of a genus of counterfeits called "supernotes," fake $100 and $50 bills of such exquisite quality that they are virtually indistinguishable from the real thing. They are usually only identified once they circulate back to a Federal Reserve bank equipped with the fanciest detection gear. One Treasury official reported that when he looked with a magnifying glass at the back of a supernote, he saw that the clock-tower hands on Independence Hall, for example, were sharper on the fake than on the genuine article.[5] Another anticounterfeiting cop put it in even starker terms: "Supernotes are just U.S. dollars not made by the U.S. government."

Investigators with the Secret Service, State Department, and other federal agencies all believe that supernotes come from North Korea.* A decade ago, a small State Department team was asked to solve the riddle

---

*Another theory holds that supernotes are made and used by the CIA. There are irregularities in the North Korea story, one being that if your goal is really to sabotage the U.S. economy, you should flood the market with $10s and $20s—notes that people actually use—instead of $100s, which get stored or shipped overseas. But to date this theory has few proponents.

of how a paranoid, flat-broke dictatorship with a huge trade gap was able to function at all, let alone fund its nuclear ambitions and buy luxury goods for Dear Leader. Money for food aid—even if it was being diverted, as it surely was—still wasn't enough to explain the situation. Why weren't sanctions and the dysfunctional domestic currency crippling Kim Jong Il's fiefdom as much as analysts said they should?

It didn't take long to find the answer: industrial-scale counterfeiting and narcotics. Heroin, knockoff cigarettes, fake Viagra, meth—pretty much anything and everything that could be sold on the black market is made there. These enterprises generate anywhere from $500 million to $1 billion a year for the regime.[6]

Forged $100 bills play a unique role in this panoply of the illicit. For one thing, they gel with the regime's febrile anti-Americanism and the aim to undercut U.S. global power by sowing doubts about our currency. Counterfeiting at the state level is a kind of slow-motion violence committed against an enemy, and it has been tried many times before.[7] During the Revolutionary War, the British printed "Continentals" to undermine the fragile colonial currency. American currency eventually went into a hyperinflationary death spiral—due more to over-issuing by the nascent United States than British subterfuge, but the counterfeits didn't help. Napoleon counterfeited Russian notes during the Napoleonic Wars, and during World War II, the Germans forced a handful of artists and printing experts in Block 19 of the Sachsenhausen concentration camp to produce fake U.S. dollars and British pounds sterling. (Their story is the basis for the 2007 film *The Counterfeiters*, which won the Oscar for Best Foreign Language Film.)

While the Nazis worked on their banknote blitz, the United States had another shrewd use for bogus banknotes. The U.S. military airdropped onto Japan an untold number of notes with copied artwork from the ¥5,000 bill on one side and a message in Japanese on the other, urging people to buy commodities like food and clothing and to steer clear of banks and bonds. The goal was to hit Japan's war machine in the wallet. "With saving bonds you cannot stop a child from crying," read one such note. Another said: "The military clique is squandering your tax money." These communications were less persuasive than the ones the Japanese were receiving at home: *Your God-emperor wants you to take over the world or die trying.* Still, it was a clever and relatively harmless way to try to win hearts and minds.

During the war in Vietnam, the United States produced convincing counterfeits of the North Vietnamese Dong banknotes, with a tear-away warning attached that has an ironic tint today: "The Communist Party is spending your money on a hopeless war. If the war goes on, there will be nothing for you to buy. The war is destroying your country. All your savings will be worthless."[8]

That warring countries try to exploit paper money's fragile worth is a reminder that without a supply of authentic cash—and trust in it—countries fall apart. Most money may be digital nowadays, but I don't think anyone wants to run the experiment of obliterating the integrity of the greenback with a massive flood of fakes to see just how uncritical paper money's trustworthiness has become. Do we really want to eliminate one of the last remaining tactile symbols that ties us together as one nation, under God, transacting peacefully?

Economic warfare may be part of North Korea's counterfeiting effort, but the simpler and more likely explanation is that the government needs money. It can't buy much with its nearly worthless national currency, the won. A recent attempt to raise funds revealed the level of the country's fiscal desperation, as well as the abuse Dear Leader is willing to inflict on his people: in 2009 the regime devalued the currency by 100 percent. One thousand won now only has the purchasing power of ten won.[9] Officials set a tight limit on how much of the old money could be exchanged for the new, which meant whatever paltry savings people might have had were destroyed overnight.

This disastrous policy inevitably wrecks commerce, as Roman emperors who debased their currencies can attest. Goods leave the marketplace because no one wants to sell anything if they're going to be paid with a medium of exchange that doesn't have value, or that they don't believe has value, which is essentially the same thing. With that, every-thing breaks down: paying, buying, accumulating wealth, and, most of all, any hope of forging a more prosperous tomorrow. The change in value is called *revaluation*, but it could just as easily be called kleptocracy. By comparison, raising funds by counterfeiting the currency of a more stable economy looks downright humanitarian.

Supernotes are not super forgeries because of any technological prowess on the part of the North Koreans. It's a matter of equipment. The North Koreans are apparently in possession of the same kind of in-taglio printing press used by the Bureau of Engraving and Printing, and the notes are printed on similar high-tech paper.[10] A leading theory is that in 1989, just before the collapse of the Berlin Wall, the press (pos-sibly presses) made its way to North Korea from a clandestine facility in East Germany, where it was used to make fake passports and other secret documents. That same year, a teller at the Central Bank of the Philip-pines noticed that the paper of a $100 bill that had crossed her desk didn't feel quite right. She reported it to the authorities, and soon the U.S. Secret Service opened a file labeled "supernotes."

For almost seventy years, the design of Federal Reserve Notes was essentially unchanged. Bureaucratic inertia, perhaps, but today this con-sistency is almost sacred—and carefully guarded. It's a symbol of eco-nomic might and stability. Perhaps the connection between unchanged banknote design and economic stability was never taken as seriously by banknote users as government officials might have thought, but what-ever it meant, that streak ended in 1996.[11] The supernote problem forced a redesign of the dollar. That remake, and another that followed a decade later, incorporated new security features like microscopic printing. The newer series notes also have vertical security strips, which you can see if you hold the note up to the light. Under an ultraviolet lamp, this strip shines pink for the $100, and other colors for other denominations.

Then there's the shifty ink. The 1996 series twenties, fifties, and hun-dreds have ink that jumps from green to black, depending on the angle at which you hold the paper. The technology has its roots in the U.S.

space shuttle program, in a special material used to coat the shuttle's windows to block cosmic rays.[12] The United States buys the ink from a Swiss company—so much for Buy American—and is the exclusive customer for the color-shift combo of green to black. Not long after this deal was struck, however, the North Koreans bought the rights to the green-magenta combo, which to the untrained eye can look a lot like green-black.[13]

Within two years after the first redesign, a newer supernote model was found in circulation, and supernotes copying the 2003 series have also been confirmed.[14] At one point during the investigation, an undercover FBI agent obtained a bulk order of supernotes at a 70 percent discount. (In this maze of values, counterfeiters sell their wares for a fraction of face value because the risk is borne by the buyer.) The first Secret Service agents he showed them to thought they were real, and it was only later, after a detailed analysis by experts in Washington, D.C., that the notes were identified as forgeries.[15] There are now at least nineteen different versions of supernotes.

In 2005, two U.S. undercover investigations, dubbed Royal Charm and Smoking Dragon, netted about $4 million in supernotes from North Korea. The 2007 conviction of a Taiwanese man who had been caught laundering millions of dollars' worth of supernotes in Las Vegas casinos suggests the mainstreaming of the 1996 and 2003 reissues hasn't brought an end to this scourge. Chen's package of counterfeits in San Francisco showed that the supernote hasn't been eradicated and may be going strong.

◆

BUT WHAT DO YOU REALLY CARE that Dear Leader fakes C-notes? On one level, it's little more than black comedy: forging the currency of the evil capitalists because your own currency is nearly worthless. The absurdity reaches its pinnacle in light of the North Korean concept of *juche*, or self-reliance—a "philosophy" conjured by Dear Leader himself.[16]

Supernotes also provide delicious ammunition for rhetoric in Washington. In his typical staccato bravado, President George W. Bush said in 2006: "North Korea's a country that has declared boldly they've got nuclear weapons. They counterfeit our money. And they're starving their people to death."[17] It's one thing for North Korea to hurl missiles over our ally, Japan, sink a South Korean navy vessel and its crew, shun talks to promote peace, bomb a South Korean island, and point guns at our servicemen and women stationed on the southern edge of the Demilitarized Zone. But plagiarizing our *money*? That is just low.

Yet how different is Kim Jong Il's counterfeiting, really, from the decision to spend $700 billion in borrowed money to kick-start economic growth, from creating more than $1 trillion out of thin air to help clean up the housing bubble crisis?[18] That may sound blasphemous, but Americans have a long tradition of skepticism about money creation, forgeries or otherwise. In 1837 John Quincy Adams said that the only thing separating counterfeiters from bank directors is that the former are more skilled and modest. "It requires more talent to sign another man's name than one's own and the counterfeiter does at least his work in the dark, while the suspenders of specie payments brazen in the face of day, and laugh at the victims and dupes, who have put faith in their promises."[19] Back then, of course, there wasn't a single clearly defined national currency. Yet today's efforts to defend against counterfeiters are vestiges of bygone eras of confusions about banknotes' authenticity and suspicion about the alchemy of money creation.

Through this prism, Kim Jong Il is merely adding a few million drops into the ocean that is the money supply. Depending on how finely you slice it, supernotes *are* real money—medium of exchange, store of value, unit of account, and so on. Illicit, sure, and they do hurt the Little Guy if he accepts one and then loses money because of it. But they can be traded for goods and services. The only thing that neutralizes the value of confiscated supernotes is that they're stuck in a filing cabinet somewhere at the headquarters of the U.S. Secret Service. Wander down this alley far enough, and you'll eventually bump into two questions that share an answer: What is real? What is value? Whatever we believe it to be.

What's most dangerous about supernotes is not, in fact, the attempt to devalue your savings or undermine the currency, but what the North Koreans hope to procure with them. According to the House Task Force on Terrorism and Unconventional Warfare, supernotes aid the regime's effort to acquire nuclear materials.[20] That's probably why we don't hear much of late about counterfeiting from Washington. You've got to pick your battles, and nukes are the obvious priority here.

Officials estimate that about three of every 10,000 U.S. banknotes are counterfeit. Most of those are poor-quality forgeries, usually printed on inkjet printers by meth addicts who, on their third sleepless night in a row, get the bright idea to bleach a pile of $5 bills, scan a $20, and then re-print the image of the $20 on the bleached paper. (The Secret Service says more sophisticated bleach-based schemes in Colombia, Nigeria, and Italy have produced half-decent fakes.)[21] Other estimates suggest that counterfeits constitute as much as 30 percent of the stock of U.S. dollars circulating in Africa, Russia, and parts of Eastern Europe.[22] The true figure, although ultimately unknowable, falls somewhere in between.

The Secret Service says it has been seizing, on average, $3 million worth of supernotes a year over the past decade or so. In comparison, it seized $113 million in all counterfeit U.S. currency in 2005, and $177 million in 2009.[23] Mind you, that is just the fakes that get discovered within the United States. Since the supernotes were first detected, at least $45 million worth believed to be of North Korean origin have been detected in circulation, and the regime pockets an estimated $15 to $25 million year from them.[24] (Some other official estimates of the supernotes in circulation are much higher—up to several hundred million dollars' worth.)[25]

Meanwhile, counterfeiting operations elsewhere are ramping up as well. Over the past decade, Colombian authorities, with support from the U.S. Secret Service, seized about $239 million in counterfeit greenbacks and busted almost 100 printing operations. But like a game of Whac-A-Mole, this pressure has just pushed the forgers to set up shop elsewhere. Since the arrival of a Secret Service unit in Peru in 2009, investigators have already netted more than $20 million in bogus notes and terminated more than a dozen printing operations.[26] Anyone want to wager whether El Salvador or Honduras will be the next hot spot? As a Secret Service representative explained to Congress during testimony in 2010, production and distribution of counterfeit notes is going global.[27]

Yet an absolute value for the number of counterfeits in existence has never really been the core threat—nor will it ever be, as long as the banknotes' direct impact on the economy is *de minimis*. A few hundred million in counterfeits sounds massive, but compared to the $1 *trillion* worth of banknotes that are out there, it's a barely perceptible few onehundredths of a percent. The real danger, nukes notwithstanding, is the sign I saw the other day at an ice cream shop not far from where I live: "We do not accept bills over $20. Sorry for the inconvenience." I asked the server why. "We get a lot of counterfeits here," she said. "Not that I would know if I was holding a fake or not."

This is lost confidence in a nutshell, and it's scary. In 2004, Taiwanese bankers and government officials began pulling millions of supernotes from circulation after detecting a small number of counterfeits. The Central Bank of Taiwan had decided, perhaps recklessly, to deliver a public warning about the fake $100 bills, telling people to have them double-checked at their local bank.

Oops. Thousands of Taiwanese citizens who had been readying for the summer travel season, exchanging Taiwanese dollars for greenbacks, suddenly flipped out. According to the State Department, people dashed to the banks to trade in several hundred million dollars, most of which were legitimate. It was, in no uncertain terms, a run on the U.S. $100 bill. A scramble to mollify concerns finally convinced people that the panic was unjustified, but the episode was a shock to law enforcement and overseers of the currency. And not just in Taiwan, although there was strangely little public discussion of the matter in the United States, other than testimony from one or two officials who had been closely tracking the supernote situation.

A run! When stocks of Bear Stearns crashed on March 13, 2008, the details of the firm's financials mattered little. What mattered that day was the rush—the herd's evaporating confidence in the stock and the contagious fear about being stuck with worthless shares. It's not crazy to think that a few miscalculations and miscommunications in Taipei could have led to more widespread doubts about the $100 bill, and similar runs elsewhere.[28]

◆

COUNTERFEITING AND ANTICOUNTERFEITING efforts have all kinds of hidden costs. One economist who has tried to look closer at those costs is John Chant, a retired professor from Simon Fraser University in British Columbia. Canadians have an interesting relationship with counterfeiting, in large part because of a pot-smoking twenty-six-year-old computer whiz from Ontario.[29] A decade ago, Wesley Weber began counterfeiting Canadian $100 bills with convincing precision and then mass-producing them. At the peak of the operation, Weber's counterfeits were surfacing all over Canada, and even showing up in the United States and London. When the fakes became pervasive enough, people started refusing all CA$100 bills. Between 10 and 15 percent of the retailers in and around Toronto and Montreal posted notices to customers that they wouldn't accept any CA$100s, and throughout the country people were turning away CA$50s and CA$100s because of rippling suspicions.[30]

Investigators later estimated that Weber had pushed upwards of $7.7 million worth of bogus currency into circulation. By 2001, one out of every 290 notes in Canada was believed to be a fake, Weberian counterfeit or otherwise.[31] Weber himself laid low—at first. Five months after he and his friends had perfected their counterfeiting technique, he still hadn't tried to pass a single note. But his friends did, at Home Depot, at Canadian Tire, and at other local stores. No one noticed. So Weber too began to spend, a little at first, and then a lot. Before long he owned a Ferrari, BMW, two SUVs, and a Mustang convertible, as well as a slick condo in Toronto.

By the fall of 2000, Weber was spotting his paper creations taped to cash registers at businesses around Ontario. At the same time, a friend had obtained a letter from the authorities highlighting the deficiencies in Weber's notes, which Weber promptly set about remedying. Soon, he was literally overwhelmed with cash: $300,000 in a safe, bundles of bills stored in cabinets, and even a $100,000 block of bills stashed in the freezer.

The whole enterprise expanded at a speed that perhaps Weber himself hadn't expected, and the success made him paranoid. He eventually decided to start selling bills in bulk to "a Middle Eastern fellow"—for twenty-four cents, and later just twelve cents, on the dollar. One night the following summer, while Weber and his crew worked away in the lakeside cottage they'd converted into a print shop, the authorities hammered on the door. Before anyone really knew what was happening, it was over. (The cops had staked out the cottage months before and installed surveillance equipment.) Weber pled guilty and was sentenced to almost six years, during which, by the way, he developed a keen interest in the stock market.

In a country like Canada, with a smaller population and therefore fewer banknotes in circulation, Weber's $7.7 million in fakes constituted a non-negligible amount of paper. Canada's paper money is more vulnerable to a counterfeit-led confidence crash, compared to that of a country like the United States, which has a far larger population and volume of paper money to support it. In 2004, the Bank of Canada released a new CA$100 as part of a new line of bills. But the damage to the reputation of the country's high-denomination paper was not so easily undone. Some stores closest to the epicenter of Weber's operation still won't take CA$100 bills, and in 2011 the Canucks rolled out yet another one-hundred-dollar bill.

One way to consider the myriad costs of counterfeiting, says economist Chant, is to think about inflation. If I hold money, inflation takes some of its value away and transfers it to people who hold debt. Why? At the end of the year, the value of their debt has gone down, while the value of my money in hand has also gone down. The role of a central bank is to take precautions against this decreasing value. "Inflation at high rates erodes belief in the *acceptability* of the currency. If counterfeiting is rife, it too can be destructive to that same faith," Chant told me. The rub with counterfeiting is that acceptability can suffer a blow even if the only thing that is rife is overblown concern about counterfeiting, as was the case in Taiwan.

But the true costs of counterfeiting only start with the losses incurred by people who unwillingly accept fakes. Chant once tried to examine the costs associated with efforts to prevent counterfeiting. One such cost falls to businesses, organizations, and government agencies that have to take steps to avoid accepting counterfeits, which they more or less all do. Casinos, for example, have counterfeit detection technology on site. Staff at currency exchanges, banks, and anyplace else where paper money is frequently handled need to be trained to avoid taking phony bills. All of that costs money.

More nebulous, but much greater, is the cost governments incur to battle the enterprise of counterfeiting—the "hidden costs of suppressing it," says Chant: expensive banknote design, inspecting circulating currency, reissuing new series, and prosecuting and imprisoning counterfeiters. Yet to arrive at any kind of meaningful figure for these costs, says Chant, you would have to add up all the prevention costs at the treasury, law enforcement agencies, central bank, private sector, and so on. "Maybe someone has done a cost-benefit study, but I don't know of any. If they exist, they will be buried in confidential files somewhere."

◆

BY THE EARLY 2000S, as supernotes surfaced in more and more countries, overseas banks began asking the U.S. Treasury what was being done to remedy the situation. The supernote had become an embarrassment for Washington, and at some point a dollar redesign became inevitable.[32] Not that there were many options; state-sponsored counterfeiting is a diplomatic stumper. What do you do—order airstrikes on the presses? Send in Blackwater?

Yet a reissue doesn't necessarily solve the problem. In fact, it brings a whole new set of risks. Think about it from the perspective of the central bankers and anticounterfeiting officials. Frequent reissues can boost confidence by showcasing the issuers' commitment to reliable paper money. On the other hand, there's no better time to move your product—to launder your counterfeits—than when the government issues a new series, because that's when the public is most confused about what's legit. *Not that I would know if I was holding a fake or not.* Even talking about redesigning currency can create doubt. Yet if enough counterfeits exist, or if those in existence are getting enough press, redesign is the only reasonable way to deal with the scourge of doubt.

On April 21, 2010, in the Cash Room at the U.S. Treasury building in Washington, D.C, the captains of the Federal Reserve, U.S. Treasury, U.S. Secret Service, and the Bureau of Engraving and Printing gathered with bankers, journalists, and economic security types to unveil the new $100 banknote. (Six months later, the release would be delayed due to that gazillion-dollar printing snafu.) The event—pageant, really—received obliging media coverage but wasn't exactly page-one material.

The unveiling was an exercise in conjuring faith as carefully choreographed as a mega-church service. "Individuals, businesses and governments around the world put their confidence in our currency," said the secretary of the Treasury, Timothy Geithner. "They use the dollar because they know that it is backed by the most sophisticated anticounterfeiting technologies known to men, that the design can't be stolen or replicated."[33]

Washington's top financial wizard was dutifully shoveling it. Making money always has been, and always will be, an endless arms race. Outsmarting counterfeiters, like terrorists, is impossible. The security wizardry moves an inch, and counterfeiting soon follows, and on and on.[34] "You know, we just can't rest," said Douglas Crane, the vice president of Crane & Co., in a radio interview a few years ago. The Massachusetts-based firm is the Bureau of Engraving and Printing's sole supplier of the

souped-up paper used to make our cash supply, and pressure from counterfeiters is great for Crane's business.[35]

Federal Reserve Chairman Ben Bernanke was next up after Geithner.
He gave a speech full of the obligatory blandness that is supposed to keep
us all calm about the state of our financial affairs: "A sound currency is
the bedrock of a sound economy," he told the crowd. "Therefore, the
United States government must stay ahead of counterfeiters and protect
the integrity of our currency."[36] What I couldn't help but wonder while
watching the video of the event is whether anyone present found this
trumpeting the currency's *integrity* a bit disingenuous, considering the
scope and scale of the nation's fiscal woes.

In a video about the redesign posted on a government website, a crisp
new $100 bill turns slowly in space to the sound of a crescendo-ing an-
them of revolutionary war-era drums, horns, and strings. As Ben
Franklin's dimply visage moves across the screen, security features are
announced in all-caps: "3-D SECURITY RIBBON," "BELL IN THE INKWELL,"
"PORTRAIT WATERMARK," "SECURITY THREAD," "COLOR-SHIFTING 100." At the
end of the demo, this solemn guidance: "The new $100 note. Know its
features. Know it's real."

Good luck with that. The security thread, which shines pink under
UV light, is more than a decade old, yet most people still don't know
what it is. Watermarks, those shadowy images that appear when you
hold a note up to the light, have been around for longer, so they've become more recognizable. That's not to say, however, that anyone other
than a Secret Service agent could distinguish between a fake and a real
one, and crooks have had decades to practice forging them. Neurosci-
entists have even demonstrated that when it comes to banknotes, most
people simply can't distinguish real from fake.

If most of us are unfamiliar with, and rarely look for, the old features,
what's the likelihood that we'll really learn and want to inspect for the
new ones? After all, turning in a counterfeit hurts no one worse than
yourself because the authorities will just take it. You're better off passing

it on to someone else, although I say that from a purely economic perspective, and not as an accomplice to some future passer's crime.[37]

The same is true in most countries. In India, I met a man who received a fake 500-rupee note (worth about $11) from a bank ATM. When he turned it in, the teller ripped it in half and said, "Thank you. Next!" If economics explains how rational people respond to incentives, surely central bankers know that the public has little motivation to be on the alert for counterfeits. *Don't ask, don't tell* is more like it.

True, turning in a fake gives you the satisfaction of doing the right thing, assuming you believe protecting the integrity of your national currency is more important than buying dinner. If you get caught knowingly trying to pass a counterfeit, you could get hit with a fine of $15,000 or face ten years in prison. In reality, the Secret Service is really only interested in the printers. Legally speaking, though, you're still taking a risk.

The no-reimbursement policy is based on the premise that exchanging fakes with real notes would open the floodgates, creating an incentive to produce forgeries.[38] Criminals could make bogus notes and then have someone else turn them in for real ones. Yet there is little or no evidence to support this policy; it's merely an assumption about how we behave, and if there's one thing behavioral economists know, it's that people don't behave as predicted. (Japan, which has one of the lowest rates of counterfeiting in the world, is an exception to the no-reward rule. People who turn in a fake there are eligible for an "honorarium," roughly equivalent to the bogus bill's value, and only if the forgery is from a batch of counterfeits not yet known to the authorities.)[39]

Still, you've got to hand it to the Feds—or to the material scientists, really. The new $100 bill has some technological razzmatazz, especially the Liberty Bell inside the inkwell floating just beyond Franklin's shoulder. Tilt the note and the green bell emerges from the copper-colored inkwell. Tilt the note once more and it vanishes. Pretty cool, for a piece of paper.

So is the blue 3-D security ribbon. Microscopic lenses in the material create the effect that tiny 100s and bells are moving. A Crane consultant told me how dazzled he was the first time he saw a prototype. "It was really a quantum leap. I'm a chemist and physicist, yet I had no idea how it worked! After the explanation I understood, but still . . . amazing."[40] Tilt the banknote up and down, and tiny 100s and bells move left to right. Tilt the paper back and forth, and it looks like the bells and 100s are moving up and down. It's an elegant solution, pioneered by an optics engineer who, after having sold his invention to Crane, is no doubt now living the good life on a tropical island somewhere.

The engineering is that much more impressive because this strip of optical wizardry can, at a reasonable price, be woven into the paper's cotton fibers, and can withstand the crumpling, folding, soaking, and other physical abuse that banknotes must endure.

Yet just how counterfeit-proof is the new $100 bill?

Two months after the unveiling, in a spotless conference room on the eighteenth floor of a skyscraper in Tokyo's Gotanda neighborhood, I met with a team of holography and secure documents experts at Dai Nippon, one of the world's most famous printing firms. A man named Kenji Ueda leaned across the gray meeting table to hand me a gift card that Dai Nippon had made a few years ago for a major department store chain.

The image was a rough outline of the continents in blue, dotted with pink, yellow, and silver crescents. When I tilted the card left to right or up and down, it looked like blue 3-D spheres moved inside the continents. The illusion of motion and depth was powerful, even though my brain knew full well it was dealing with a two-dimensional image. That card is printed with something called a "lens array"—not the microarray of the moving bells and 100s on the new C-notes, but close. And that, the Japanese experts say, is the problem.[41]

"You can pass it," Ueda said flatly, using the lingo of law enforcement. In poorly lit environments like bars, casinos, or taxis, it would be hard to distinguish between this visual gimmickry and the movement created by the technology on the new \$100 bill, which means counter-feiters may use lens array to mimic the new \$100, if they aren't busy doing so already.

The next morning, at the National Printing Bureau, Japan's equivalent to the Bureau of Engraving and Printing, I inquired again about the new \$100 banknote and "the most sophisticated anti-counterfeiting tech-nologies known to men." Again an engineer passed me a sample docu-ment, handing it across the table with both hands like a business card. This one was a white-and-blue polka-dotted piece of microlens paper that when tilted mimics the 3-D feature of the new \$100 bill.

He bought it at a stationery store. "They will use it," he said, referring to counterfeiters. "I would say the motion feature is like a C or a C+." Perhaps no one in the world can copy the nanotechnology underlying the great American 3-D security ribbon—not yet anyway. But that doesn't mean they can't mimic it closely enough. A counterfeiter, re-member, does not aspire to duplicate. He only needs to pass off his prod-uct undetected.

Even if counterfeiters aren't aiming to forge the new \$100 bill, they have other denominations (and older \$100s) to work with. Thanks to advances in desktop color printing, forgers now have the capacity to cre-ate high-quality imitations with off-the-shelf illustration software, in-stead of specialized training in inset printing and lithography. Between 1995 and 2002, digitally produced fakes in the United States went from 1 percent to 40 percent of all counterfeits seized.[42] By 2009, more than 60 percent of the counterfeits passed in the United States were made do-mestically by people using desktop technology.[43] One source that I can't name said that if we could do away with cash, most of the Secret Service caseload would vanish because the majority of agents' time today is spent chasing and busting two-bit "meth-heads" playing around with inkjet printers.

The banknote manufacturers and central banks have tried to engi-neer defenses against inkjet counterfeiting, such as color-shifting inks that aren't available on the open market. Another defense is something called the EURion constellation, an antiphotocopying trick that consists of small marks or design items on banknotes positioned at a set distance from one another, like stars in the sky. Because image-processing software like Adobe Photoshop makes what is essentially a mathematical picture of whatever you've scanned or photocopied, the software can be programmed to look for these specific patterns.[44]

If it detects the EURion constellation, Photoshop will abort and deliver an on-screen warning about counterfeiting laws. (Try printing the Wikipedia page on EURion and see what happens.) This seems like a victory for the guardians of paper currency, until you remember that the Internet is full of puzzle addicts and hackers. Almost as soon as EURion was detected, D.I.Y. enthusiasts began finding ways to end-around it. The system does deter many of those less sophisticated would-be counterfeiters, but it's hardly much of a defense against more deliberative and tech-savvy operatives.[45]

In the decade ahead, we're bound to see still more innovations that will make for neat little stories about the latest banknote security tech, while failing to miss the bigger point. One engineer I interviewed wants to rig bills with a kind of scratch-and-sniff feature, except instead of producing an odor, the scratching would produce a brief glow, like the little sparks of blue you see when peeling back a piece of Scotch tape in the dark. (I can already see the snappy public awareness campaign and government videos: Light Makes Right; or maybe, No Glow = No Go.) Scientists at Dai Nippon in Tokyo are working on holograms that look like they're straight out of a 3-D movie. Other researchers have found a way to mimic the iridescent patterns on the wings of butterflies and have already floated the idea of using this innovation for security printing.[46]

The technology quest must be fun for the engineers, but I feel sorry for the cops and central bankers who have to spend their careers speaking out of both sides of their mouths. They have to make us simultaneously vigilant about counterfeits and ignorant of them. Put another way: *Please keep a sharp eye out for this threat, even though it isn't a threat because we have everything under control. Our currency is totally trustworthy.*

A public that's blasé about the threat of counterfeiting is a public that trusts its paper money, and that's good for the economy. It also means almost never double-checking the cash someone hands you. In many ways, the universal acceptability of U.S. dollar bills is a testament to both anticounterfeiting efforts and the economy's relative stability. Confidence is contagious.

How strong would our confidence be if every time we received a Federal Reserve Note, we pulled out a portable ultraviolet lamp for a quick inspection? The few times I've held a $20 bill up to a light to look for a security thread, I could never keep a straight face; I felt like I was parodying a movie scene. There is also something uncouth about checking a banknote, a sign that you don't trust whoever just gave it to you.

Agents with the Secret Service or the Money Forgery Unit at Europol don't want citizens to be anxious about the authenticity of dollars or euros. Yet the public is also the first line of defense against forgeries. The cops want us to know the security features—for which the government, central banks, and you have, after all, paid a fortune—but they have to hope we never really find any. While confidence in the currency is good, overconfidence can morph into complacency. If a surge of fake $20 or $100 bills were to suddenly arrive on the market without anyone noticing for days or weeks, the bad money could spread so far that it would be much harder for the cops to find its source.

There's just no way to maintain vigilance against counterfeiters without casting doubt. This irreconcilable tension only exists, of course, as long as we use cash. Until that changes, we have no choice but to settle in and watch the theatrics and massive expenditures as the overseers of the economy try to keep us believing that nothing is wrong and everything is real.

◆

NO ONE CAN REALLY KNOW how much counterfeiting it takes to undermine an economy's banknotes or, more accurately, the public's confidence in them. Likewise, we don't get to know how much the government spends trying to prevent that from happening. All we have is the government saying *Trust us: we are spending your money wisely*, and a handful of extremely secretive and rich companies telling us *Trust your government: whatever they're paying us, it's worth it.*

Although countries like the United States, China, Russia, and Japan have nationalized banknote production, most other countries contract with private suppliers. Even those that produce their own paper money buy materials from these companies, as the United States does from Crane. While most companies that influence our everyday lives pay untold millions of dollars to cram their names and logos down our throats, few people know the names of the firms that make some of the most ubiquitous objects in the world. And they like it that way. De La Rue in Britain, Crane in the United States, Giesecke & Devrient in Germany, Oberthur Fiduciaire in France, Securency in Australia, and a smattering of smaller ones. That's it.

One curiosity about the banknote business is that some of the most high-tech physical money circulates in countries that can least afford it—places like Nigeria, Bangladesh, Nicaragua, Papua New Guinea, and Kazakhstan. In the words of the trade publication *Currency News*: "There sometimes appears to be an inverse relationship between the vulnerability of a country's currency and the sophistication of the new [banknote security] features it adopts."[47]

Why is this? Not because criminals are lining up to counterfeit the Bangladeshi taka or the Nicaraguan córdoba, that's for sure. One explanation is that the manufacturers give poorer countries discounts in exchange for what equates to free advertising. The notes are mobile billboards, displaying the latest technology to central bank officials elsewhere, especially in wealthy countries. In 2010, the rotating chairmanship of the Organization for Security and Cooperation in Europe fell to Kazakhstan. In advance of this apparent honor, the National Bank of Kazakhstan wanted to do a little strutting. Because colorful, high-tech paper money is considered a sign of economic prosperity—and a lot simpler to institute than, say, an effective healthcare system—Kazakh leaders decided to go all-out on a new banknote series.

The 1,000-tenge note (worth about $6.80) is loaded up with at least a dozen anticounterfeiting features. One industry expert calls the bills, printed by Giesecke & Devrient—company slogan: "creating confidence"—a technological "tour de force." Yet studies have shown that most people don't recall more than a couple of the security features on their bills.[48] True, some features are intended only for cash-handling machines and authorities. But without a rash of counterfeiting to fight, and banknote supply contracts and expenditures all hidden behind a curtain of secrecy, such a huge investment looks suspicious.

What did the Kazakhs spend on this new beauty? "Unfortunately, information on the costs of the National Bank for the production of this bill is classified," Gaziz Shegenov, director of the Bank's Cash Handling Department, wrote me in an e-mail. Then again, Shegenov and company might have gotten a deal. If you have a new material or security feature ready for a circulation trial run, testing in a country that isn't necessarily a big-ticket customer poses less risk than rolling it out for the first time in a wealthy country.

Perhaps it's no surprise that the reputation of this industry isn't squeaky clean. In the past, banknote manufacturers have allegedly resorted to shady practices, such as spying on each other and even counterfeiting other countries' banknotes to lure a potential customer away from a competitor.[49] The year 2010 saw some particularly unflattering reports about these firms and their government partners.[50] The delay in the release of the new U.S. $100 banknote was an expensive embarrassment for the nation and its suppliers. Ditto for the latest euro series, also delayed, and a new high-tech series of Swiss francs featuring a three-ply "paper-polymer-paper substrate" that goes by the name Durasafe. In Britain, the country's Serious Fraud Office descended on De La Rue to investigate accounting irregularities and allegations of falsified documents.[51]

Recent events in Australia are an order of magnitude more salacious. Two years ago, a whistleblower from the banknote materials firm Securency went to the press with a tale of the company bribing foreign officials. Actually, he first went to the authorities, but they either ignored or buried his complaint, so then he went to the press. Whereas the other moneymakers are companies that date back generations, Securency, launched in 1996, is the industry newcomer, and in many ways a revitalizing force, much in the way a young gun on the tennis circuit re-energizes the old guard. Australia was the first major country to have plastic banknotes, and the goal for Securency was to export this technology. No one had ever successfully challenged the hegemony of paper, and it was both an engineering achievement and a source of pride for Australians that a local firm, half-owned by the country's central bank, was leading this advance.

Plastic notes are more durable than paper ones, less susceptible to tearing and water damage especially. Over the past twenty years, Securency has nudged its way into markets once dominated by the paper giants. The dream was to bring polymer banknotes to the world. But to make it happen, company executives apparently bribed foreign officials to sign up Securency as their supplier. The whistleblower, and a subsequent investigation by reporters with *The Age* newspaper, alleged that Securency had bought official favor in Nigeria and Vietnam, probably in Malaysia, and possibly in other countries as well. To help seal the deals, company officials also furnished their potential business partners with prostitutes—paid for, one can only assume, with cash.

In the fall of 2010, the Reserve Bank of Australia announced plans to sell its stake in the company, presumably to distance itself from the scandal. But the damage had been done. The whistleblower had already confirmed that the company's link to the central bank had been key to scoring new contracts, right down to the RBA logo printed on the business cards of Securency reps dispatched overseas. Company officials have cried foul, claiming that multi-million-dollar "commissions" (read: payoffs) are simply how the business of moneymaking gets done. The scandal was still unfolding at press time, with nine former senior executives connected with the RBA facing charges, including Securency's former deputy chairman.[52] Just imagine for a moment if the Federal Reserve were embroiled in this kind of fiasco.

If the bribes and other unscrupulous mischief really represent business as usual for those who make the authentic versions of paper money, you've got to ask: Who's really being defrauded with this endless loop of corporate and government spending on still more banknotes saturated with still more security bells and whistles? It's as if cash casts such a captivating spell over the human psyche that we don't want to bother considering its price. As it turns out, that's just one of many ways it messes with our heads.

CHAPTER 4

The Loyalists

*All that it is and it has, money surrenders fully to
the human will, becoming totally absorbed within it.*

—GEORG SIMMEL, *PHILOSOPHY OF MONEY*

A few years ago, Fox radio and television personality Dave
Ramsey coined the term *plasectomy*. It loosely means to
part with one's credit cards, preferably in dramatic fash-
ion. "Plastic surgery," quips Ramsey, although there is nothing cosmetic
about this procedure. Why it isn't *plastectomy* remains a mystery.

As one of the country's most popular personal finance coaches, Ramsey preaches common-sense advice about living within your means. At
live appearances he lectures to thousands of people who pay as much as
$220 a ticket to watch him pace on stage and tell them what they've al-
ready read in his books, and probably learned from their parents ages
ago: avoid debt.[1] Ramsey will introduce credit cards to a pair of sharp
scissors, and the congregants will applaud. There is no baptism or con-
vulsing at Total Money Makeover, but there is more than a whiff of the
Pentecostal.

And it's no wonder, considering the uncomfortable relationship between religion and money, especially lending. Lending at unreasonably

high interest rates—usury—has been a no-no to the devout for millennia, and a no-no to the common-sense ethicist for just as long. The evolution of bank lending and financial institutions is in many ways a story about finding theologically palatable strategies to bend the rules so that lenders could profit from interest without infuriating God.

Doing business with outcasts already beyond salvation was one of the more convenient solutions. Today, because banknotes are representations of IOUs, depending on your reading of the Koran or Bible the only way to avoid trading with these sinful pieces of paper is to transact in gold. A twenty-first-century take on this restriction is the gold-dispensing ATM.[2]

The brainchild of a German entrepreneur, the Gold to Go ATM accepts your paper money or credit card and delivers small gold bars or coins. A prototype was unveiled in 2010 in the lobby of a fancy hotel in the United Arab Emirates, and a second one has landed at a mall in Boca Raton, Florida. The roughly 1,000-pound machine can stock up to ten different products and comes with optional molybdenum steel armor. Maybe next we'll have ATMs dispensing jugs of crude oil.[3] Better yet, why not just fess up to your lost confidence in the international monetary system and stock the machine with blankets and bullets?

The other reason a splash of religion melds with Ramsey's shtick is that we're epically on the hook. Americans own 610 million cards—about two per person, including kids—and owe on them $850 billion, give or take.[4] Then there's the federal deficit, but let's not go there. Ramsey's idea of the plasectomy has injected a little levity into the demoralizing topic of debt enslavement.

People who've dealt with the difficulties of debt have taken plasectomy to the next level in terms of aggression, and the violent fruits of their labors can be observed on YouTube. If you're ever feeling blue about debt, personal or national, watch a few of these home videos of plastic haters chopping up credit cards in kitchen blenders, blowing them up with fireworks, piercing them with a bow and arrow, and attacking them from behind a shower curtain to the screechy soundtrack from *Psycho*.*

My favorite YouTube selection is a mock hunting show called *Huntin' Plastic with Everett Sonstegaard*.[5] In an exaggerated Appalachian drawl, Sonstegaard explains the subject of today's expedition: a silver-colored MasterCard taped to a watermelon. "Now, this specimen was harvested last year," he says, loading ammunition into a shotgun. "I'd say it's a two- or three-year-old one with 19 percent interest. They can get much bigger than that, even twice that size . . . meaner and nastier specimens."

The scene cuts. Sonstegaard is now wearing noise-canceling earphones, creeping through the woods. "I think we can spot one right over there." A moment later, he takes aim. The camera holds on the Master-Carded watermelon resting on a brush pile. *BOOM!*—the melon explodes in a shower of wet red guts, replayed again in slow motion. "Well, as you can see, this was a clean and humane kill. . . . Next week, we are going to teach you how to clean and dress your kill."

◆

LET ME BE CLEAR: this exposition about cash versus electronic money is no valentine to plastic. I use credit cards because they're relatively convenient, Bank of England gift shop notwithstanding. I'm also addicted to the perks, and, of course, there is cash's filth factor. I'm all too aware, however, that plastic is a marvelously efficient catalyst for personal debt, and all the hardship that spills from it. As consumer protection watchdog Elizabeth Warren succinctly puts it, these companies "pick the pockets of the most vulnerable—young, old, and working people with spotty

---

* Not that a nationwide halt to borrowing and buying more stuff would necessarily cure our financial woes; if only it were that straightforward. Because the U.S. consumer accounts for about a fifth of all global economic activity, a sudden cure to our debt addiction could have tectonic effects on the global economy, which might damage our financial situation much more than our prodigal ways.

credit records."[6] Credit cards also beloved by criminals who steal identities, money, or both.

In the public eye, credit cards have become the de facto antipode of cash, even though they're not; they're just one of many different payment tools, and a rather outmoded one at that. But it's hard to imagine society willingly pulling the plug on cash before untangling our feelings about these two different forms of money.

In 2003 the CEO of Barclays, one of the most powerful banks in the world and a big-time issuer of credit cards, made an odd public confession. "I do not borrow on credit cards; it is too expensive."[7] For practitioners of plasectomy, compulsive debtors, and pretty much anyone who has ever been in financial trouble or merely attempted some belt-tightening, step No. 1 is to cut up the damn cards. Then, set a budget and use cash so that you can stick to it. Perhaps you'll even employ what members of Debtors Anonymous call "the envelope method." For each of your monthly expenses—rent, utilities, gas, groceries, etc.—withdraw the necessary amount of cash from your savings account, and then put each in an appropriately labeled envelope. Get clarity about where your money is, what your expenses are, and how much you have.

When you pay with cash, proponents argue, even though that paper no longer has intrinsic value, the physicality of the exchange is akin to transactions of yesteryear that involved money of weighable worth—of trading something for something. This salience is an advantage for cash as far as keeping spending in check. The expenditure, the loss of funds, the relinquishing—whatever you want to call it—is just that much more in your face. The numbers printed on the paper tether banknotes to the idea of value better than plastic or other electronic payment methods do, or at least we've been conditioned to think so. Using a credit card, in contrast, creates the feeling of getting something for free. It also doesn't provide fixed denominations: walk into a casino armed with three C-notes and you know you could lose, at most, $300. Walk into a casino with a credit card, and you could lose your house. Cash is clear.[8]

For most of my year shunning banknotes and coins, I didn't miss this clarity. Perhaps on a dozen occasions, when I met friends for dinner or drinks, we would run into the hassle (for them) of me not having cash with which to pay someone back. But that is only because someone else beat me to the punch, snapping down a credit card before I could, for they too usually lacked any cash. Two friends in particular were especially generous during such episodes, shrugging it off with a "you get the next one." They know who they are.

Just as often, though (or so I'd like to think), I was the one treating. I too have that basic impulse to grab the restaurant check (or so I'd like to think), or at least the wish not to be a mooch. And I too want the extra airline miles. The Federal Reserve estimates that the average American consumer is armed with $79 in cash at any given time, a figure I find to be an astounding overestimation, no matter how bulletproof the wonks' methodology may be. True, nobody's circle of friends is a representative sample of the American public, but more often than not the people I know don't have paper money with which to reimburse the person who happens to step up and pay with plastic. Not that I could have accepted it. Most of the time, my friends and I just split the charge on two or three cards, or, more recently, use our phones to send each other money. But more about phones replacing wallets a bit later.[9]

I've long since been hooked on the convenience of plastic. In the world of self-employment, the record of transactions is key during tax season. And I like the benefits. I know they're a savvy marketing invention that helps banks and other businesses keep pawns like me loyal, but as someone who travels a lot, I don't care. I get some "free" trips out of it, so there is some value in there, even if it's not as much as I'm led to believe.

Unfortunately, while the need to borrow is the true cause of debt—to cover payments that are absolutely necessary or otherwise—debt is often exacerbated by credit cards. Why? A generation of behavioral economics research has demonstrated that standard predictions of how we treat and handle our money have woefully misread *Homo sapiens*. We aren't perfectly self-interested. We don't hold consistent preferences. A tax incorporated into a price tag on supermarket shelves makes us more frugal, whereas an equivalent tax added at checkout is virtually ignored. We spend the same money differently depending on whether it's labeled *credit*, *rebate*, or *bonus*, and willingness to pay is heavily influenced by the payment method. When it comes to moola, the technical term for us is "cuckoo."

As early as the 1970s, scientists were trying to decode plastic's hypnotic power.[10] Even among wealthy people, 15 percent of participants in one pioneering study failed to pay their monthly balance to zero. Three-quarters of respondents from another survey "said that credit cards made it too easy to buy things that they may not really want or can't really afford." Despite awareness of this hazard, the card's Manchurian power was too potent to resist. Those same subjects reported that the primo benefit of the card is that it enabled them to "buy without having the money and pay the bank back over time."[11]

Talk about a linguistic pirouette: *buy* without having the money. How is it that a language as marvelously expansive as English still doesn't have a simple verb describing the act of acquiring something on credit?[12] It's not *buying*, no matter what the salesperson would like you to think. I hereby nominate *curchase*. As in, *I recently curchased a new car*.

Even when credit cards only exist at the periphery of our experience, they can boost our willingness to fork over funds or borrow. In another landmark experiment, subjects entering the classroom where the research took place happened to see an American Express logo on a desk. The experimenter feigned that this was irrelevant, removed the paper with the logo, and then proceeded to ask subjects how much they would be willing to pay for an array of items listed in a catalog.[13]

The subjects had been "primed," exposed to something without thinking about it directly. Merely by "decorating the experimental setting" with this visual equivalent of a subconscious whisper—*credit caaard*—willingness to pay jumped 50–200 percent compared to the control group.[14] The credit card effect, as it's known, has been demonstrated time and again, and is perhaps best encapsulated by the cheeky research paper title "Always Leave Home Without It."[15]

Scientists have also found that when using a credit card, people don't recall their expenses as well as they do when using cash. Sticking to a budget is that much harder if the experience of spending, of relinquishing those funds, doesn't register as powerfully in your head.[16] All money is fiction, but apparently this form of it is that much more ethereal. That is, until you get your statement and think, *Holy shit. I did what?* Cash and electronic money may both be liquid, but they differ in their degree of slipperiness, and the fact that we're more spendthrift when using plastic reinforces the opinion that cash is less complicated, safer, and somehow more upstanding.

It might make us more honest, too. Dan Ariely, a professor of psychology and behavioral economics at Duke and the author of the bestseller *Predictably Irrational*, ran a set of experiments showing that people are apparently more ethical when dealing with paper money as compared with other objects that have the same dollar value. In one experiment, he covertly placed six-packs of Coca-Cola in refrigerators located in the common area of college dorms. He wanted to see how fast they would vanish; that is, how fast students would steal them. In other refrigerators, he placed six $1 bills. After seventy-two hours, all the Cokes were gone, but not a single greenback had been lifted.

Ariely is careful to point out that these results are not a part of his goal to prove the immorality of students at a certain college, or, for that matter, his fellow man. Rather, they reveal hidden biases that we all possess to some degree. Many people, for instance, have no problem helping themselves to pens or notepads from the office, or to using the office copier for personal use, yet they would never help themselves to the contents of the petty cash drawer. In another study, Ariely's research team found that business travelers from New York were more likely to expense a gift for their kids that they picked up at the airport in San Francisco, compared with a gift bought back in the Big Apple. We can't even cheat consistently.

In another study, Ariely and colleagues showed that people are dishonest when offered a monetary reward for correct answers. Not much of a revelation there. But they also discovered that the cheating was more than twice as likely if the *form* of the monetary reward is something other than cash. Even when the researchers explicitly told subjects that the tokens earned could immediately be traded for real cash with the person just across the room, cheating was still much more prevalent. Cash may be the currency of crime, but somehow banknotes and coins make us behave a little less crooked.

The reason, says Ariely, is that when stealing involves money that is one (or many) steps removed from cash, we more easily rationalize dishonesty. The veiled monetary value makes the morally reprehensible act "fuzzier" than a straight-up holdup, and that allows us to wield our impressive powers of justification. At the office, we might tell ourselves that disappearing staplers are simply part of the larger cost of doing business; what company *doesn't* expect employees to take a few items home? Plus, don't you deserve some trifling office supplies, after all those years of loyalty to the firm? It's not like you're walking off with a company car. With the stolen Cokes, the rationale is even easier: if there are any what's-mine-is-yours communities left on Earth, they are college dormitories.

These findings help us to understand the thinking—or lack thereof—that goes on in the minds of villains like Bernie Madoff, the architects of the Enron scam, and even bankers who sell legal but toxic assets. Ariely ventures that these people, and millions like them, wouldn't mug an old lady on the street, and he's probably right. Fuzzy up the transaction, though, and it brings out the worst in us. "We need to recognize that once cash is a step away," writes Ariely, "we will cheat by a factor bigger than we could ever imagine."

It would be foolhardy, though, to jump to the conclusion that this handful of findings about behavior provides a meaty defense for keeping cash around. Cash itself isn't more honest, despite its associations with

Abe Lincoln and God. It all comes back to the salience of the form, and the fact that we've been acculturated to behave more honestly with this particular one. We've all been taught that stealing a thing, anything, is bad, and physical money is just a thing. But that doesn't mean the more honest behavior we exhibit when dealing with cash can't be recreated, or reengineered, in future technologies. Imagine a smartphone app, for instance, that showcases, through vivid images and sound, the act of transferring value between your checking account and the merchant's.

Besides, I don't think cash keeps us as honest as Ariely suspects. For one thing, greenbacks sitting in a fridge are a weird thing to encounter, unless you're that congressman from Louisiana who hid his bribe money in the freezer. The circumstances of that test are atypical enough that the results are an iffy gauge of typical behavior. More significant is the fact that he used $1 bills. People don't pick up pennies off the street anymore, and many would not hold up traffic to fetch a quarter, and morality has little or nothing to do with those decisions.

For students at one of the best colleges in the country, who might just have an inkling that dollars sitting in a fridge are part of a trick or experiment, what is there to gain by stealing $1 or, at most, $6? Perhaps this experiment says more about inflation than it does human behavior. I'd like to see how honest cash makes people when researchers use $50 bills as bait, and leave them someplace where subjects don't have to wonder if the money belongs to a friend living across the hall. Still, Ariely is right that white-collar criminals who would never steal a wallet but have no qualms about stealing millions from a pension fund are, to use the technical term, assholes.

◆

WHEN IT COMES TO MONEY'S FORM, our cognitive foibles don't begin and end with plastic versus paper, or the morality of stealing soda. One of our most fundamental hang-ups is conflating the face value printed on a price tag, menu, or banknote with the real value of something—the bundle of goods or services we can acquire with it. There is even a name for it: the money illusion, made famous by an economist named Irving Fisher. In his 1928 book, *The Money Illusion*, Fisher describes how physical representations of money can be a confusing, even misleading, measure of value.[17]

We get duped into thinking banknotes have value equivalent to the numbers printed on them, not a gauge of something else's worth. Back when we had the gold standard, people could at least imagine money as a specific amount of something earthly. Now everything is, quite literally, relative. For people living in countries that have more recently experienced rip-roaring inflation or currency crises, this relativity is easier to grasp. One week 10,000 pesos pays the rent, the next week it can't buy a tank of gas.

The money illusion in the modern age can have a bizarre influence on our decisions. Because we have a built-in bias for bigger numbers, we presume that the higher-priced wine, automobile, restaurant, college, or hotel will offer better quality, better value. Economists have even shown that the placebo effect of a pretend medication (vitamin C pills, for instance) is stronger when the price of the "drug" is higher.[18] The money illusion also helps to explain why we value a $100 gift card or check as less than an equivalent amount of cash, which is to say we are more apt to spend it. The artifice with gift cards is that they have no value, so we act as if they're play money. To economists, a restaurant coupon worth $100 equals $100 in cash, equals $100 in a bank account. Yet these different iterations of $100 are not at all equal when measured by the yardstick of human behavior.

We also treat cash differently depending on the denomination. Anyone who has ever felt reluctant to break a $100 bill, or rummaged through a purse for the satisfaction of paying with exact change, will recognize this instinct. Twenty times five may equal one hundred always and forever to mathematicians, but in the mind, five $20 bills do not equal a $100 bill. In the opposite direction, we're more willing to part with coins than we are an equivalent amount of bills, and this tendency has been demonstrated among populations from the American heartland to eastern China.[19] Following the 2007–2008 financial crisis, one scientist joked that the Obama administration, as part of its stimulus package, should issue more $1 coins, or even $2 ones, because peoples' willingness to spend coins would spur spending.[20]

"A coin symbolizes man's free will," wrote Jorge Luis Borges. Yet our predispositions and inconsistencies suggest otherwise. If you don't think these forces impact how you spend your money, it's only because you haven't spent much time with people like Priya Raghubir, a professor of marketing at New York University's Stern School of Business. One of Raghubir's recent studies looked at how we treat different national currencies. Most people assume that Americans traveling abroad spend more in a country like Thailand or Argentina, where prices are cheap compared to prices at home. But Raghubir and her fellow researchers have found that how a price appears has such a powerful influence that it can usurp our rational understanding of the real price—the real value. They dubbed this phenomenon the *denomination effect*.

In Thailand, transactions are often conducted with 500- and 1,000-bhat banknotes, and the key is that those are multiples of the paper money denominations at home in the United States. As of October 2011, 1,000 bhats would buy you about $32. "But you latch onto the fact that this is 1,000 *somethings*," says Raghubir. Although you know, at the intellectual level, that numerical value is distinct from that money's purchasing power, the large number will trick you into thinking prices in Bangkok are steeper than they really are. As a result, Americans in Thailand are far more frugal than predictions of rational economic decision-making would suggest.*

What happens when the situation is reversed? Raghubir found that Americans transacting in Britain or Bahrain, countries where U.S. dollars

---

*Perhaps policymakers in countries like Thailand ought to rejigger their cash denominations to capitalize on this aspect of our irrational selves, so as to boost visiting foreigners' willingness to spend.

are represented as a *fraction* of the local currency, spend more. These aren't just quirks of the American psyche, either. During the implementation of the euro, the new currency was valued at a fraction of the national currencies it was to replace (except in Ireland), so that two Deutsche Marks, for instance, equaled one euro. Again, Raghubir found people were spending much more with this new money, almost as if it were Monopoly® money.[21] It's the money illusion cross-pollinated with currency confusion. "People are unable to calculate the exchange rates, even if the calculation is trivially easy!" All those zeroes on the restaurant menu in Bangkok or on a Thai banknote block us from thinking clearly.

Perhaps nothing is more cuckoo, though, than cash's role as happiness elixir. In the years ahead, as physical money fortifies itself against an onslaught of new technologies and critics, one of its most formidable defenses may turn out to be emotional, not economic. For starters, there is the notion that dealing with cash encourages honesty, at least when it comes to our reluctance to steal $1 bills versus cans of Coke.

But a recent series of studies involving pain illustrates physical money's true mental charms. When people are exposed to cash versus slips of blank paper, they're better insulated from a particular type of social pain. In one experiment, participants played a computer game in which they were asked to pass a ball around to other people who were also playing the game. But the fix was in. The test subjects never got the ball, like kids ostracized on a playground.

Past investigations have shown that even this seemingly simple exercise leads to empirically significant feelings of rejection. In this scenario, however, subjects who handled banknotes before the game started were less affected by the experience of exclusion. The socially painful event was less painful for the cash handlers, which is a roundabout way of saying that handling cash warms the heart, or at least bolsters the ego. And it does so even when that money isn't our own.[22]

The same researchers then decided to up the stakes. After having subjects count out either banknotes or blank paper, the scientists had them put their fingers in hot water for thirty seconds. Cash, it turns out, is like a suit of armor. The money counters didn't think the water was as hot as the paper counters did, and those who handled the banknotes reported feeling less pain. It's as if every interaction with cash, at the subconscious level, takes us back to the sensation of reaching under a pillow the day after losing a tooth, and bumping into the cool metal of a fifty-cent piece. Cash feels *good*.

Summarizing the results of these investigations in an article for the journal *Science*, researchers concluded that material money appears to make us feel less pressure to be included or liked by others, shields us from feeling emotional or physical pain, reduces feelings of rejection, and promotes feelings of independence and self-sufficiency. The other side of this coin is that the money handlers in the studies tended to be more distant from others, less helpful, and less inclined toward teamwork.

With cash that is rightfully ours, these emotional forces are only magnified. When a waiter or store clerk gives you $8.75 in change after settling your bill, maybe you leave the $3.75 as a tip and put the fiver in your wallet, that nice new burgundy wallet bought during the memorable autumn shopping day with your sister. You align it just the way you like next to photos of your kids, your personalized credit cards, your driver's license, and your gym membership card. Or maybe you prefer a money clip, the one your grandfather gave you when you were a boy. Using the clip, you never think about how unhygienic banknotes are, let alone about tax evasion or bank robberies. No, you think about your suave grandfather—how the money clip is part of what made him cool—a man's man, like Sinatra or McQueen. ("Men carry cash," is how *Esquire* magazine decided to open its 2009 cover package entitled "How to Be a Man." I'll bet Kim Jong Il saved a copy of that one. Dave Birch? Not so much.)

Besides, we've wired cash into our cultures. It's not just tipping and tooth fairies—it's passing the plate at church or during Hindu *Aarti* offerings. It's Hanukkah geld, donations at Shinto Buddhist shrines, and a shower of coins during Persian weddings. The intricate and extensive role of paper money in Japan is especially interesting because it runs contrary to the widespread belief that Japan is speeding toward cash-lessness. In Tokyo's bustling day-glow hotspots like Shinjuku or Shibuya, high-tech cash substitutes are indeed easy to notice—stored-value cards, for example, with cutesy names like Suica and Pasmo, as well as cellphone-based payment tools and countless types of gift cards that act as a kind of pseudo-cash.

Yet during my trips to Japan, whenever I duck into the basement of one of the massive department stores to browse among the vendors selling assorted green teas, sweet-bean cookies, rice crackers, and square watermelons, I mostly see customers paying with cash or the occasional credit or debit card. Like people throughout the world, there is a sense among the Japanese that not having at least *some* cash on hand could turn a tricky situation into an emergency. What's more, cash gifts are almost a national obsession, required for all kinds of special occasions like weddings and graduations, and on holidays like New Year's. The custom is to give crisp new banknotes, except in the case of a condolence for the family of someone who has died. In that situation you have to give old banknotes, indicating to the recipients that you know this is not a happy time.

None of this bodes well for the anti-cash crusade. If people throughout the world like this form of money, if it's so intertwined with culture, if it hurts more to part with it, and if it gives us a buzz merely to handle it, who in his right mind would want to abandon it, other than maybe that Manhattan restaurateur who wants to keep poor people away?

If the choice were really this kind of oversimplified either–or, I'd probably stick up for cash. But the future of how we pay will have all kinds of options. We can already see some of these better tools for transacting. PayPal's app for smartphones nukes the need for having cash on hand to divvy up a restaurant bill. We can just "bump" phones to "flash" (e-mail, zap, zip, send) the funds to each other right there and then, and be finished before the waiter returns with a credit card receipt to sign.

Not that we'll need to sign for much longer. Soon enough, you won't even need a plastic card with a magnetic stripe or a chip to hold data.

Cellphones equipped with tiny antenna wirelessly transmit payment for something with a quick tap on a reader device at the cash register. By 2014, transactions conducted via wireless connections from our phones are expected to total $1.13 trillion.[23] Initially, most of these new technologies will only provide alternative ways to make a credit card charge, but that too is changing, as users turn to person-to-person methods that cut out the middlemen, the cumulative effect of which is fewer tack-on fees and less friction in our economic lives.

But one worry with new digital tools is that they will further separate us from the act of spending, pushing us in the direction of less responsible financial decisions, if that's even possible. I don't buy that fatalistic view because we can use findings from behavioral economics to better ourselves. As disheartening as it can be to learn about how irrationally we treat money, the upside is that these insights can guide the development of future forms of money and financial devices. We can design systems that coax us into making wiser choices. This isn't Huxleyian enemy-state social engineering—it's just smarter tools, like automobiles that adjust to icy driving conditions, or coffee pots that shut off after a certain amount of time so that you don't set fire to the kitchen.

A service as basic as an e-mail reminder to pay a bill on time is a simple example of just such an attempt to compensate for human frailty. A more substantial instance of applying behavioral economics findings to everyday life is default participation in 401(k) plans. People are both myopic about financial planning and plagued by their own inertia, and they keep putting off signing up for a retirement savings program even if they want to be in one. So policymakers recently made retirement savings an opt-out program instead of an opt-in one. Presto: more Americans now save for retirement.

In his discussion about cheating and how we can be "dishonest without thinking of ourselves as dishonest," Ariely provides a quick aside about ways these tendencies could be fixed. We could label office items at work with a price, for example. That might reduce peoples' habit of helping themselves (although it could also backfire because it makes an employer look so distrustful). But what if we used more targeted language when talking about stock options and mortgage-backed securities, to eliminate the fuzziness of the values involved, and any morally suspect decisions that may be embedded within them? What if we started using words like *curchase*? Knowing what we know about ourselves, we can manipulate our biases about money for the better. The personal finance tools that we now use, or have at least come across, provide clues as to how this can happen. Consider something as unsexy as Quicken, the desktop software for financial organization, and how much it helps people budget and keep track of spending, all without having to store cash in categorized envelopes.

More recently, there are services like Mint.com, which pull together your various accounts, credit cards, investments, home loan, and the like, into one easy-to-digest website or smartphone app. Mint puts your net worth right at the top of the screen. If you're like millions of homeowners in the United States, that means a negative number is now a very salient part of your everyday life. Might that influence behavior, such as willingness to pay, in just the opposite way that those gold- or platinum-colored credit cards hypnotize us into spending more than we should? We can't yet answer that question because these apps—and the everyday use of apps—are still so new and evolving, but I would bet yes.

An app I want to see will recreate the salience of relinquishing paper money, or cleverly simulate the pain in spending currently only associated with cash. Maybe you'll see images of banknotes on the display, and receive an audible message of caution about discretionary spending from a Ben Franklin impersonator. If you find you still have trouble controlling your spending, you could program your mobile wallet to halt transactions after spending a certain amount, or to require you to sing an embarrassing song in order to make the transaction go through. It's a bit like the Gmail feature Google offered a few years ago. People leery of sending drunk e-mails could turn on a filter of sorts, which makes them perform a math problem before sending the composed message. If the user is too slow or can't get the right answer, Gmail won't send the potentially regrettable message.

Because we can hack our behaviors for the better, we shouldn't underestimate our ability to decipher our biases, work around them, or capitalize on them. It would be a mistake to reject future payment tools or new forms of money out of hand, just because today's tired old credit cards boost willingness to pay and undergrads at one university don't steal single dollar bills out of shared refrigerators.

And as this new generation of technologies cuts into that category of transactions for which we still think cash is useful, another, completely different, pressure on cash is coming from the changing landscape of currencies. If notes and coins represent denominations of national currencies, what will happen to cash in a world in which fewer and fewer countries bother to have one?

CHAPTER 5

The Patriot

Goddam money. It always ends up making you blue as hell.

—HOLDEN CAULFIELD IN *THE CATCHER IN THE RYE*

*H*elvitis *Fökking Fökk!* Loosely translated, this Icelandic expression means "Oh, hell fucking fuck." I've seen it emblazoned on T-shirts in a hip Reykjavik clothing shop, local economists and academics told me about it, and even a friend who works at Iceland's national hospital mentioned it. Now here it is again, on the wall of the café where I'm finishing a plate of soggy French fries.

It started with a placard carried by a bearded man who, together with several hundred people in this country of just 300,000, spent several chilly autumn days in 2008 protesting outside the country's central bank. Iceland had just suffered what was the most spectacular banking collapse in the history of the world. The expletive on the man's placard became something of a catchall pronouncement for everything that went wrong.

From this spot at Café Paris I can see the Parliament building, as well as the statue of Jón Sigurdsson, the father of Icelandic independence. Sigurdsson is also the face of the 500-króna banknote. Adorning the café wall are fourteen large prints created by a local artist and his son depicting an abbreviated history of Iceland and the recent economic crisis. Each one is painted in a vibrant Dick Tracy-meets-manga style and is accompanied by a small explainer in English.

They start with warring Vikings striking out from Europe. The fourth panel shows a man in a V-neck sweater, smiling and toasting a glass of red wine with the skyline of a big city behind him. The caption reads: "More than a thousand years passed until we Icelanders returned to Europe. This time, we didn't bring swords or shields, our arsenal was laced with money. But it wasn't our own money for we borrowed it from large international banks."

The next panels depict the crash, with a man seated on the edge of a skyscraper, smoking a cigarette, and, if not contemplating suicide, certainly at his wits end. Understandably so. Almost overnight, Iceland's stock market lost 90 percent of its value, and the country as a whole was saddled with debts amounting to roughly ten times the GDP, or all the money of the state.[1] For a sense of scale, Iceland's $12 billion GDP is about $4 billion less than Nike's annual revenue. The panels after that portray the protests, including the forlorn-looking man wearing a hoodie and carrying his now famous sign.

The investment bankers blamed for the crisis are known locally as the Viking Raiders, or "the forty, plus two women." They had embarked on a global shopping spree with borrowed money, gobbling up assets including a power plant in India, part of a European airline, and a pro soccer team in England. How did they do it? With lots of borrowed money denominated in foreign currencies. Those assets hypnotized them into thinking they were earning real money. With appreciation, they were, sort of—provided you don't mind blurring the definitions of *equity* and *money*. One Icelandic economist summarized it this way: "The banks were trying to lift themselves off the ground by grabbing the hair atop their head and pulling up. It doesn't work." Yet for several years it did work, at least on paper. Iceland's banks were hoisting themselves up by their hair, much like a pyramid scheme can create the illusion of viability.

In the days after the financial collapse, Icelanders found that everything they needed to buy—gas, prescriptions, clothing, groceries—was three or four times more expensive, while the loans on their homes and cars had suddenly doubled or tripled. After growing grotesquely inflated with lousy assets, the country's three main banks imploded. But their failure didn't just leave a discrete mess. Because the banks had amassed debts far exceeding Iceland's GDP, they pulled down the entire economy, causing the króna to lose more than half its value against other currencies and sending the government to the brink of bankruptcy. Some Norwegian commentators floated the idea that Norway should assume its neighbor's debts and effectively buy back its former colony.[2]

Icelanders are now considering joining the European monetary union, which will mean abandoning the króna in favor of the euro. Many economists and financial journalists say this is inevitable, or were saying it before the sovereign debt crises in Greece, Ireland, Spain, and Portugal rattled the world's confidence in the euro. That debate will continue, but, sooner or later, Iceland will probably sing the króna's swansong, joining a growing number of countries and territories that have dumped, or are thinking about dumping, their national currencies.

One idea for the monetary future of the world is to nuke all but a few of the most influential currencies. It's not as radical as it sounds. Panama, El Salvador, Ecuador, and East Timor have all officially adopted the U.S. dollar, and in countries from Uruguay to Cambodia, the Caribbean to the Caucuses, the dollar is accepted just as regularly, if not more so, than the local currency. The situation is similar with the euro. Estonia is the most recent addition, at number seventeen, to join the common currency club. Latvia is on deck, and a handful of countries around Europe use, but aren't technically on, the euro. In other cases, it may come as a surprise that tiny nations or subnations still have their own currencies. On October 10, 2010, the islands of the Dutch Antilles in the Caribbean finally said goodbye to the Dutch Antillean guilder, which had been used locally despite the fact that the Dutch themselves had long since replaced their guilders with euros. Disney Dollars are used by more people than some of the world's smallest currencies, and, in case you're itching to know, the dobra, issued by the tiny island nation of São Tomé and Príncipe, is the national currency with the least amount of circulating cash.

As this process of currency consolidation unfolds, however slowly, it's a safe bet that the likes of the Malawi kwacha, Azerbaijanian manat, and Icelandic króna will go the way of the wampum. The road to cashlessness will be paved with the banknotes of dead national currencies. For economists and policymakers, the topic of halting national currencies is intertwined with the difficult, if not wrenching, question of relinquishing monetary sovereignty. What I want to know is perhaps less complicated but more elusive: what might it mean for a country and its people to kiss their currency goodbye?

The final panel in the series at Café Paris ends on a hopeful note. Mimicking the famous photograph of U.S. soldiers raising the Stars and Stripes over Iwo Jima, camouflage-clad soldiers in the painting raise the Icelandic flag on the shore of Reykjavik harbor. The national flag is blue with a red-and-white cross stretched across its length. As flags go, it's a handsome one. Coins and currency notes are similar symbols of the state, used to make us feel connected to it, and to one another.

◆

THE NEXT MORNING I step off a yellow city bus in a suburb south of Reykjavik, and walk downhill from a small shopping plaza. It's a strangely mild winter day with drizzle interrupted by occasional sunbursts. The road curves left, leading into a quiet neighborhood of Lego-like houses with blue and red roofs and lingering Christmas decorations. To the east, the developed environment abruptly ends, minus a few roads weaving out into a dark volcanic landscape dotted with small cinder cones. It looks like the setting of a *Mad Max* sequel set in the cold.

A few minutes later, Kristin Thorkelsdottir's house comes into view. A capsized trapezoid, the house is almost like a bunker, but cheerful. The side facing the street is covered with light-blue corrugated tin (over a more insulating material, I presume), and the sides are a bright purple.

I walk around a handful of stunted evergreen trees and mossy rocks and climb the wooden steps to the door.

Sipping coffee and eating chocolate cookies in her brightly lit studio, Thorkelsdottir recalls the task she describes as infusing paper with a most usual kind of value. "It was a great privilege when the central bank contacted me about the redesign of the banknotes," she says. The year was 1977, and the Icelandic government, following an ugly episode of inflation, had secretly decided to issue new banknotes and coins, and revalue the currency in the process.

Governments, especially those of wealthy countries that try to assert their civility and stability, take pride in the condition of their physical money, and part of the mythmaking of being a wealthy and civilized place with a healthy economy is to have sharp new banknotes equipped, of course, with first-rate security features. Switzerland, that bastion of banking and tax-evasion tradition, doesn't let banknotes circulate more than a few times before shredding them and reprinting new ones.[3]

Thorkelsdottir has short-cropped white hair, long silver earrings, and red rectangular glasses. She looks like a gentler version of Dame Judi Dench. To lead Iceland's paper money overhaul, she was the obvious choice. One of the most famous artists in the country at the time, she had already impressed the governors of the central bank with her design for a commemorative coin marking Iceland's 1,100-year anniversary in 1974. (If you don't have one of those commemoratives, I know some people who can hook you up.)

She started by thinking about the macro vision. "I introduced two themes for the Bank to choose from. The first was about Icelandic scientists and the outdoors. The second was portraiture," or more specifically, portraits of dead Icelanders who embody the country's "culture and its tradition of scholarship." Because the art on past banknotes relied heavily on images of industry, namely cod fishing and sheep farming, and probably because Icelanders were getting a little sick of being known to the rest of the world only for cod fishing and sheep farming, the bank bosses opted for the culture theme.

But Thorkelsdottir had a minor problem in that she didn't really know what that culture was, or who might best symbolize it. She spent a week at the tiny National Museum, perusing the portraits gallery and speaking with historians to learn about the individuals who typified what it means to be Icelandic. And so it came to pass that Iceland's banknotes today include intricate portraits of: Sigurdsson, the grandfather of the country's independence movement; a famed manuscript collector who went around the countryside gathering texts written on calf skins, which otherwise would have been eaten by mice or turned into shoes; a renowned bishop and architect; and a seventeenth-century woman known as a trailblazing artist and teacher. "I wanted to show that we have these heroes and a rich history," Thorkelsdottir explains.

The joy of the project, she says, was in the exactitude, finding just the right artifacts associated with the different individuals and using them to create two-dimensional objects that would portray the character of her homeland. She was given tacit support from the bank governors to spare no expense to get it perfect. They make the money, after all. She took her time finding just the right antique desk to model, and research-ing period-specific fabric patterns and fonts. She even hired a bearded man as a model and had a costume and wig made for him so that she could better draw the portrait of the chubby bishop featured on the 1,000-króna note. For the image with the manuscript collector, she wanted to have a full bookcase in the background, so she consulted with an expert on book-binding for tips about how the spines of those mi-nuscule books depicted on the bookshelf of her bills should appear.

"The banknote is like heritage in your hand," she says. "It lets you read the culture of the country." It has been this way with physical money for centuries. Struck into coins and embedded in the fibers of that high-tech paper are stories—micro-histories that animate the past, and that provide the bearer with a sense of that place's identity. Words, a dictionary editor once told me, are a palimpsest. Their etymologies contain the shadows of words and people from ages past. Banknotes are too, I suppose.

It was only when Thorkelsdottir commented about heritage that I suddenly remembered that for years, without an overt plan to do so, I would often save a banknote or two from a trip abroad as a souvenir for my father. Physical money isn't just a tactile representation of the currency; it's also a representation of the place, a snapshot of life there, or at least design taste there, mixed with a kind of cultural highlight reel. Looking back on this habit, perhaps I brought the bills back for my father because I wanted him to know, if only just a little, what everyday life was like in these countries I was visiting, and there's nothing as everyday as the notes and coins in peoples' pockets.

Different cultures value banknotes differently, though, as far as art is concerned. From a designer's perspective, Thorkelsdottir says, "you even see that some cultures don't care much about elegant design." She says this with a nod and a wink toward me and the greenbacks of my homeland. She is not alone in her lackluster opinion of the look of the most coveted currency in the world. Among design buffs, Federal Reserve Notes score low marks for a handful of reasons, one of which is that they are so busy—"a cake that has been decorated to within an inch of its life," as one designer put it.[4] A *Gawker* critic said the new $100 bill "looks like a god damn child's crayon scratch pad."[5] And it's true: So many fonts and swirls and micro-patterns and micro-swirls and drawings and facial hair and borders and textures and codes and now splashes of color—it's almost enough to make a man long for a simple piece of plastic or a chip implanted in your forearm.

Those who emphasize functional design like to point out that U.S. banknotes are all the same size, unlike notes in most other countries. That uniformity puts nearly 4.5 million blind or visually impaired Americans at a disadvantage. A court order following a lawsuit filed by the American Council of the Blind in 2002 has forced the Treasury to remedy the situation. Treasury lawyers actually had the gall to appeal the lower court's ruling, claiming the costs of accommodating the blind were unreasonable; apparently the purpose of cash is to promote commerce among those who can see it. But in 2008, the U.S. Court of Appeal for the District of Columbia struck down that argument, accused the Treasury of exaggerating its cost estimates, and again ruled that U.S. banknotes aren't accommodating the needs of all citizens.[6] To date, the government is still assessing how to implement this now mandatory fix.

Yet there is method to the perceived madness of America's uni-sized and detail-saturated notes. Remember: the goal with banknotes is to get the transacting public using them by convincing people that this worthless paper represents real value. Maintaining the same look of the greenback since 1928, and the same basic coloring since the Civil War, may not appeal to those with an eye for elegant lines or visual balance. It does appeal, however, to those who comprehend just how much rides on confidence in the U.S. dollar, and the necessity of engineering that confidence *into* the banknotes.

It's all about perceived stability, which means protecting the value of banknotes not only against the devaluing influence of counterfeiters, but also by broadcasting a message of the issuer's stability through time. What you're really trying to conjure on the banknote is faith in the government. The fact that all U.S. currency ever issued is still acceptable legal tender, coupled with the consistent look of our paper money through the generations, is central to the mission of monetary image-making.

Still, all the high-minded language in the world isn't going the make U.S. banknotes any prettier, and the recent design tweaks don't exactly help. As one designer put it, additions like the purple fives are "as inelegant and clumsy as a denim patch on a satin dress."[7] In 2009 a "creative strategy consultant" in New York named Richard Smith started a contest called the Dollar ReDe$ign Project. ("It's time to ReBrand the Buck!") There's nothing official about it—it's just one of those clever ideas born online that went viral. Swift economic recovery, Smith writes on the website, requires "a thorough, in-depth, rebranding scheme—starting with the redesign of the iconic U.S. Dollar."

Looking through the collection of different entries to Dollar ReDe$ign is thought-provoking in that it reminds me how thoroughly programmed I am to recognize the greenback as something unique, almost holy. These designs, in contrast, with their variable colors, new images, and celebration of Americana from Martin Luther King and the Grand Canyon, to Amelia Earhart and the moon landing, smack of absurdity. Some of the mock-ups incorporate familiar faces and "legacy features"—the requisite bald eagle, cheerful FDR, pyramids, Franklin's dimply mug—yet these too just look so . . . *off.*

The greenback is one of the most instantly recognizable images in the world. Yet are the machinations of currency and paper money so foreign to Americans today that we can't conceive of a design overhaul? Why are the Swiss OK with it but Americans, who live in a country born out of currency revolution and self-reinvention, are stubbornly resistant to it? Maybe we reject profound change to our physical money (or government officials reject it for us) because it's another one of those lines of thinking that could invite unsettling thoughts about conjured value and a global financial system riding on circulating promises.

It's a little like how retiring the penny isn't just about pennies because it gets you thinking about inflation, which can lead to outsized fears of inflation that end up harming the economy. If your job were to keep the economy stable, would you be eager to conduct a dollar redesign? Remember how badly Coca-Cola botched it when the company rolled out New Coke? Rebranding can be risky for a product or a company. Imagine what it could do for the currency that is the backbone of the international monetary system.

Designing paper money, says Thorkelsdottir, is unlike designing anything else in the world. Banknotes have this strange functionality in that few things are as commonplace, yet many people have strong emotional relationships to physical money. For people who relish travel, or even hold low-grade curiosity about landmasses in other time zones, there is a mysterious allure to the banknotes and coins of other countries. What else could explain why so many corner stores, diners, and bars have pinned wrinkly banknotes from dozens of nations on the wall like postcards or passport stamps? As Thorkelsdottir puts it: "Banknotes tell stories of history, but they also are history."

Right about this time in our conversation, I expect Thorkelsdottir to express some wistfulness about the possible end to the króna, about national soul, about an uncle who collects banknotes—*something*. Instead, she is a portrait of practicality. "I want money to stand for what it is, for the value it represents," she says. "If we have to take up the euro because of today's situation, it's probably for the best. To insist on the króna would be like smacking your head on a stone over and over."

Perhaps this lack of sentimentality is a consequence of the country's recent economic nightmare—a national reckoning about money and a new prevailing ethic to be practical above all things. Or maybe this no-nonsense worldview is something Icelanders have always had, a requirement for survival in such a harsh landscape, and it was only a tiny group of investment bankers who recently turned their backs on this heritage. Whatever the reason, if I was looking for someone to say that killing the national currency is akin to burning the flag or a heartbreaking loss in the World Cup, I wasn't going to hear it here. "I actually use plastic most of the time," adds Thorkelsdottir. "Money is just a tool," she says, "and the credit card is more convenient."

As it happens, Icelanders are more addicted to electronic cash and payments than any people on earth, making Iceland something of a frozen paradise for anti-cash mavens. An American expat in Reykjavik told me he once saw a couple of local children selling homemade cookies on the street, much like American kids set up lemonade stands, except that the young Icelanders had debit-card readers on hand. This widespread adoption of a card-based system makes economic sense: analysts have found that using cash in Iceland has a per-transaction cost that is five times higher than using a card. If that sounds abstract, think about it this way: it's expensive for businesses and governments to ensure that ATMs, cash registers, and banks in every remote fishing village have correct change, whereas all you need for electronic payment is electricity and a phone hookup.[8]

As Thorkelsdottir shows me some of her first pencil sketches for the banknotes redesign, I think of my conversation the previous day with an Icelandic economist, who reminded me that it was George Washington who said: "It is not a custom with me to keep money to look at." Not long from now, Thorkelsdottir's creations will move from immortalizing the history of this country into their humble place within it.

But maybe not just yet. Iceland is currently facing the prospect of more inflation, and the country is at least a few years from joining the euro. (Possibly more than a few, with the euro currently stuck in the mud, and countries like Sweden noticeably enjoying the economic benefits of not being on the euro.) Perhaps another round of revaluation is in the forecast. So I ask, 90 percent in jest, whether the recent financial collapse means the Central Bank of Iceland will retain Thorkelsdottir's services once more, this time to design a 10,000-, or perhaps even a 20,000-króna note?

"I can't answer that," she says.

"But you're not retired, right?"

"Right."

◆

IN OCTOBER OF 2008, the króna suffered a near fatal crisis of faith. Because those three private banks' losses dwarfed the national economy, the central bank couldn't come to their rescue as lender of last resort. Despite the alchemy of money creation, central banks are still limited to creating money in their national currency. Issuing more króna to try and absorb the banks' gargantuan debt wouldn't have worked because those króna couldn't *buy* anything. Iceland was forced to approach the International Monetary Fund hat in hand and accept a last-minute loan from Russia to stave off bankruptcy.

Before the crash, the króna was strong—a source of national pride, and only getting stronger. It was so strong that Icelanders were buying or taking loans in other currencies—often euros, Swiss francs, or Japanese yen—because the interest rates were better. For those with trading savvy, there was money to be made bouncing between currencies or in investment deals involving a series of conversions.

But what Icelanders failed to notice was that no one was investing in *their* currency. This point was driven home for me after my year without cash. I still had about $20 worth of króna burning a hole in my wallet. When I asked at a few currency exchanges on the streets of London or at airports far from Iceland whether they buy Icelandic króna, the tellers looked at me as if I'd asked them to exchange red feathers for U.S. dollars.

When the bottom fell out of the króna, loans denominated in foreign currencies more than doubled, because twice as much of the domestic currency was suddenly needed to pay back those loans in euros or yen. The banks had built not just a house of cards, but a house of króna. As an Icelandic friend put it: "We were stuck with a currency that is like a sack of rotten potatoes. No one wants it and it's worth nothing." It's important to note that the króna has since recovered much of that lost value. Nevertheless, many experts insist that Iceland and countries like it are no less vulnerable to this kind of currency crisis today than they were in 2007.

During my week in Reykjavik, newspapers reported that vandals were tossing red paint on the homes and cars of Viking Raiders who hadn't yet fled to England or the Continent. With their wages still paid in króna, Icelanders were losing their homes, cars, and small businesses, unable to make their now-ballooned loan payments. At the national hospital, hours and wages had been reduced, while administrators cut costs by slowing admissions, blood testing, drug sourcing, and diagnostics. Then again, at least Icelanders will now be eating a little healthier. In 2009, McDonald's decided to close its three restaurants in Iceland. No one was going to pay 780 króna—more than $6.00—for a Big Mac.[9]

◆

IN AUGUST OF 2007, at the apex of Iceland's dash for financial-sector stardom, an American named Benn Steil flew from New York to Reykjavik to recommend euthanizing the króna. Steil is an economist with the Council on Foreign Relations. That spring, he'd written a provocative article for *Foreign Affairs* in which he argued that modern economics

has "failed to offer anything resembling a coherent and compelling response to currency crises." Yet a viable strategy is staring us in the face,
he says, and it has been around since it was first described by a Nobel
Prize–winning economist in the 1960s: killing national currencies.
"Governments," he writes, "must let go of the fatal notion that nationhood requires them to make and control the money used in their terri-
tory." The Icelandic króna and dozens of currencies like it, Steil asserts,
should be abolished, and replaced with regional currency blocks.

Steil delivered his 2007 address to Icelandic bankers, government officials, and academics in a gray-and-purple conference room at Reykjavik's Hilton Nordica. Presenting alongside him was the former finance
minister from El Salvador, who had shepherded his country through the
dollarization process. Ditching the króna, Steil asserted, would help in-
sulate the tiny nation from the shock of future currency crises, because
the currency's value couldn't get tossed around like leaves in a wind-
storm, and local companies would no longer have to pay exchange fees.

The speech was received like an insult to Icelandic manhood. The
head of Iceland's Central Bank said: "This is not El Salvador." Iceland,
he said, doesn't need to climb aboard the euro the way Latin American
countries might need to piggyback on the dollar. The Hilton event ended
cordially, though a bit awkwardly. Then Steil and his wife, together with
the Salvadorian official and his wife, enjoyed a three-day weekend tour-
ing waterfalls and glaciers in the Icelandic countryside. "That part was
nice!" Steil admitted. Thirteen months later, the banks collapsed and the
króna was pancaked.

In the age of globalization, what does it mean, really, to be from one
country and not another? We have some easy answers, along the lines
of language, shared history, cultural references, and geography. I grew
up cheering for the Red Sox, not the Hiroshima Carp, so that adds to
my American-ness. I had to learn about the Federalist Papers in high
school. I pay taxes and vote here. I've consumed innumerable gallons of
Ben & Jerry's Ice Cream, watched *Happy Days,* and listened to both Nir-
vana and the Beach Boys. When I see coffins draped with the Stars and

Stripes, the sight fills me with a kind of reverence that other images of coffins don't. All of these things, some minor, some major, contribute to my sense of being part of this country.

Greenbacks do too, whether I like it or not. The coins and banknotes of a place are one of the few remaining touch-points of national identity left in our increasingly digital world. The monuments, symbols, and famous people splashed on them help reinforce this sense of nationhood. But as representations of the currency, they do more than that, because the currency is both the fabric of the economy and the stitching of the state. Even Marco Polo saw this in China, as the currency pulled a vast kingdom together under one umbrella of economic organization.

In recent times, though, having a national currency, at least for smaller countries, is looking more and more anachronistic. At the minimum it should be up for debate. Steil told me that when he lived in Europe in the 1990s, the old saying was that to be a country you needed an airline, a stock exchange, and a currency. By the twenty-first century, that was hardly the case: airlines had merged or gone bankrupt, stock exchanges had consolidated, and the euro had become the dominant currency of the continent. In the years ahead, more and more small countries may decide to quit their currencies and adopt that of a more powerful neighbor (the Australian dollar in parts of Oceania, for instance), band together with nearby countries to form a currency block (e.g., the East African Monetary Union), or jump aboard an international powerhouse like the U.S. dollar or the euro.

All kinds of factors could sway this decision: runaway inflation, fear of currency crises, too little infrastructure to manage the cash supply, an unexpected rash of counterfeits, hope of greater competitiveness in global trade, and the wish to put an end to potentially dangerous speculation about the currency's worth next week or next year. Steil points to relatively strong economic growth and stability in countries like Ecuador, El Salvador, and Panama, which have all officially adopted the U.S. dollar. Even where the local currency still reigns as far as officialdom is concerned, "spontaneous dollarization" is widespread.

More than half of the bank deposits in Latin America are denominated in U.S. dollars.

Steil's thesis hinges on the fact that most monies in the world are unattractive to people who live outside the countries where those currencies circulate. Notaphilists may keep Icelandic króna in their collections, and my dad still has the Samoan, Cuban, and Egyptian banknotes I once gave him, but investors won't hold these currencies as a store of wealth, says Steil—"something that will buy in the future what it did in the past." The same goes for the Argentine peso, and doubly so for currencies of absolute-shambles countries. Know any friends who are denominating their kids' college savings accounts in Somali shillings? Exactly. At the same time, while all countries conduct trade to grow their economies, smaller ones eat extra costs for perpetually converting from the local currency into something else. There's also the fact that countries generally need U.S. dollars to repay their creditors.

Dumping the national currency would also protect people from harmful manipulation of the currency's value by corrupt or incompetent public officials. As Nobel Prize–winning economist Milton Friedman once put it, in the "socialized industry" of providing the people with a transactions medium, "governments are inefficient, produce a poor product and charge a high rent for it."[10] More recently, Harvard financial historian Niall Ferguson has written that "from the very origins of coinage, rulers sought to establish and exploit monopolies over currencies. This, more than anything else, helps to explain the many inflations and other monetary disruptions in history." Which begs the question: would a handful of regional currencies, or even a single global currency, help to prevent such disruptions, and by extension improve prosperity?

As for citizens in the United States and Europe, when other countries adopt the dollar or the euro, we profit from seigniorage—or the government does, anyway. By putting more money into circulation—inside or outside our borders—the Fed pockets the interest generated from this process, so it's really no skin off our backs, provided those countries understand that the United States will never make monetary or economic policy decisions because of conditions in some other country that happens to use our currency.

This idea of pulling the plug on small-country currencies was making all kinds of sense to me, right up until the insanity in Greece began to unfold only a few months after my visit to Iceland. Greece's crushing debt was partly the fault of government officials who cooked the country's books so that the nation could meet the standards of economic stability necessary to join the euro a decade ago.[11] The International Monetary Fund, a kind of global credit union, had to intervene, as did other European countries, to the tune of a $145 billion loan to prop up Greece and prevent the common currency from coming unhinged.[12] Ireland was the next one to fall, and, at press time, Italy is looking shaky. In a matter of months, the euro transmuted from a shining success of international cooperation and integration into a beast with renegade appendages.

The financial press was soon reporting high-level discussions in Athens and elsewhere about quitting the monetary union.[13] The spreading crisis was a bitter validation of the opinion espoused by the likes of Paul Krugman that the euro is a premature experiment gone horribly wrong.[14] Economies in a fix can't be fixed, Krugman and many others argue, without decisive government action. The wealthy countries of the monetary union had to bail out the broke ones, while the countries most hurt by the crisis, now without their own central banks, lack any ability to jiggle the handle of their economies by issuing money, shifting interest rates, absorbing toxic assets, devaluing out of trouble—*something*. For Iceland, having a sovereign currency was suddenly seen as an advantage. It didn't help the people whose house loans are denominated in euros, but the weaker króna meant the country could be more competitive with its (now cheaper) exports.

At the moment, the euro looks like a suit that is five sizes too small, and Steil's *Foreign Affairs* piece calling for currency unions seems distinctly out of sync with the times. Maybe the króna and other tiny-country currencies have a future after all. But other leading currency experts assert that this is a short view of the euro situation, and that after this period of turmoil it'll bounce back stronger than ever.

As Steil and his sympathizers see it, countries with their own currencies invariably walk in monetary step with their major trading partners: Mexico's currency generally tracks to the U.S. dollar, Sweden's krona closely follows the value of the euro, and so forth, and this is the case no matter how autonomous those countries' central banks may think they are, and no matter how patriotic the artwork adorning their banknotes may be. As Olafur Isleifsson, a professor of business at Reykjavik University, told me: "We didn't have monetary independence before. The central bank moves were all forced moves, like in chess. Monetary independence is a phantom." I kept hearing this basic idea whenever I spoke with people about ending small sovereign currencies in favor of regional ones, but the debt fiascos in Europe show that this is anything but a definitive forecast of what lies ahead.

For economists, this dispute cuts to the core of the most macro question there is: what monetary system offers the best route to a more prosperous future for the most people? Starkly different answers to that question reveal how divided scholars are about what it takes to keep economies healthy, and even about the utility of sovereign currencies. As if the stability of the whole show wasn't tenuous enough already.

Nevertheless, the fact remains that more countries, especially biggies like Turkey, want to adopt the euro. (Poland and the Czech Republic, also in line, slowed down their efforts to join in light of the debt crises, but analysts say these countries will eventually join as well.)[15] Leaders in these countries and elsewhere are convinced that the advantages of getting hitched outweigh those of going it alone. Icelanders who are now worrying that the safe harbor of the euro may not be as safe as they once thought may end up favoring a currency union with some of their solvent Scandinavian neighbors.[16]

A third way to buttress the value of a national currency is to tether its value to that of another one that is more stable. This strategy has worked for a number of countries, and some experts argue that the availability of this tool can make the idea of regional currencies look like a moot point. Why terminate the central bank's ability to manipulate the money supply in an emergency if you don't actually have to? Steil says this approach is still precarious and can end up robbing people of their money: "Which would you prefer. One: I give you $100. Two: I give you a hundred pesos, with a promise to redeem them for $100 if you ask? Option two is a currency board or 'hard peg,' which is what Argentina did until 2002." That was when the Argentine government reneged on its promise to redeem pesos for greenbacks. So much for your 100 bucks.

Steil is hardly the first person to have thought about regional currencies, or to challenge the government imperative to issue money, but he's one of the most vocal. The concept of *optimal currency areas* was coined by economist Robert Mundell in the early 1960s, and since then there have been a handful of campaigns to bring the idea into practice—a few of which are slowly moving forward, in Africa and the Middle East most notably.

On the one-world money front, there are scattered dreamers out there, outfits like the Single Global Currency Association, and supporters of something called the Terra TRC (for Trade Reference Currency). In the 1940s, the legendary John Maynard Keynes conceived of a supranational currency that he called the Bancor.[17] The idea can be likened to the constructed language of Esperanto—one common tongue for all humankind. Why not one money for one world? Supporters of Esperanto believe it could someday reduce miscommunication and, by extension, promote world peace. Backers of a single Earth currency envision a great smoothing of transactions, an end to damaging currency speculation, and less economic turmoil, which could mean greater prosperity for all.[18]

While Esperanto struggles for credibility, some economists seriously consider how a one-world currency might happen, albeit in a highly theoretical future.[19] One idea is for this new currency to be an expanded version of something that already exists: Special Drawing Rights. SDR is really a crossbreed of four of the world's most significant currencies, and it's used for particular kinds of settlements at the IMF. Perhaps the SDR is the embryo of a new global currency. Not that this would be a geopolitical walk in the park. "No global government . . . means no global central bank, which means no global currency. Full stop," says UC Berkeley economist Barry Eichengreen.[20] And a world government, lest we forget, is an apocalyptic prospect to a hell of a lot of people.

At the same time, however, many Americans' image of the future incorporates this idea of a global currency—one Tolkienesque coin to rule them all. According to a Pew Research Center survey, 31 percent of Americans think an asteroid will smack into Earth by 2050, but 41 percent of them said they expect to see a shift to a global currency. We have it in our minds that dramatic change is on the horizon, even if the variable currencies and colorful cash we currently trade in and travel with seems like a permanent aspect of modern life.

◆

MY LAST DAY IN REYKJAVIK, I make my way to a sparkling new twenty-story office tower by the waterfront. Friends had told me about it: an outsized eyesore from Iceland's meltdown. It's now virtually empty. I pass two construction workers in the lobby, but neither pays me any attention as I walk to the elevator. When the doors open onto the top floor, I walk into an empty gray-carpeted suite with windows looking down on the mini city and across the water to bluffs in the distance. In front of one window, four metal chairs are aligned side by side facing out to the Reykjavik harbor.

Visiting a place like Iceland and thinking about money is different than doing so in a megalopolis like New York or London. There, everything is money. Not necessarily in the "greed is good" sense, but in the way that a cityscape is entirely manmade. Virtually every square inch of it involves economic activity, and in each office, apartment, restaurant, gallery, and bar, commerce is king. In a place like Reykjavik, though, you can look right past the city onto inhospitable wilderness. Gazing out at the stark volcanic landscapes, the social forces that give money its value come into focus. Among the untouched rocks and snow, banknotes can't buy you jack.

After leaving the ghostly office tower, I meet coin expert Anton Holt in the lobby of the Central Bank of Iceland. A broad, mustachioed white-haired man of fifty-five years who reminds me of Captain Kangaroo, Holt is the curator of the Numismatic Museum at the bank, as well as the curator of the nation's coin collection, so long as the government doesn't sell it off to raise a little dough.

We're the only people here today who are interested in old forms of money; meanwhile, a steady flow of stern-looking men in suits files in and out of the bank, talking into cellphones as they steam purposefully past. "The IMF guys," says Holt. "These are the save-our-bacon meetings."

Holt leads me through a currency tour beginning with dried fish and swatches of wool used as money back in the day, currencies of Iceland's original sagas. The first coins were *silfur* arriving via trade with the rest of Europe, but they were always in short supply and were less practical than commodities like ewes, wool swatches, and fish. It wasn't until 1874 that the Danish monarchy finally granted Icelanders the right to have a bank and issue their own currency.

Soon we are on to banknotes, first supplied by a private bank and backed by gold, and then later print runs, emergency issuances, the inflation years of World War II, and, finally, Thorkelsdottir's designs. "All of this tells you the story of Icelandic independence," says Holt. "You only need to delve in a bit to see that with most countries, the money is the country and the country is the money." The word *króna*, he reminds me, comes from the Danish word for *crown*, as in the sovereign. The same word has been used for centuries in Norway, Sweden, Denmark, and Iceland. In 2000, when the government of Denmark held a referendum about whether to adopt the euro, opponents asserted that abandoning the króna would be an insult to the queen. How persuasive this royalist line of reasoning was is anyone's guess, but the Danes said no to the euro.

"Most countries don't give it much thought, but these notes and coins, they speak to national identity," says Holt. Yet when I ask if joining the euro and no longer having an Icelandic currency will be a blow to that sense of nationhood, Holt, like Thorkelsdottir, expresses little interest in nostalgia. "I hear people at work talk about 'when the króna bounces back.' I am like: 'Are you crazy?' It's not bouncing back." As a coin collector, though, surely a part of him will mourn the loss of Iceland's sovereign currency, right? "Oh forget that! Are the French any less French because they use the euro? The currency was never, and should never, be an ego thing. It's only a tool. The króna as a source of pride—this is only something people bring up now because we might lose it."

Couldn't the same be said about cash?

CHAPTER 6

The Traitor

No, they cannot touch me for coining; I am the king himself.
—WILLIAM SHAKESPEARE, *KING LEAR*

On a sunny October morning, Bernard von NotHaus shoots west out of Honolulu in a beige Toyota Camry. He has a habit of seeking eye contact, which right now means looking over at me as he rambles through his wandering monologue. With each head-turn the car swerves, but von NotHaus always manages to return his attention to the highway just fast enough to jerk the car back into line.

He may be an enemy of safe driving, but von NotHaus hardly looks like the domestic terrorist federal prosecutors say he is. He wears a black-and-vanilla Hawaiian shirt tucked into light pleated pants with a thin black belt. His delicate wire-rim glasses frame a narrow, almost gaunt face, and his hair curls up in a wave of gray and silver that he pulls into a tiny ponytail. Aside from some arthritis, the sixty-seven-year-old man who calls himself the Monetary Architect makes a point of mentioning his good health, in light of the decades of motorcycling, freewheeling romantic exploits, and bountiful drug consumption, all of which he recalls often and fondly. "I never expected to live this long. Really. I mean, we once drove a truck into the lobby of a hotel!"

After von NotHaus finally accepts the idea that I'm not an undercover FBI agent, which takes a while, he is smiley and magnanimous. His speech, although saturated with shouting and f-bombs, also contains a hearty dose of self-deprecation and Hawaii-isms—*mellow, cool, mahalo*—giving an overall impression of a dude impervious to stress. Which is remarkable, considering that he's facing criminal charges for conspiracy, counterfeiting, mail fraud, and—get this—"one count of uttering, passing, and attempting to utter and pass, silver coins in resemblance of genuine U.S. coins in denominations of five dollars or greater." He has lost, or temporarily lost, possession of hundreds of thousands of dollars' worth of other peoples' money, including his own mother's, and one of his sidekicks has been in jail for more than a year. Two months before I meet him, von NotHaus himself was incarcerated for five nights after violating the terms of bail that allow him to hunker down in Hawaii while awaiting trial.

Past Pearl Harbor we turn north toward the town of Waipahu. We pass a Chinese food restaurant called the Golden Coin before entering a small industrial park. Von NotHaus pulls into a space next to a tan-and-blue building that is part factory, part warehouse. Yellow hibiscus blossoms intermingle with a chain-link fence across the street. Inside, we greet the owner of Pacific Mills, Inc., Bud Gregory, who mills precious metals into wire and sheet material used for making jewelry.

The machining shop is filled with rolling dies, presses, and an oily smell. What we've come to see is the gray six-foot-tall machine set in the corner, which looks like a three-ton hourglass. This is the tool of von NotHaus's chosen trade and life passion: minting. "It looks fantastic! Oh, I could just kiss this baby," he says, and then he does, wrapping his arms around one of the press's thick columns. According to FBI agents and federal prosecutors, this coin press is also a mechanical accomplice to von NotHaus's crimes.

Because the press was recently refurbished, it isn't quite ready to mint coins again; a few parts still need to be put back in place, and it has to be moved off of the temporary blocks of wood it's sitting on. As soon as that happens, though, Gregory, who leases the manufacturing arm of von NotHaus's minting business, can get back to filling orders. But not von NotHaus. "I'm not allowed to mint anything," he explains, holding his hands together as if cuffed. This sanction is another term of his bail, as are unannounced visits from a parole officer.

Coins have always been a part of von NotHaus's life. Growing up outside of Kansas City, he inherited a modest collection from his grandfather, and his mother instilled in him a respect for the value of silver, giving him silver coins as gifts and lecturing him about the metal's penchant for appreciation. "I saved every one of those real silver quarters," he says, referring to U.S. Mint quarters that, before 1965, contained 90 percent real silver. (At press time, with silver at $39 an ounce, one of those quarters has a melt value of more than $7.)

For more than thirty-five years, von NotHaus and his girlfriend, Telle Presley, have run a business called the Royal Hawaiian Mint Company, using this press to make coins for a variety of customers. In the mid-1970s, von NotHaus ordered the press, nicknamed Hammer, and had it shipped from California. He and Presley tried to run the mint business on the Big Island, where, according to von NotHaus, they lived next to a treasure trove of hallucinogenic mushrooms. But the operation proved difficult; merely finding reliable electricity for the powerful press was problematic. So in 1983, just in time to commemorate the twenty-fifth anniversary of Hawaii's statehood, they moved the business and family—sons Random and Xtra—to Honolulu, where the Royal Hawaiian Mint has been located ever since.

Von NotHaus and Presley joined the small club of custom minters that exist all over the world, producing merchandise for war veterans, country clubs, historical societies, academic institutions, and anyone else willing to pay for specialized coins or medallions. None of this is illegal. Over the years, von NotHaus's business has produced coins celebrating Hawaii's statehood, commemorating icons of Hawaiian history like Captain James Cook and King Kamehameha, saluting winners of the Hawaii State Numismatic Association Medal, and marking the fiftieth and seventieth anniversaries of the attack on Pearl Harbor, a coin commissioned by the Pearl Harbor Survivors Association. The association wants him to do the seventy-fifth anniversary commemorative as well. If he's not in jail, he will.

The minting business was the perfect way to blend his love of Hawaii and his infatuation with precious metals. Coins sell themselves, in a way, but von NotHaus has a knack for marketing the combined benefits of metallic value and artistry. When he isn't on a tirade about sovereign currency and inflation, and merely holding forth on the minting process and the craft of coin design, he speaks with unencumbered glee. In the blue-carpeted showroom at his store, von NotHaus shows me a white plaster mold, about a foot in diameter, featuring the head of Hawaii's Queen Liliuokalani, which became the image on one of his coin issues. "Look at the flowing hair. I mean, the hair is one of those elements that often comes out looking shitty. But this is just exquisite!" For decades, von NotHaus has worked with a reclusive sculptor in New York who develops the cast that, after substantial editing demands from von NotHaus, eventually becomes the master die for punching out a coin series. "Look here, on Liliuokalani's necklace. See what we've done with the pendant? Look at that. Beautiful."

Back at Pacific Mills, I ask if I can see some of the coins—the Hawaii Dala in particular. The Dala is one of the coins that got von NotHaus in trouble, although I don't recommend using the word *coin* in front of him. "DO NOT CALL THEM COINS! Coins are made and issued by the government. Do I look like the government to you? The whole idea of this *private voluntary barter real-value currency* is that it is not the government! Never call them coins!" I am permitted, however, to call them *pieces, specie, silvers,* or *Liberty Dollars.* The diction gymnastics are ridiculous because, obviously, they're coins. Yet von NotHaus's unusual legal case rests partly on parsing such terminology, not to mention use of the symbol "$" and minuscule numerals pressed into coins. For charges that include uttering prohibited utterances about coinage, no detail is too arcane.

A moment later, Gregory returns from his office with a small box containing a dozen plastic cases, each housing a single coin. He hands me one. The picture is of Hawaii's revered King Kamehameha, standing proudly in a warrior headdress, left arm raised as if he's about to address his loyal subjects. Turning it over to inspect the other side, I read *HAWAII DALA* across the top. Hawaii's state seal floats in the middle of the image, with the words *Liberty Dollar* on the left, and *$20* on the right. Below the seal: "Twenty Dollars: one ounce .999 silver minted in USA," with a tiny *RHM* trademark symbol.

"This was minted on this press—on Hammer, right?" I ask. Von NotHaus nods.

Because Gregory is the one often punching out coins for the mint, I ask why he's not in trouble with the Feds. If the government says these so-called pieces are possibly counterfeit and infringe on the U.S. Treasury's exclusive right to mint coinage, isn't Gregory an accomplice to von NotHaus's crime?

"The reverse," both men reply in stereo, referring to the other side of the coin. Gregory hands me another one. King Kamehameha again, and the coin is the same size, weight, and composition. But turning it over reveals an image of a traditional Polynesian boat and the state motto in large capital letters: *UA MAU KE EA O KA AINA I KA PONO* (The life of the land is perpetuated by righteousness). This coin also has "1 oz .999 silver RHM," but—and here's the crux—no denomination, no "$" symbol, and no declaration of a dollar value. Gregory never minted the suspect Hawaiian Dalas, Liberty Dollars, or Tea Party Dollars. He only produced what he calls collectibles, like this one with the boat.

I hold the two silver pieces in the palm of each hand, as if their heft might offer some clue as to their variable consequence. Then I place the two side by side on the table, alleged counterfeit on the left, knickknack on the right.

"That is what they're pissing over!" yells von NotHaus. "I mean: Do I look like a counterfeiter to you?"

◆

WHAT IS IT THAT MAKES private currencies sound somewhere between unscrupulous and ridiculous? Reflexive patriotism, perhaps, or possibly willful ignorance about the difference between money, currency, and national currency. You may have heard the term *legal tender* before, but many people often misinterpret it to mean that government-issued money is irrefutable always and everywhere. But you're not legally bound to use coin of the realm, as those cashless airline cabins make clear. You're only required to accept it as payment for obligations already denominated in dollars. Yet when I show people the Liberty Dollar, they bounce it a few times in their hands before saying something like: "Yeah, but is it real?" Have we latched so tightly onto central bank-issued currency, in electronic or tactile form, that it's now the only kind of currency we can conceive of as being legitimate?

What we can legally do with, or to, U.S. currency is rather confusing. Overt satire is usually fine. On the streets of Washington, D.C., you can buy spoof greenbacks, bills with Bill Clinton's picture on the "sex dollar" ($6) note or a smiling Ronald Reagan on the $10,000,000 bill. These slips usually only have (bad) art on one side, and they clearly aren't intended to defraud. U.S. Secret Service says: you're good to go.

Not always, though. In the early 1970s, a novelty manufacturer in Massachusetts decided to start selling a coffee mug festooned with a caricature of President Nixon on a $3 bill. The Secret Service seized the merchandise from retailers and confiscated 2,000 mugs at a warehouse in California. Despite the dubious legal grounds for this crackdown, the company didn't challenge the seizure, citing the economic might of its opponent as rationale for backing down.[1]

Are you allowed to light legal tender on fire? In 1994 two British artists torched £1 million in a remote corner of northwest Scotland. The event received significant media attention, but the authorities were apparently unmoved; no laws were being violated. Public reaction was mixed, with locals expressing more of a sense of incredulousness than anything that might resemble admiration for creativity, or praise for a grandiose gesture meant to kindle discussion.[2]

On this side of the Atlantic, burning banknotes would violate the section of Title 18 of the U.S. Code prohibiting "mutilation of national bank obligations." You may be able to marshal a free-speech defense, but in light of von NotHaus's offense of illegal utterances, I wouldn't be so sure. The situation is analogous to the flag-burning debate, although the economic implications of a flag-burning epidemic probably wouldn't be as serious.*

Private currencies are legal too, and, once you start looking for them, quite common. Up until the Great Depression, local currencies could be found throughout the country as people realized that there was an inadequate supply of money to facilitate exchange. Before that, during the Free Banking Era of the nineteenth century, private banks issued notes backed (or supposedly backed) by real coins or bars of metal inside their safe rooms. Once the Federal Reserve and the dollar came to reign, however, most local currencies died or were snuffed out by the Feds.

Now they're bounding back. Referred to as *alternative* or *community* currencies, a few of the better-known examples are the Ithaca HOUR, issued in Ithaca, New York; the BerkShare in western Massachusetts; and the Brixton Pound, which circulates in a district of London. (The award for best local currency name goes to one in Japan called *fureai kippu*, which loosely translates to "caring relationship tickets.") The philosophy behind alternative currencies is the financial equivalent of eating locally. By focusing consumption on food grown or raised nearby, you reduce, or at least get to say you reduce, bad things like factory farming and greenhouse gas emissions, while also eating fresher food and supporting local businesses.

The locavore approach to money is supposed to have similar benefits for your neighborhood economy. Instead of taking your hard-earned salary and using it to purchase a table made in India, brought to you by

---

*Longtime New Yorkers may recall the case from 1987 about a homeless woman who was institutionalized for, among other things, running into traffic and "tearing up money and urinating on it."

way of a credit-card payment on CrateandBarrel.com, why not use your community currency to buy a table from the furniture-maker on Main Street? He in turn uses his BerkShares to buy bread from the baker next door, and not from Walmart or Costco, which would send a portion of that payment into corporate coffers located far, far away. Some of these local currencies use paper bills, while others have an open central database recording transactions so that users can track what they have or owe, and which area businesses accept the currency.

Most alternative currencies are, at the end of the day, souped-up barter exchanges, whereby person A exchanges services with person B for x amount of tokens, which are then used to buy something from person C. To most of us that sounds a lot like regular old money, and in terms of function it is. But it's distinctly not the same as sovereign currency because the country's central bank doesn't control the supply of it and you can't pay your taxes with it, although the IRS says you do have to treat earnings in alternative currencies as taxable income. Most alternative currencies have an exchange rate with dollars or other national currencies, which is how taxes are calculated, at least in the United States.

The alternative currency idea branches in a number of directions and, not surprisingly, most are blossoming online. These virtual currencies are used primarily to buy virtual goods in online games, be it property, weapons, farm equipment, or special powers. In 2011, Facebook rolled out something called Facebook Credits. Like other virtual currencies, these credits have a dollar value and are used to buy and sell things in games and other applications. You buy them with good ol' U.S. government money, usually online, but Facebook has also made them available in the form of gift cards. It's not unlike buying tokens at Chuck E. Cheese, using them to play skee-ball, winning tickets, and then using the tickets to buy toys. Except that Chuck E. Cheese doesn't have 800 million customers like Facebook does. If the marketplace of goods available for purchase through Facebook expands, as it's forecasted to, it's hard to imagine what you *won't* be able to buy with your Facebook Credits.

Like any electronic payment service, most virtual currencies provide a way to transact that doesn't involve government-issued tokens representative of an amount of money. It's not national currency, but it has an exchange rate with currency of the realm that makes them close cousins.

Yet these currencies also have the potential to steal revenue from governments. A few years ago in China, a virtual currency called the QQ coin was taking off. Sold by an Internet company at the price of 1 QQ for 1 Chinese yuan, the coins were being used by tens of millions of gamers to buy virtual goods to meet their online needs, as well as real-world merchandise.[3] The business was booming, and government silence on the matter was interpreted as tacit consent. But then QQ crossed some unspecified line, perhaps one as simple as the number of users or transactions, or maybe someone finally estimated government revenue lost due to transactions in this non-yuan currency. Whatever the trigger, in 2009 the Chinese government banned the use of virtual currency for transactions involving real goods.[4]

The allure of virtual currencies can extend beyond commercial necessity and convenience. A few summers ago, a computer scientist from the University of California at Irvine named Yang Wang spent some time in China and Japan, looking at peoples' relationships to digital money. While in Beijing, he met a man who, like so many millions of people, had become addicted to the online videogame World of Warcraft. In the game, you buy stuff with accumulated gold coins—weapons, magic powers, armor, and so on. But earning gold often requires patience with in-game tasks that some people consider tedious or boring, compared with other in-game exploits that require more gold. So why not just pay someone else to do the menial work?

The industry is known as gold farming. Teens and twenty-somethings, usually in Asia, sit at computer terminals for hours, earning virtual gold for clients who might live 40 or 4,000 miles away. They settle up with an online payment, of course, denominated in some sovereign currency and often paid for with a credit card or via PayPal.

The economics were interesting to Wang the computer scientist, but even more so were the details of some of the transactions. The middle-aged man from Beijing, for instance, had once arranged to purchase some in-game gold from someone he met online. Unbeknownst to the buyer, the seller was a twelve-year-old boy in central China. The seller said he couldn't accept payment by mail, probably because his parents might get suspicious. For the man in Beijing, then, the question arose: how to pay for his World of Warcraft gold?

On New Year's Eve a few years ago, the Beijing man got in his car and drove hundreds of miles for a rendezvous at an Internet café. He met the kid, and they sat down at neighboring computers to log into the game. He got his gold, and he paid the kid with cash, yuan worth about $150. Then the man got back in his car to begin the drive back to Beijing. A costly, borderline farcical rigmarole, right? But the guy from Beijing conveyed to Wang that the whole thing was like an adventure. "It was just the opposite of the inconvenience you would expect to hear about," Wang later told me. "Virtual currency isn't just about accounting and denomination. It's extending the game experience into real life, mixing together these elements of personal entertainment and empowerment."

Currencies connected to social networking take this idea of redefining transactions to a new level. Projects like Hub Culture, Bitcoin, and Superfluid are trying to blend the interconnectivity of social networks with alternative currency models (although who knows if they'll still be around by the time you read this). At Superfluid, users trade in Quids, which, as the website explains, are not dollars. "They're placeholders for favors." Hub Culture's currency, Ven, is an attempt to bridge the divide between virtual currencies and real-world goods and services. People in the network transact in the "local" currency, which is priced from a basket of major sovereign currencies, commodities, and carbon futures. Your Ven can be exchanged for one of the major national currencies based on the same floating exchange rates that govern the value of world currencies against one another. Bitcoin has captured peoples' imaginations because the money supply is determined by an algorithm, not bureaucrats or economists, and there is a cap to the number of Bitcoins that can be created: 21 million.

Two related experiments are the Wuffie Bank and Serios. Wuffie has tried to set up a currency based on reputation, as determined by an algorithm that measures the influence we have on others via our social networks. Serios is a currency of attention, based on the idea that in the age of information overload, an incoming e-mail loaded with 100 Serios is of more value than one loaded with just five Serios. Or think about the "Like" button on Facebook: when someone clicks this button on an article, product, or online video, she is assigning a tiny additional value that wasn't there before.[5] In the summer of 2011, the publishers of *Longshot* magazine decided that instead of making readers use a conventional paywall, they would ask for payment in U.S. dollars *or* by sharing the site with others via social media. After all, both have value. Could these kinds of reputation, attention, or networking values ever be convertible—used in a way resembling currency in the dollars sense of it? Sounds a little vague, I know. Then again, so does "In God We Trust."*

A broad goal shared by these initiatives is peer-to-peer transactions. Keep the government out of it, as if we are neighbors swapping a rake for a batch of homemade brownies, but by way of some medium of exchange that ensures this is not just barter but commerce conducted with a fungible currency. As author Douglas Rushkoff put it in a *Wall Street Journal* interview, centralized currencies were developed and perfected by monarchs centuries ago to prevent peer-to-peer transactions. By issuing currency, the government provides the people with a convenient medium

---

*As the writer Stephen Squibb put it in August 2011, just before President Obama signed the now-famously-feeble debt deal: "Considered against the great encyclopedia of human promises, no religious gospel nor philosophical ideal, no scientific theory nor legal precedent, no testimony of love nor vow of hatred has ever been so widely or deeply believed as the full faith and credit of the United States Government today." (http://nplusonemag.com/origins-of-the-crisis)

for conducting exchanges. But when using government money, there's also a built-in transaction between the individual and the central authority. The money people want for purposes of transacting, says Rushkoff, is "also being used by speculators to extract value from communities." Fiat currency just isn't good at both reinforcing the economic power of the government and promoting transactions between individuals.

So what, then? Replace the dollar? Not necessarily. The democratization of currency that we're witnessing is about innovating monetary systems that are more efficient and valuable for use at times when government currency is suboptimal. Encouraging or using alternative currencies doesn't have to be some kind of wholesale revolt against government-issued money, which has—let's not kid ourselves—helped catalyze an astonishing rise in prosperity over the past century.[6]

On the surface, this potential phantasmagoria of new currencies—Facebook Credits, Brixton Pounds, World of Warcraft gold, Ithaca HOURS, Bitcoin, Ven, Apple Seeds (I just made that one up)—may appear like an inefficiency disaster in the making that could never possibly compete with the omnipresent and omni-accepted power of the almighty dollar. *Less* convenient systems are the last thing people want, or will accept. But there is a relatively easy answer to this critique: digital technology. Software could calculate currency conversions on the fly, so that transactions would be as easy and as fast as today's payments. Faster, even.

One of the most provocative currency ideas I've seen is one based on something that has, and always will have, real and unchanging value: energy. More specifically, kilowatt-hours. These are the units in which your power company calculates your bill: 100 kWh is how much energy you need—exactly—to keep a 100-watt light bulb illuminated for 100 hours. Gold may be history's most famous currency, but at the end of the day its value is still only built on our faith in it, and that value isn't constant because we, the fickle creatures that drive markets, are not constant.

A kilowatt-hour, however, is constant in the physicist's sense of the word. To those who worry about what holds value, and about the long-term fate of national currencies, the idea of energy as currency is enticing. We can't know what our dollars or euros will be able to buy in twenty-five years, but we know we'll need to heat our houses and power our electric cars, and that the amount of kilowatt-hours to do so on some future date equals the amount it takes to do so now.

But energy units are anything but fungible. How could you ever use them as a medium of exchange when their only two states of being are consumed or lost?

A couple of months ago, I received a few dollars off my electricity bill. It was a gift of sorts, for the purpose of a demonstration. A PhD chemist, pilot, patent attorney, and inventor from Virginia named Robert Hahl had made it happen. "In 2006 and 2007, I got interested in how the economy and the financial system works," Hahl told me. But whereas this baseline curiosity would compel most people to read a book or three, Hahl decided to see if he could upgrade the whole thing.

He started something called Kilowatt Cards, a prototype system for turning kilowatt-hours into a currency by way of paper representing an amount of electricity. The cards are just like gift cards, which can be used to pay for ten kilowatt-hours of electricity consumption. The difference between these cards and, say, gift cards for Best Buy, is that these cards are for something everyone needs, which means they could easily be traded and, at least in theory, circulate as a type of currency.

Hahl sent me a few Kilowatt Cards—he's giving them away free for the time being, to help spread the word. They're simple white slips of paper the size of a business card, with a red logo and an authentication code. Entering that code into a website will void the value on the card so that it can't be used more than once, although in the future distributing and trading these credits, as well as authenticating them, could just as easily take place digitally.

Here's how it works. You can't send the cards to your local utility to offset your bill. Instead, you *redeem* them by sending them to Kilowatt Cards headquarters, which is to say Hahl's home in Virginia. Think of it like redeeming your gold from the goldsmith's shop with a paper receipt, except that instead of gold coins, you get lighting or heat. Hahl makes the arrangements to pay 10 kWh worth of your electricity bill, in U.S. dollars. If you don't want to redeem the power just yet, you can pass the Kilowatt Cards to someone else in exchange for goods and services.

Because the currency is units of energy, holding them doesn't risk a loss of value from inflation. I'm breezing through a lot of the details of Hahl's vision, but this is the gist. And there are, as you may have surmised, major hurdles to ever making this kind of system viable. One is the variable cost, denominated in whatever currency, of delivering electricity to homes and businesses in different locations. Another challenge is limiting the issuance. Hahl says this is easy enough: he only issues as many electricity coupons as he can pay for from the sale of commodities "that represent real labor and energy," such as grain and firewood. That sounds fine, if not a little rustic, but what if a future overseer of this currency is less ethical, or just a regular old banker who falls victim to the temptations of over issuance?

Still, Hahl's model is compelling for at least attempting to address the puzzle of value by way of a currency that is useful *and* stable, something few other currencies could ever claim. "Government currency, company stocks—they're all just electrons," says Hahl. "I'm not especially bitter—but it is crap. The train of thought for me was: what could make it real?" It may sound quixotic, but the scientist in Hahl sees real-world proxies indicating that his scheme may not be as out-there as critics presume. "Now that people are sending cellphone minutes to one another as payment, that shows that you can pay for things with useful things. The Kilowatt Card could be a universal unit of value or a currency." The key, of course, is getting people to trust it, and use it not merely as a one-time thought experiment but as an everyday way to trade.

If something like Kilowatt Cards or Ven were to ever take off, they wouldn't, or shouldn't, be a problem for the Feds. Alternative currencies remain on the safe side of the law by following some basic rules. They don't look anything like government-issued paper, and they aren't called dollars. They also use exchangeability to gain traction. Two Ithaca HOURS, for example, will cost you $20. Put another way, Ithaca HOURS are coupons that have a $US value.

Disney Dollars may sound childish, but they too constitute an alternative currency. They only work locally or within a specified community, and they exist to promote spending; holding onto them won't do you much good after you've returned from your Orlando vacation. On the other hand, you may have incentive not to convert your Ithaca HOURS into something else, because of a built-in discount that some alternative currency designers employ to encourage use. The local bike shop or computer guy may offer 10 percent off to customers paying in the local currency of choice.

It may be tempting to belittle alternative currencies as limited, unrealistic, or maybe a little hippie-ish, but they do work, so long as they don't run into a counterfeiting problem, and so long as the supply of this money is intelligently controlled so as to avoid inflation (or worse). That's why Bitcoin's algorithmic approach to steering the money supply is captivating, although wild fluctuations in its value in the summer of 2011 suggest to some that *The Economist* is correct: "Bitcoin is technically sophisticated. As a monetary system, it looks primitive."[7]

Alternative currencies are at a disadvantage due to their limited connection to the banking system. Credit is money too, after all, but there aren't really loans out there denominated in Ven or Bitcoin, let alone Kilowatt Cards. Nevertheless, nothing but perception makes the issuing authority of the U.S. government more legitimate than the Ithaca HOURS Circulation Committee. Both supply users with real money, and both do their best to wisely steer monetary policy in a way that, they hope, promotes growth and avoids inflation.

Looking at the Kilowatt Cards, Liberty Dollars, Ven, and Facebook Credits all sitting on my desk and desktop makes me think back to something digital money swami Dave Birch told me in London. Alternative currencies aren't coming from people espousing a single political, economic, or even religious philosophy. New ideas about money are uniting people on the right, who are worried about deficit spending and a heavy government hand; libertarians like von NotHaus, who more forcefully oppose sovereign currencies; and über-progressives seeking a monetary system that relies less on frenzied speculation and plundering natural resources than today's consume-to-the-gills market capitalism. Each of these innovating groups and subgroups is nibbling around the edges of government's monopoly on currency issuance. A rainbow of new value possibilities awaits.

The groundswell of interest in alternative currencies has also created unlikely alliances. The private currencies E-gold and GoldMoney, for example, are online accounts from which people can make payments against gold bullion stored in a company vault. The founders of these and similar businesses have partnered with a group of Muslim business-men to promote their currency in the Islamic world, under the name E-dinar. As one proponent of this e-styled return to a gold- and silver-backed medium of exchange told *Wired*, suicide bombings aren't the way to fight Western capitalism. "You want to be radical? You don't need to blow up the bank, just burn your bank account. And for that you are going to need an alternative."[8]

But unless gold somehow manages to reclaim (redeem?) its status as the backbone of the international monetary system, it will remain a mere commodity. Owning it means vulnerability to its market price, which makes digitally accessed gold accounts a new money scheme that isn't new at all—except for the online part. But if you're convinced that an oversupply of money in the system is a plague on the financial system, then maybe gold is your thing. For alternative currencies like the Ithaca HOUR, the risk of a mismanaged money supply is alive and well, and a misstep, or confidence trouble resulting from the outbreak of war in up-state New York, could suddenly cause the HOUR's value to plummet. National currencies run this risk too, but those who handle the state money supply have more tools at their disposal for maintaining stability, like being able to buy up hundreds of billions of dollars' worth of foul-smelling mortgage-backed securities.

Local currencies, by definition, have limited utility in a global econ-omy. Unless people start accepting them far and wide, you won't have much luck using them if you ever travel outside of town or want to buy something over the Internet sold by a company located thousands of miles away. In the case of online currency exchanges like Superfluid, the limitations aren't geographic so much as the kinds of exchanging you can do. Should you run out of trading partners willing to accept your graphic design consultation, freelance copy-editing, or massages, which seem to be the bulk of the business offerings, at some point you'll have to find a way to earn some money denominated in a currency acceptable to your power company, landlord, and pharmacy, at least for the time being. Ven are starting to show more widespread applicability—some people have bought cars with them, for instance—but the jury is very much out on these projects.

One sign that alternative and virtual currencies are gaining in popularity is how many people look to them as a preferred means of payment. As one analyst recently told *Bloomberg News*: "We have to stop differentiating between the virtual world and the real world. The virtual world is very real." Money and currency don't discriminate between what we might describe as real versus virtual currencies, the way an online avatar is virtual but a hole in your roof is real. Currency is simply that which is accepted as payment, and its legitimacy and global reach is only limited by the extent of that acceptability. Getting paid in airline miles suits a travel addict, just as getting paid in Disney Dollars may be exactly what parents planning an Orlando vacation need, especially if using them at the theme park confers some kind of discount. Getting paid in the virtual gold coins traded in World of Warcraft may be what your mechanic prefers for payment in exchange for car service, but the two of you don't yet have the killer apps to make that transaction as seamless and trustworthy as today's predominant methods of exchange. They are coming, though.

As far as government authorities are concerned, your alternative currency adventures—whether with units of energy, goods in cyberspace, old-fashioned paper, or holographic representation of those giant stones from the Micronesian island of Yap—won't be a problem as long as your currency doesn't look like government-issued notes and coins. Don't use it to conceal income, and don't advertise it as a competitor to your national currency, especially if your national currency is the U.S. dollar.[9] So if Bernard von NotHaus's Liberty Dollar is a "private voluntary barter currency," why is he facing up to twenty-five years in prison and a $750,000 fine?

◆

IN 1998, VON NOTHAUS and a handful of supporters launched—nay, "issued"—their Liberty Dollar: "a private voluntary free-market currency backed entirely by silver and gold." One of the organization's brochures lays it out in simple language. "It is real gold and silver money that you can use just like cash wherever it is accepted voluntarily for everyday purchases at your grocery store, dentist, or gas station."[10] It's also "100% moral, legal, and constitutional."

Von NotHaus trumpeted the kind of community-minded ideals that have boosted efforts like Ithaca HOURS, but the group's primary selling point, popular among the far right, was about protecting oneself against the shrinking value of the U.S. dollar. Liberty Dollars, they declared, are better than worthless government paper because "Liberties" are made from, or backed by, precious metal. The "$" stamped on them was like an exclamation point. Or a middle finger.

One afternoon in Honolulu, I meet von NotHaus at the offices of the Royal Hawaiian Mint, on the seventh floor of the Waikiki Trade Center, a drab office building just blocks from the beach. Over his desk hangs a framed drawing of a faux greenback, with a portrait of a dinosaur and, in the same font that we're so accustomed to seeing "United States of America," the words "Hypnotized State of America." The serial number is UOOOOOOME.

Within minutes after my arrival, von NotHaus shows me an album full of famously worthless Weimar Republic banknotes. "You can read all this Austrian economics crap, but they all lack a real-world solution. I'm not a hairy fairy intellectual do-nothing asshole. I'm just an everyday asshole—a regular guy with a great idea. And it's totally legal!" When the Liberty Dollar started, silver was trading at around $5 an ounce. Von

NotHaus was stamping $20 on his one-ounce silvers, though. Coining adds value to the spot price of a metal because coins are prettier and easier to carry. He added the denomination, he says, to give the pieces a "suggested face value" that would get people comfortable transacting with this novel currency.

In the parlance of Wall Street, von NotHaus is what's known as a gold (and silver) bug, a devout believer in the value of precious metals. Mainstream bug theology rests on the conviction that detaching the value of the dollar from a real substance was a horrible decision. Without anchoring money to something tangible, the value of paper and cheap coins is no more real than a unicorn. Gold and silver, they argue, have been used *as* money for so long that they essentially *are* money. Or, in the words of titanic British philosopher John Locke, "silver is a matter of nature different from all other."

Many bugs stop there, content to invest heavily in gold or silver because they view precious metals as a safe haven for assets, especially when the economy is struggling and currency values teeter. But others go further. In their eyes, we need to return to the gold standard. They believe fiat currencies backed only by government promises are essentially garbage—"only the ghost of money," as Thomas Jefferson put it. Because governments have historically failed to limit the supply of money in the system, these critics say "fiat trash" invariably erodes the population's wealth by diminishing the purchasing power of the bucks people have. In a word: inflation.

At various points during our conversations, von NotHaus impresses upon me the notion that silver and gold equal "real money." His most memorable attempt to emphasize this point goes like this:

"Are you real, David?"

"Yes."

He then gestures to the silver bullion bars, spread out on his office table at right angles like dominos of various sizes.

"If I grabbed one of those silver bars and clocked you in the face with it, what would you do?"

"Bruise," I said, unsure whether this was the answer he sought, but fairly confident it was correct.

"OK, yes. And?"

"Retaliate?" I said.

"Yes! We live in a physical plane, David. The markets—they are *physical*. You can order a shirt online, but the damn shirt still has to get shipped to you." I nod quietly, deciding not to mention the estimated $3 billion spent on virtual goods last year.[11] In a way, it's not wrong to say that metals, corn, or other commodities possess intrinsic value because it's so supremely unlikely that their market price will ever be $0, and because some of them can be eaten or used for making or doing things in the real world. But they're still just forms of money with fluid value like any other. As with banknotes, physicality alone says nothing about an object's value.

Ignoring the fact that the majority of economists today would echo, in one way or another, economist John Maynard Keynes's opinion that the gold standard is "a barbarous relic," and Adam Smith's declaration that gold and silver are "utensils, it must be remembered, as much as the furniture of the kitchen," and never minding that money is really more like a verb than a noun, von NotHaus and millions of metal-heads across the globe still believe precious metals are value incarnate.*

Not to suggest that this is an absurd idea. Central banks own about 18 percent of all the gold ever mined. In recent years the central banks of India, Russia, China, and other countries have been gobbling it up, although no country owns nearly as much of the shiny stuff as the United States—8,133 tons, according to the Treasury, socked away at Fort Knox, the New York Fed, and probably some secret bunker alongside Dick Cheney's G.I Joe collection.[12] In the spring of 2011, Utah actually legal-

---

*Investment guru Warren Buffett famously observed that gold "gets dug out of the ground in Africa, or someplace. Then we melt it down, dig another hole, bury it again and pay people to stand around guarding it. It has no utility. Anyone watching from Mars would be scratching their head."

ized gold and silver currency. You can now take your silver $1 American Eagle to Salt Lake City and spend it on something worth $1 or less. "You'd be a fool," U.S. Mint spokesman Tom Jurkowsky told the *New York Times*. "But you could do it." You'd be a fool because the silver content makes that coin worth about $38.[13]

A return to the gold standard, or a gold and silver standard, is one of those perennial ideas that may sound throwback-ish, until you remember that we've only been ticking along with a fiat currency system for about a century, and only forty years with the complete separation from gold. It's also something of a puzzler that fiat currencies are the way of the world, yet central banks themselves hoard so much gold.

Still, even distinguished economists who are gravely concerned about the dollar and the global economy's dependence on it say that a return to the gold standard is a bad idea.[14] For one thing, there just isn't that much of it, a limitation to reviving the gold standard that could, theoretically, be overcome if we were to transact digitally in ever-smaller fractions of an ounce. More fundamental and technical criticisms of the gold standard have to do with the inflexibility that handicapped economies of old. You can't easily feed the beast of the money supply if there's a finite amount of money.

Another concern about the gold standard is that it can make prices drop when the economy is chugging along. That can make the money in your wallet more valuable to you than spending it, which could create dangerous deflation. The key here is not that the gold standard itself is a wacky idea, but that a return to it would be akin to a monetary Hail Mary pass. On the other hand, it's bizarre, if nothing else, that one of the most oft-touted advantages of fiat currency is that it can be used to rescue countries from financial ruin, and not necessarily that it's a stable vehicle carrying us into a more prosperous tomorrow.

The dystopian worldview held by hardcore gold (and silver) bugs usually falls short of an invocation of Satan, but like those who believe going cashless is a harbinger of the End of Days, reverence for precious metals and a return to the gold standard is reinforced by the conviction that a Weimar-scale hyperinflation is just around the corner. Von NotHaus gives us a year, maybe two. Monetary doomsayers have been saying this for many years now, if not decades, but gold bugs cling to this vision of collapsing empire as if the forecast itself was a gold ingot. Then again, since the crisis beginning in 2007, when trillions of dollars' worth of value suddenly vanished, such dire predictions of calamity no longer feel like Nostradamus nonsense.

Von NotHaus's original aim was to capitalize on the belief that precious metal in your hand is the only true form of wealth, as well as that renewable resource known as antagonism toward government. (In 2009 he also started minting and selling Tea Party Dollars.) "People are unhappy with the government, but they don't necessarily know why," he says. "It's not the Democrats or the Republicans. It's the fucking money! Period. They're taking the value of the money! That takes the values out of society, and before you know it you have massive debt, which means massive criminality. Immorality."

His fury over fiat currency makes it that much more insulting, and tragically ironic, that von NotHaus faces charges of counterfeiting. He says it took him twenty-three years to engineer precisely how the Liberty Dollar would work. "Do you have any idea how hard it is to develop a private currency based on a commodity with an ever-changing price?" His goal seemed straightforward enough: make it inflation-proof and rescue the nation from self-destruction. "This is an important step to give people power to control manipulations of currencies," he says.

That public-spirited line is reminiscent of what PayPal co-founder Peter Thiel is said to have told his employees in the early days of the company, when they were trailblazing a new online system for sending and receiving money. By having one's money in an online account, Thiel claimed, people would be able to bounce between currencies. "It will be nearly impossible for corrupt governments to steal wealth from their people through their old means [a.k.a. devaluation or stealth taxes] because if they try, the people will switch to dollars or pounds or yen, in effect dumping the worthless local currency for something more secure."[15] Yet few people would consider Thiel to be some kind of clown.

The Liberty Dollar combines money in the time-tested sense of tangible worth, a specific weight of gold or silver, with more modern features, including membership discounts, an eLibertyDollar option, and a mysterious mechanism called a "MoveUp" for keeping pace with the market price of metals, even if those prices happen to move down (a prospect von NotHaus does not like to discuss). The reason for the MoveUp is that if the price of raw silver or gold soars so far above the face value von NotHaus has stamped on the coins, no one will want to spend them. They'll just hoard them, or sell them for their intrinsic metal value.

So von NotHaus came up with some special rules—it's his currency, after all—whereby the value of the Liberty Dollar is hooked to a base figure. One ounce of silver equals $20, for example, which was the working base value for a while. If the market price of silver goes up high enough and for long enough, as it did a few years ago, von NotHaus bumps up the base accordingly. Following the MoveUp, owners of Liberty Dollars have the option to mail in their coins and, for a small minting fee, have a one-ounce $20 coin transformed into a one-ounce $50 coin. Snap: you just more than doubled your money. If you don't send in your Liberty Dollars, you're essentially cheating yourself out of free money, while giving a monstrous tip to someone in the future who accepts your $20 coin as payment and then promptly mails it in to have it turned into a $50.

Ask von NotHaus what happens if the price of silver or gold goes down and his explanation goes serpentine. "The currency can't be used if it doesn't have value. You can't barter a car for a chainsaw if you can't measure their worth." What I think he means is that people need a commonly recognizable unit of account; we think in dollars, at least for the time being. But that hardly suffices as an explanation of the full ramifications of a MoveUp that actually moves down. I press the point, and this time von NotHaus starts yelling about real value and the "giant gorilla" of government.

Since its inception, the Liberty Dollar has been run by a nonprofit called NORFED, short for National Organization for the Repeal of the Federal Reserve and the Internal Revenue Code (later renamed Liberty Services). Von NotHaus was the point man, but the upstart currency had an office in an Indiana strip mall, where a few employees filled orders for coin purchases and filed paperwork for people who wanted to hold Liberty Dollar warehouse certificates for silver or gold stored at a facility in northern Idaho.

New users join the club when they pay a fee to become Regional Currency Officers, a privilege that allows them to buy Liberty Dollars at a discount, say $18 for a Liberty coin denominated as $20. They in turn recruit "associates" and local merchants to participate by accepting the currency as payment. When using the Liberty Dollars, though, the idea is for participating merchants to make change based on that $20 face value, which means the silver coin you just bought for $18 (in greenbacks) now has buying power equivalent to $20.

For the first five years or so of its existence, the Liberty Dollar flew under the radar of both the government and the public at large. In scattered communities around the country, usually small towns, transactions were being mediated with these shiny silver rounds. How many users is impossible to say, but von NotHaus enjoys proclaiming that the Liberty Dollar is America's second most popular currency. He says upward of $50 million worth of Liberty Dollar–denominated silver and gold pieces were circulating by 2007, with more than 250,000 supporters. But bear in mind, the source of these figures is a man who believes the 9/11 attacks were a government operation, and that a mysterious "frequency machine" can cure all diseases.

Still, from Arkansas to Illinois to California, citizens were buying and using the Liberty Dollar. Some may have accepted it just for novelty's sake, and the majority of Liberty Dollar transactions probably had little to do with monetary insurrection. The pieces look stately, adorned with Lady Liberty, "USA" and "Trust in God" on one side, and the liberty torch and lots of official-looking text on the other.* If people weren't tricked into thinking the coins were government money, they might have been taken by the idea of owning a little silver or gold. Or maybe a friend or neighbor was atwitter about this newfangled currency, and, so, what the heck? Why not trade it for your proffered haircut, pizza, or an antique lampshade? It's not like doing so is going to matter in the grand scheme of things, right?

When, exactly, the Feds finally took interest in the Liberty Dollar is uncertain, but in 2004 von NotHaus appeared in a segment on the Learning Channel, filmed in Washington, D.C.'s, Constitution Garden, across the street from the temple itself—the Federal Reserve Board. In the clip, von NotHaus brags about the currency's silver backing and public support. "After five years of doing this, people take the currency readily!"[16] To show the Liberty Dollar in action, the television crew filmed von NotHaus at a local sandwich shop. Leaning on the counter, hands clasped, he places his order.

"Hi. I'd like to have two turkey and Swiss and one ham and Swiss."

Then he reaches his right hand toward his pants pocket, brushing back the bottom of his tan suit coat like a magician, and takes out his money: a Liberty Dollar and a wad of Federal Reserve Notes.

"I have a ten-dollar silver," he says, smiling as he passes the coin to the woman at the cash register. The greenbacks stay in his left hand.

Her voice is somewhat muffled, but it sounds like the sandwich shop lady says: "We don't accept—what is *this*?"

"It's the new ten-dollar silver piece," says von NotHaus.

The woman shouts to her co-worker to come and take a look at this thing.

---

*The "888.421.6181" and "NORFED.ORG" on the coins reduces that aura of the bona fide.

The next thing you see is von NotHaus walking away from the counter and straight toward the camera, box lunches in hand. "Just like that. Used every day, throughout America."*

If he was trying to provoke a reaction, he succeeded; it just took a couple of years. In September 2006, the U.S. Mint issued an unusual press release. The Department of Justice had determined that using Liberty Dollars as circulating money—as opposed to using them as, say, miniature coasters—was a federal crime. Copies of the warning were mailed to von NotHaus and the people at the NORFED office, who in turn shared the news with their Regional Currency Officers and the media. If any of them had concerns about the legal consequences of their actions, this would have been the time to bow out of the business and shelve their precious assets just like any other investment or keepsake.

They didn't. Instead, they pursued a golden opportunity. In the fall of 2007, Ron Paul's campaign for president was gaining unexpected momentum. The Texas physician and longtime statesman adamantly opposes the Federal Reserve system, and for this, gold bugs consider him a veritable deity. Von NotHaus saw the underdog's campaign as a chance to advance the cause, a potential source for profit, or both. In the fall of that year, Liberty Services ordered thousands of copper, silver, gold, and platinum coins featuring the likeness of Ron Paul. If von NotHaus's past media appearances and inflammatory rhetoric had been meant to needle the government, the decision to mint and distribute Ron Paul Dollars was like shoving a thumb in the Treasury's eye.

---

*In Honolulu, I asked about this episode at the sandwich shop, and whether he was disingenuously representing the Liberty Dollar as government-issued money. After recounting precisely how the Learning Channel opportunity came about, and how serendipitous it was that he was to be in Washington, D.C., the same day as the production crew, von NotHaus said he didn't remember what he said when buying the three sandwiches. But when transacting in Liberty Dollars, he says, you don't want to deliver the whole spiel. "The waiter doesn't want to hear it, nor do the people waiting in line behind you!"

On November 15, 2007, at the Evansville, Indiana, offices of Liberty Services, employees were readying to mail out the first batch of 60,000 Ron Paul Dollars when FBI and Secret Service agents arrived and shut everything down. Other agents descended upon Sunshine Minting in Coeur d'Alene, Idaho. Sunshine is the U.S. Mint's primary supplier of planchets, those flat faceless metal discs that the government transforms into legal tender. The Idaho firm was also under contract to produce Liberty Dollar coins and safeguard bullion on site—the silver behind Liberty Dollar silver certificates. That autumn afternoon, when computers, cash, invoices, and order forms were confiscated from the office in Indiana, the agents in Idaho hauled away what von NotHaus says was more than $1 million dollars' worth of silver, gold, and copper.

Paul's campaign staff claimed to have no affiliation with NORFED or the renegade currency, but the spillover media attention had its benefits. Gold bugs, Paul supporters, and down-with-the-Fed types were galvanized by news that NORFED had been raided and the Liberty Dollars seized. At a campaign event, Paul said he believes in alternative currencies in general and would like to repeal legal tender laws, but that he didn't know specifics about von NotHaus's organization.*[17]

Reports of the raid made the front page of the *Washington Post*, but it would take a year and a half before charges were filed against von NotHaus and three of his associates. His trial was bumped a number of times, with mountains of evidence, new paperwork, and procedural tit-for-tat all helping to assure that the case of the Liberty Dollar would become a monstrous drain on Department of Justice time, manpower, and money. "I'm just on ice down here," von NotHaus said of his legal limbo, the confiscated assets, and his customized sanction against minting.

---

*In an e-mailed newsletter to "supporters" (and curious reporters), von NotHaus says Paul's office contacted him back in 1999. The two men had an unsatisfactory meeting, he says, although since then, according to von NotHaus they have dined among the same company on three different occasions. You can also find a picture online of Paul, looking less than thrilled, standing next to von NotHaus, who is dressed in Revolutionary War–era garb, pointing a sword at the camera.

◆

BEFORE VON NOTHAUS'S TRIAL, I contacted two specialists to try to grasp the nuances of the situation. One of them was Walker Todd, a lawyer and economist who worked at the Federal Reserve Bank of Cleveland, and before that as a lawyer with the Federal Reserve Bank of New York. (For the record, Todd himself has advocated for a return to the gold standard.) The second is David Ganz, a coin specialist and longtime government legal consultant in matters of the U.S. Mint. In 1974 Ganz was lucky enough to be among a contingent of 120 members of the public who were allowed to view the gold inside the Fort Knox Bullion Depository.

"A lot of people will say that believing in gold instead of believing in fiat dollars is archaic or wacky," said Todd. "But look what happened just yesterday with the announcement from the Fed." This was late September 2010. In response to the suggestion that the Federal Reserve would soon inject hundreds of billions of newly conjured dollars into the economy, the price of gold shot up by more than $20 an ounce, on its way toward $1,300 an ounce, and $1,500 not long after that. "Some economists worry about the quality and quantity of money in the economy," said Todd. "Bernard and the Liberty Dollar people are basically operating in that reality. But it's distorted as they practice it."

One prong of the government's case against von NotHaus, Todd explained, is that the whole thing was a Ponzi scheme. Nestled within the discounts for signing up users, commissions, price differences between silver bought and sold, adjustable base value, and re-minting fees for a MoveUp are red flags that indicate, in the words of the prosecutors, "a scheme and artifice to defraud." Von NotHaus vehemently denies this, of course, saying that the Liberty Dollar is a single-tier referral system, just like when people put an Amazon.com button on their websites and get a small percentage from referred sales. David Ganz agrees: "You'd have to be a moron to believe that the average person would be confused by this," he told me, meaning tricked into thinking Liberty Dollars are government-issued currency.

But it's the other prongs of the government case, said Todd, that could have more profound implications for our understanding of what cash and currency are, and just how much private innovation will be permitted by the state in the future. Paradoxically, von NotHaus's first mistake was to forge his alternative currency out of such an old-fashioned technology: coinage. Few other private or alternative currency issuers bother with coins—only paper, if they supply anything tactile at all. This enables them to avoid tangling with the U.S. Mint, or running up against the Constitution's clearer prohibition against (literally) minting money. Only the government can do that.

Metal is sort of the point with the Liberty Dollar, though, especially if you're the mintmaster of the Royal Hawaiian Mint and an ardent gold and silver bug. "Bernard is not a counterfeiter by any definition," said Ganz. Yet the fact that Liberty Dollar "coins" look somewhat like U.S. Mint coins is precisely how government lawyers would try to nail von NotHaus on the counterfeiting charge. There is precedent. In 1995 a U.S. District Court in Washington, D.C., rejected an argument made by lawyers representing J.S.G. Boggs, the artist who drew banknotes and transacted with them. Despite the fact that Boggs's works were never used to defraud, and never functioned as an alternative or competing currency, the judge said Boggs was in violation of the law prohibiting the making of "obligations" in "similitude" of U.S. currency. It's the currency version of *Don't tread on me*.[18]

In Todd's view, if NORFED had only issued Liberty Dollar silver certificates, and then an electronic version of the same, it's possible the group may not have faced legal challenges. "Private coinage schemes in the past usually ran aground when issuing notes," he said, "because they didn't have the silver or gold to back them. As far as I know, Bernard did have the gold and silver." As long as that paper doesn't look anything like greenbacks, it would probably be legal. Probably, but the boundary between *alternative* and *competing* currencies is starting to look fuzzy.

"I think where Bernard went off the rails was when he added the denomination," said Todd. Von NotHaus may have been asking for trouble with the likeness of Lady Liberty, the phrase "Trust in God," and even the familiar size of his coins. But it was denominations that signaled his intention for the currency to circulate in competition with the fiat currency of the land. Further indication of that intention was advertising materials ("it's meant to be spent") and von NotHaus's own writings and media appearances, like the Learning Channel segment. Whether his personal hostility toward government institutions influenced law-enforcement officials is unknown, but printing and selling T-shirts that read "The U.S. Mint Can Bite Me" probably didn't engender much sympathy. "He is a person who is annoying people in very powerful positions," said Ganz.

One aspect of the case that is striking is how forcefully the government asserted, at least in its indictment, the Treasury Department's supreme authority over money, and especially over the realm of coinage. "Say you decide to privately mint coins," said Todd. "And say you're mindful to keep any denominations or dollar signs off of them, and you only sell them at the fair-market value for silver or gold. That is basically what the Franklin Mint does." Private enterprises like the Franklin Mint "skate inside the law" by referring to their products as *medallions* or *collectibles*, and avoiding features suggestive of circulating currency. "Many analysts would say that is legal, as long as it only contains the metal's weight on its face. There shouldn't be anything wrong with that."

With the Liberty Dollar crackdown, however, even that activity may be called into question. "Treasury now seems to be arguing that it has the exclusive right to all coinage of any kind. This was surprising," said Todd, as was seeing a nineteenth-century statute dusted off to support the argument. "That was like watching your grandfather's old shotgun being brought out of storage and shot after 100 years."

Ganz said he believes the Liberty Dollar is legal. "If Bernard can't make a coin based on this theory, then the U.S. Mint can't either." A few times in the past, the U.S. Mint made coins that had not been authorized by Congress. Although they were soon canceled, the people behind this essentially illegal money were never considered counterfeiters. At the end of the day, said Ganz, this is about intimidation, about dissuading people from getting into the admittedly unusual business of monetary innovation. "If you had it in your head to do an alternative currency, would you do it now, knowing about this case? In that sense, [government prosecutors] have done what they set out to do."

In the original indictment, prosecutors point out that Congress has the power to mint coins as money "and to regulate the Value thereof." And they go on: "Congress has the concurrent power to restrain the circulation of money which is not issued under its own authority in order to protect and preserve the constitutional currency for the benefit of the nation. Thus, it is a violation of law for private coin systems to compete with the official coinage of the United States." Strangely, though, the judge decided that the version of the indictment that went to the jury would not include this paragraph, suggesting, albeit subtly, that there may not be a constitutional prohibition against private citizens making and trading in their own metal coins.

Perhaps we should be thankful that government lawyers prosecuted von NotHaus to the fullest extent of the law. Could it be that the "incredible insight into multigenerational information" von NotHaus says he's privy to courtesy of LSD and too many mushrooms really has bestowed on him enough power to singlehandedly torpedo the U.S. economy? If so, please put that man in a cage and banish his funny money. I'm all for alternative currencies, just as long as they don't undermine faith in the monetary system we're all now living with, for better or for worse.

Congress's power to prohibit the circulation of money "not issued under its own authority" makes sense, especially in historical context. This law was solidified at the end of the Free Banking Era. To successfully carry out the transition from being a nation with myriad monies into one nation under the greenback, Congress had to enforce a tax on privately issued notes so that no one would want to use them, and the discounted national currency would become the dominant currency of trade. It worked, and the courts upheld the constitutionality of this power.

But where is the line between "protecting and preserv[ing] the constitutional currency for the benefit of the nation" and permitting alternative currencies used in farmers markets, or virtual currencies like Ven or Bitcoin? "Bernard went up to the line that Treasury permits, and he tried to push it," said Todd.

During my conversation with Todd, I asked why the government decided to bust the Liberty Dollar when it did, in 2007, instead of years earlier—when von NotHaus was conducting his subversive transactions outside the Federal Reserve Board in 2004, for instance. He could only flip the question back to me: "It's reasonable to ask if there was some publicity event that forced the Treasury's hand."

The day of the raids in Idaho and Indiana, just as all those thousands of Ron Paul Dollars were about to be shipped to Liberty Dollar members around the country, Bud Gregory, the machining expert in Honolulu who presses coins for the Royal Hawaiian Mint, got a call from the owner of Sunshine Minting in Idaho. Gregory knew of the guy, but they had never met. "He asked me sort of out of the blue how things are going. I said, 'Uh, fine.' Then he says, 'Well let me tell you what's happening here. I've got the FBI and Secret Service going through my place. Do you know why?' I said no. He says the Feds are going through all of Bernard's stuff from the Liberty Dollar and the Royal Hawaiian Mint."

Gregory hadn't been minting Liberty Dollars, so he and his business weren't in jeopardy, and he never got his own visit from the Feds. Still, he was in shock. He immediately called a friend who'd been selling Hawaiian Dalas in his store, told him there might be trouble, and recommended that he pull the coins from his showcases. "My buddy starts insisting there's nothing wrong or illegal about the Dala or the Liberty Dollars. I told him that's not the point. 'They're about to become a lot more valuable! You don't *want* to sell them now.'"

Sure enough, soon after the busts, Liberty Dollars were selling for hundreds of dollars on eBay. Some observers used the surging price to suggest that the government's action had backfired. It brought attention to arguments about the potential weakness of government-issued currency, inspired contributions to Ron Paul's presidential campaign, and added value to the very coins the Treasury was trying to exterminate. Von NotHaus also spins this piece of the story in a positive light. "The accusation that people are left holding the bag—that is crazy. People are selling Liberty Dollars for *hundreds* on eBay. They're bidding up in a free market. It's a *free-market* currency."

But the high prices paid for Liberty Dollars auctioned online pose a fundamental problem for von NotHaus: they signal that people are buying Liberty Dollars as memorabilia, like Confederate currency or Olympic pins. Instead of spending them, people are putting them on the mantle or in a cabinet with other keepsakes. As the philosopher Georg Simmel put it, money must move. "When money stands still, it is no longer money according to its specific value and significance."[19]

I'd brought this point up with von NotHaus when we went to see the coin press. "It isn't really a currency if people are just buying it like a collector's item, and not transacting with it."

"Fuck you and your 'it's not a currency,'" said von NotHaus. "The only reason it's not circulating is because of the damn raid! And it'll always be a currency. The government can send me to jail or run over me with a bus. That won't change a thing. The Liberty Dollar reveals the lie about government money."

◆

ONE EVENING IN HONOLULU, after another seminar on von NotHausian economics, von NotHaus and I decided to walk from the offices of the mint down Seaside Avenue to the hotels and shops of Waikiki. The global credit crunch, recession, and lumbering recovery have been tough on Hawaii. When money is tight, vacations are one of the first things people decide to go without.

Yet the scene this evening in October 2010 is hardly so bleak. Droves of tourists stroll past restaurants browsing menus, posing for photographs next to illuminated palm trees, and spending their hard-earned dollars (read: yen exchanged for dollars) at Armani, Fossil, and Louis Vuitton.

Not exactly the kind of scene to make people think about an imploding monetary system.* On the other hand, opening the *Wall Street Journal* this morning, it was hard not to be reminded of the prophecies that make gold and silver bugs so bullish. "Central Banks Open Spigot" and, on a later page, "Gold, Oil Lead Rally on Fear of Currency Devaluations."[20]

The Hawaii von NotHaus knew thirty-five years ago is hard to envision, but one thing that is the same is Waikiki's grand dame, the Royal Hawaiian. The pink hotel first opened in 1927, designed in the Spanish-Moorish style that has made it an architectural icon in all the ways that Oahu's hotel towers are not. "Remember, I studied architecture in college," says von NotHaus, inspecting ornately painted beams above archways facing out onto the Pacific.

Our table at the Mai Tai Bar is set amid tiki torches and a crowd of other visitors, many of them wearing newly purchased Hawaiian shirts. At the Sheraton next door, guests sit at white-clothed tables on the lawn, watching luau musicians and dancers. Tickets to the show are expensive, says von NotHaus, noting with pleasure that we get to "cockroach" the luau—his term for getting something without having to pay for it.

We order mai tais and burgers, and von NotHaus launches into stories about seeing Santana at Diamond Head in the early 1970s, his 1985 trip to Japan as a goodwill ambassador, the Free Marijuana Church of Honolulu, which he founded ("The service is inside your head!"), and how Hawaii is special because everyone is a minority here.

Von NotHaus washes down his mai tai with a pint of Guinness. Listening to the gentle rhythms of the ukulele, he briefly sets aside his megalomania and revolutionary ramblings and begins talking like a person who's getting on in years and contemplating his mark on the world.

---

*When investment giant Bear Stearns went under and thousands of Wall Street traders were sent packing, just-fired employees walked out onto the streets of Manhattan and were shocked to see all the people strolling and shopping—simply going about their daily lives as if they had no clue of the catastrophe underway. ("Wall Street Vérité," *The New Yorker*, October 11, 2010)

"I don't really have a lot of piss and vinegar left in me, you know? I'm trying to do everything I can to get those people their money back."

By *those people* he means Liberty Dollar investors/participants/supporters/suckers/early adopters. One associate sent von NotHaus pretty much his entire pension, $260,000, to buy Liberty Dollars, and now he doesn't know when he'll get it back, if ever. Another enthusiast sent von NotHaus tens of thousands of dollars to convert into Liberty Dollars. That money arrived the day before the raid, so von NotHaus's colleagues didn't even have time to make the silver purchase. "So now he's out of his property, his silver, and his money," says von NotHaus.[21]

And von NotHaus's ninety-one-year-old mother had what he says was 16,000 ounces of silver locked up in her son's private currency experiment—about half a million dollars' worth. In the summer of 2010, when he was caught violating the terms of his bail for minting and selling Hawaiian Dalas, Tea Party Dollars, and other derivatives of the same model he was already in trouble for, he had to borrow $1,000 from his mother so that he could report to the judge in North Carolina to accept his jail sentence. (The charges against the Liberty Dollar group were brought in Asheville, North Carolina.) "I have like $72 in the bank," he says. "I'm paying her back in weekly installments" with money earned from sales of commemoratives from the Royal Hawaiian Mint.

"That must be pretty painful," I say.

"It is. But she trusts me. So do all the other incredible people who believed in the Liberty Dollar."

In recent years, and especially in the wake of the raids and subsequent charges that put a stop to the Liberty Dollar, von NotHaus has become both a media whore and darling. He craves the podium, while those who give it to him get the dual benefit of his unconventional ideas and non-existent filter when it comes to articulating them. They also like quirky stories, and what's quirkier than trying to supplant "real" money with D.I.Y. silver coins stamped with "Trust in God"?

The weird thing is that I find myself admiring von NotHaus. It's not the conspiracy theories, obviously, or even the Liberty Dollar per se.

Anytime someone tries to sell you something by shouting that it isn't a scam, you've got to worry a little. The Federal Reserve's conjured dollars, seigniorage profits, and offloaded debt in the form of government-issued paper may sound like a scam too, but a confusing and inflationary system isn't necessarily a deceitful one.

Von NotHaus's claim that the Liberty Dollar could compete with U.S. currency the way Federal Express competes with the U.S. Postal Service doesn't hold much water, either: while there are no laws against delivering packages, there are laws, however obtuse, against too much monetary mischief. His questions about money's worth are refreshing, but I worry that so much slandering of the national currency will create a kind of self-fulfilling prophecy of undermining it, when it fact it may be the best system we could ever come up with. And it goes without saying that I disagree with the idea of reverting to some old form of physical money.

Yet I appreciate von NotHaus the dreamer. Here is a person who decided to scrutinize one of the most omnipresent elements of our lives and then ask: why does it have to be this way? Then he had the audacity to propose something else. His "solution" may be offbeat, but who else is out there, badgering the establishment about the form, meaning, and value of modern money?

The Samoan fire-dancer is now onstage at the luau, and von NotHaus keeps looking over my shoulder to watch. The statuesque man, covered from his midsection to kneecaps in dark tattoos, spins, throws, stomps, and claps to the music, with his two torches whirling in hypnotic circles. I look back at von NotHaus, who's now hunched over his drink, the fire from the dancer reflecting in his glasses. He's crying a little.

"All these people whose property was seized in the raids—they really wanted to do something good for the country," he says. "I'm just the point person. And I'm not going to cop a plea. This is my last hurrah. I've got to crow as much as I can."

When I ask if he feels guilty, he snaps back into firebrand mode. "Guilty for what? That is a bad word, David. I haven't done anything wrong. I've done everything possible to keep this above board and the government *HAS NO CASE.* Now I'm doing everything I can to get people their property back." He insists that all of his supporters still stand by him and his private currency, and indeed it's hard to find Liberty Dollar associates complaining that they were ripped off.

◆

IN MARCH 2011, a federal court convicted von NotHaus of conspiracy and counterfeiting. Following the verdict, the lead U.S. Attorney for the government said: "Attempts to undermine the legitimate currency of this country are simply a unique form of domestic terrorism." She went on: "While these forms of anti-government activities do not involve violence, they are every bit as insidious and represent a clear and present danger to the economic stability of this country. . . . We are determined to meet these threats through infiltration, disruption, and dismantling of organizations which seek to challenge the legitimacy of our democratic form of government." Von NotHaus will appeal, of course, while federal prosecutors work to take (by forfeiture) an estimated $7 million in Liberty Dollar coins and bullion.

Yet this latest round of post-conviction publicity has also renewed discussion as to whether the government may have gone too far. A new team of lawyers from Virginia has volunteered to help von NotHaus with an appeal. Who knows? Maybe the guy really is on to something big, or at least paving the way for someone else to do so. Or maybe he needled the establishment in just the right way, provoking the rest of us to think a little more about how it all works. "All government currencies are going down, David," he told me that night at the luau. "They came after me because they don't want competition."

CHAPTER 7

The Revolutionaries

E pluribus unum
"Out of many, one"

Sonu Kumar owns a dusty electronics repair shop on a
rutted dirt road west of the Indian capital of Delhi. Sur-
rounded by ancient television sets and a few suspect-
looking VHS and DVD players loaded on rickety shelves, Kumar sits
hunched over a table strewn with spare parts.

He points a small screwdriver into what looks like an unsalvageable
transistor radio. Yet after a couple of turns, followed by a pinch with pli-
ers, a crackle of static breaks the silence. A moment later a Hindi-
language dance tune pours forth, spilling into the street.

The customer hands Kumar two crumpled 100-rupee notes (worth
about $5), which vanish into a shirt pocket. Until recently, those bank-
notes, like all of Kumar's earnings, would have stayed bunched up in that
pocket, or crammed into a hiding spot in his upstairs apartment.

On the opposite side of the road from Kumar's shop stands a cluttered
drugstore, Sharma Medicos, where owner Lakhnlal Sharma fills prescriptions and sells multivitamins, shampoo, prepaid minutes for cell
phones, and, as of a few months ago, bank accounts.

Kumar, who is twenty-one, walks over and greets the pharmacist. The young repairman places 1,000 rupees worth of bills on the counter, pulls out his cheap-o Nokia cellphone, and starts punching a few quick codes. A moment later he receives a text message confirming that his savings account with the State Bank of India has been credited 1,000 rupees. Sharma the pharmacist also enters numbers on his cellphone. The cash on the countertop is now rightfully his, as if he'd made an ATM withdrawal, so his bank account is debited 1,000 rupees. That's it. They're done. It's a decidedly undramatic exchange. Yet the technology powering this brief transaction is being heralded as one of the twenty-first century's most promising weapons in the battle against poverty. For cash, it could prove to be the angel of death.

◆

UPHILL FROM SEATTLE'S Space Needle, Ignacio Mas has just finished a call in his glassy office at the headquarters of the Bill and Melinda Gates Foundation. In recent years, the Gates Foundation has committed tens of millions of dollars to support a kind of financial innovation that has nothing to do with Wall Street's latest Byzantine products, and everything to do with the humble cellphone program Kumar used to deposit his 1,000 rupees. In November of 2010, Melinda Gates announced a $500 million commitment to further promote these kinds of advances in basic financial services, recognizing that merely having the means to sock money away empowers people, as she put it, "to use their own energy, their own talents to lift themselves out of poverty."[1]

Mas is deputy director of the foundation's Financial Services for the Poor program, and it's his job "to teach the world that cash is the enemy of the poor." Born in Spain and trained in economics at MIT and Harvard, Mas first began thinking about the relationship between saving money and money's various forms in the 1990s while working at the World Bank. He was hop-scotching the globe from one financial fiasco to the next, trying to help governments regain more stable economic footing. While on the job, he began to suspect that something was amiss about the way experts at the World Bank and other institutions assess the economic health of a given country.

One key measure looks at how much the population saves. The figure is derived by comparing aggregate savings of the country with gross national product, which matters because it provides a broad picture of what the people, collectively, can afford. "But I began to realize that that tells you nothing about who's saving," says Mas. Is it 83 percent of the population, or is it only 3 percent who have money saved in banks?" Because if it's just 3 percent, then the financial situation for the people is extremely unstable, even if the population as a whole has a large sum of money saved up.

He wasn't the only person to see it this way, and among economists today, says Mas, "there's much more of a sense that $1 doesn't equal $1. To improve peoples' welfare, you need *participation* in banking, not just money in banks." How to expand participation, he realized, was a question that required fresh thinking about the interplay between saving, cash, and electronic money. "People tend to intellectualize this stuff, but it's very straightforward. The poor are trapped using cash." Herein lies physical money's hidden cruelty: the privileged don't want it and can easily avoid it; the poor can't avoid it, and are most penalized by it. When your only option is cash, your assets are stuck in the material world. Without the ability to convert the cash into electronic money, you're completely out— excluded from banking, and thus denied a safe and reliable way to save.

A savings account of some kind won't remedy a fundamental shortfall of economic resources. But it can add a dose of financial stability where once there was only turmoil. This is banking in its most humanitarian form, even though, in the era of Occupy Wall Street, that sounds like an oxymoron. A rosy view of financial institutions might not come easily in the post–financial meltdown era, but in the developing world, banking in the uncomplicated, no-derivatives sense of deposits and responsible lending is of fundamental importance. You can't feed or vaccinate your children with a bank account. Yet having a secure means to store money and conduct transactions empowers people in ways that few other tools can.

But conventional banking means making trips to a bank branch, waiting in line when you could be out earning income, maintaining a minimum balance—all requirements that are impractical and out of reach for the poor. According to one recent study, the average cost of a bank transaction, when you factor in all of the various travel, time, and fees, is about $1. That doesn't sound like much to many of us, but for the 2.7 billion people in the world who live on an income of $2 a day, it's a huge sum.[2] So they stick with cash. (Not that costs and barriers to banking are only a problem for people in faraway lands. An estimated eighteen million Americans don't have bank accounts, and twenty million rely on payday lenders and check-cashing businesses, which owe their very existence to the fact that their customers are trapped using cash.)

The poorer you are, the more crushing the costs and risks of cash become. Everyone you know—a habitually drunk cousin, an ailing neighbor, your belligerent spouse—can beg you for a few bucks, or steal the hard-earned money that you're trying to save to pay your children's school fees. A fire or natural disaster can obliterate your meager savings. And you may have to spend days riding buses and walking to the countryside to deliver cash to, or retrieve cash from, a relative. Even if a wire service is accessible, you must endure steep fees when wiring funds, which is especially costly when you have so little money to begin with.

In wealthy countries, money, for the most part, is born in the form of 1s and 0s on some distant computer, usually by way of a bank deposit. As old-fashioned as checks are, even they represent money in electronic form. How do you spend that money? If you happen to want or need cash, you stroll to a nearby ATM. Otherwise, you use your credit or debit card, because merchants are generally equipped to accommodate your electronic money needs.

Having money in electronic form is our ticket to both streamlined commerce and financial services that help us build stability beyond the next meal or visit to the doctor: mortgages, small-business loans, interest-bearing accounts, health insurance, home insurance, college savings, e-commerce, and more. This access is a luxury we barely notice.

Countries like India, however, are so completely hooked on cash that visitors can't realistically go without it, unless they plan to remain inside their hotels during their entire stay. I was in a jetlag-induced stupor at Amsterdam's Schiphol Airport, awaiting my connecting flight to Delhi, when I suddenly realized that I would need cash in India. There was no way around it. To pay for a taxi, buy water, hire a rickshaw, employ a translator, purchase a souvenir, pay the small entrance fee to visit historic sights—to do any and all of it, I was going to need physical money. My year without cash would have to go on pause.

In the arrivals hall at Indira Gandhi International, I made my way to a currency exchange window, set a few hundred dollars in the gray crater below the glass, and requested a mix of large and small bills. (As a tourist, I expect price gouging, but there's no need to invite it by only carrying high-value notes.) The teller handed me a mountain of paper, and for a second I was seduced by the denomination effect. *So many zeroes.* A moment later the exchange-rate reality set in, and I saw the cash for what it was: a pain in the ass. No offense to Mahatma Gandhi, whose bespectacled face smiles on all of India's paper money, but the softly worn banknotes renewed that whole suite of hygiene concerns, as if their very fibers were a preview of the humidity, dirt, and sweat of this megalopolis.

For me, India's dependence on cash was a mild inconvenience. For locals, it's crushing. Cash not only perpetuates peoples' exclusion from banking and the formal economy, it also has a knack for being spent. This may sound contrary to the credit card effect, which shows that people have a harder time parting with cash versus plastic. But those studies test subjects in wealthy countries who live with both electronic and material money. When you're poor, it's cash that's most turbo liquid.

Paper money is just as tough on the state. Although India's central bank collects seigniorage like any other issuing authority, a recent McKinsey study found that if the government could find a way to make all of its payments to citizens electronic, India could save more than $22 billion a year. That would take a 20 percent chunk out of India's national deficit, or fund the country's major food aid program for two years. It would also get people saving.

The poor need better ways to save because they lead deceptively complex financial lives, and because it's almost impossible to break the cycle of poverty without money in a bank or something like it. Rural farmers receive essentially the whole year's income in one or two lump sums, which means they must stretch their earnings from one harvest to the next. Migrant laborers have the potential to earn more frequently, but usually in smaller sums, and they don't know if they'll have income tomorrow, or at all this week, which means they too must find ways to spread resources over time. As for people with menial employment, the salary may be dependable, but the amounts are still so paltry that day-to-day management of resources is as crucial as it is for the farmer who gets paid twice yearly.

Such instability guarantees vulnerability. People are climbing out of poverty all the time, but financial shocks are pushing just as many right back into it. When unanticipated hardship arrives—a sprained ankle, broken-down scooter, sick child, or flood—the economic impact will wreck a family. For the billions of people who don't have a bank account, having one could offer a chance to brace against such turmoil. Cash, in contrast, remains as inefficient and precarious as it was three hundred years ago.

Back in Seattle, Mas and I lunch at a café down the street from the Gates Foundation offices. When it's time to settle up, Mas takes a $20 bill from his wallet. I give him a surprised look. "I don't actually have a problem with cash," he says, laughing. Advantages such as universal acceptability, anonymity, and simplicity, he says, are tough to beat. And he, like me, has the luxury of choice.

Mas's indictment of cash is really an indictment of its *inconvertibility*, and the damage that engenders. By encouraging technologies that open avenues to electronic money, the Gates Foundation and other aid groups, from the World Bank to Mercy Corp, hope to reduce cash dependence while expanding access to savings and financial stability.

"But here is the key," says Mas, referring to the fate of cash specifically. If the capacity to convert tactile money into electronic money is widespread enough, cash's coveted status will diminish. "People will come to see that they don't need it. And because of its costs, they won't want it." They won't want it for many of the same reasons that people living in stronger economies don't walk around town carrying fat rolls of banknotes, and don't usually store their life savings in kitchen cupboards.

The primary barrier that has always prevented the poor from having electronic money is the old-school bricks-and-mortar bank. Traditionally, banks have had little or no interest in addressing poor peoples' needs: the deposits of the poor don't add up to much, and it will never be profitable to put bank branches in the slums and rural villages where poor people live. "But cellphones are everywhere!" says Mas, holding up his Blackberry. Phones are the solution to getting financial services to the masses—to the roughly one billion people who already have a phone but who don't have a bank account.[3] In the near future, establishing a bank account should be as easy as buying lettuce, transferring money as easy as sending a text message, and carrying cash as unreasonable as toting around a chest full of silver coins.

◆

THE MORNING AFTER my arrival in Delhi, I hire a taxi and head west through perpetually harrowing city traffic to visit a few pharmacies and shops that offer mobile banking services. Staring out the window, the deluge of stimuli dazzles and puzzles the senses to the edge of overload. Pigs and toddlers rummaging through a trash pile, wildly painted trucks belching and honking, women in immaculate saris scooping muddy water into buckets, layers of grime on every horizontal surface, impossibly cluttered stores selling chairs, toasters, bicycles, and Lay's Magic Masala potato chips. Emerging middle-class consumerism sprouts up on every square inch of the cityscape not occupied by roads, rundown apartment buildings, cows, tractors, panhandlers, green and yellow three-wheeled taxis, mangy dogs, and vendors squatting in the dirt selling limes, old shoes, and weary carnations. Savory smells one mo-ment, rancid odors the next, and the overlapping sounds of engines, laughter, coughing, music, and the occasional snort of an elephant walk-ing down the side of a ten-lane highway.

On nearly every street in Delhi I spot at least one, if not four, retailers selling cellphone airtime minutes. Whereas in the United States most mobile service is based on a monthly subscription, the rest of the world buys talk time like buying gas for a car: fill your account with minutes, or just get a few dollars worth. When you're running low, stop at a retail shop to refuel. (You can also top up online or via text message, but only if you have some form of electronic money with which to do so.)

Literally millions of shops in India sell airtime minutes. Coca-Cola may be the global distribution success story of the twentieth century, but the new coverage masters are telecom companies. In less than a decade, they have extended cellphone service and retail operations to the far cor-ners of the planet. There are now an estimated 4.6 billion mobile phones in use worldwide, with 80 percent of new connections made by poorer consumers in developing countries.[4] In India alone, cellphone adoption rates have grown from nominal usage a decade ago to nearly 700 million connections today, and millions of new accounts are opened every month.[5]

For people in the developing world, the phone embodies opportunity. In parts of Africa, farmers now receive text messages with weather updates that enable them to make more strategic decisions about what to plant or when to harvest crops for maximum yield. Another service in the works provides free healthcare advice via mobile phones to people who are un-able to get to a medical clinic, and researchers in Ohio are trying to rig cellphones so that they can be used to test children for ear infections.[6] Taxi drivers throughout the world can be in touch with customers (I kept two drivers' phone numbers on me in Delhi), fishermen use their phones to negotiate with buyers, and text alerts about mudslides, elections, or civil unrest can help people stay informed and safe. That is, as long as ousted Egyptian President Hosni Mubarak doesn't shut off the network.

Almost overnight the phone has evolved from one-trick pony—connecting two voices—into a Swiss Army knife of do-good power. (Yes, there is do-bad power too. We'll get to that.) It may sound intellectually precarious to hoist a gadget onto such a high pedestal, yet researching the ascent of the mobile phone and its potential to improve peoples' lives—in contrast to, say, the steady stream of gloomy stories about ineffectual foreign aid—makes it hard not to catch the fever. The phone has "become as essential to human functioning as a pair of shoes," declared *The Economist* in 2010.[7] Finally owning one has been likened to a get-out-of-poverty card.*[8]

The most dramatic impact from cellphones may turn out to be services that turn the phone into a mini bank branch in your pocket, thus replacing the need for material money. By 2010, there were 150 mobile money transfer or mobile banking services active or readying for launch all over the globe, and by some estimates the volume of transactions made via mobile will be $250 billion in 2012.[9] Remittance needs alone are massive, with nearly half a trillion dollars moving between family members and friends every year.

In wealthier countries, we're already seeing mobile payment tools used at Starbucks and elsewhere. In the spring of 2011, Google unveiled a service called Google Wallet. It's an app for paying—wave your phone at a retailer's terminal instead of using your credit card. This isn't the first such product of its kind, but a big push from a giant like Google

---

*One measure of the phone's potential impact is how intensely the poor spend on communication technologies. According to one recent study, those who manage to increase their income from a dismal $1 a day to a mere $4 a day start spending on cellphones over needs such as health, housing, and education. A purebred cynic could argue that the poor are buying something because of slick advertising, not out of necessity, and I'm sure marketing matters. But that conclusion underestimates the wherewithal of people who have become expert survivors. If the poor are buying hundreds of millions of cellphones, surely it's not because they've all been tricked.

gets attention and underscores the fact that a race is underway to move more commerce out of our wallets and into our phones. This exploding market will put pressure on cash. But it's people in the developing world, where the only other option has always been cash, who could deliver cash its lethal blow.

The early success story that has development experts doing backflips is a service in Kenya called M-Pesa (the *M* is for "mobile" and *pesa* is Kiswahili for "money"). It's run by a subsidiary of the huge telecom company Vodafone, and the first thing you need to know is that M-Pesa isn't a bank. It's a transfer service akin to PayPal, but you don't need an Internet hookup.

To the people of Kenya, the benefits of this service have been staggering. Instead of spending two days on buses to deliver money to grandma back in the village, you can go to a local shop—any one of the 23,000 tied into the network of M-Pesa agents—plunk down the cash you want to convert and send, and then type in the necessary codes on your cell phone. Grandma receives a text that says money has been flashed to her account, and she goes to her local shop to redeem the cash. She could also decide to keep it "in" the phone for the time being, or she could redeem a portion of that electronically stored value, in the form of purchased fruit, flour, and batteries. The shopkeeper's account is credited the corresponding amount for the groceries.[10]

After less than four years of operation, M-Pesa counted thirteen million users—more than half the adults in the country. In contrast, it took a century for the conventional banking industry in Kenya to reach five million customers. Stores offering M-Pesa are in virtually every community, with the logo advertised in windows, on flags, or hand-painted on cinderblock walls. More money already passes through the M-Pesa system in Kenya than all the Western Union transactions worldwide.[11]

Kenya's central bank has reported a drop in cash usage, and M-Pesa payments are now being accepted by a few of the country's major retailers and the national airline.[12] Other Kenyans, such as taxi drivers, load up their accounts whenever possible, so that they don't have to hold on to cash. In the earliest days of the M-Pesa experiment, an anthropology researcher interviewed a man who put money on his phone while visiting one side of Nairobi, and then, just forty minutes later, took it out again in a shop on the other side of the city. When asked why, he said he was traveling through a dangerous part of town and was leery of having cash on him.*[13]

The benefits of this kind of program extend beyond individual finances. There are signs, for example, that it could strike a huge blow against corruption. In 2010, in the central Afghanistan province of Wardak, local policemen began receiving their monthly salary as an electronic payment. When payday came and they accessed their accounts via their cellphones, many of them thought there had been a mistake. Nobody gets a generous raise out of the blue—and a 30 percent raise is preposterous. But it wasn't a raise or a mistake. Under the old system, crooked higher-ups skimmed so much off the top of the cash payments that the policemen never actually knew the true amount of their salaries. (One brazen commander complained that he was no longer getting his cut.)

It's true that cash is still part of this whole picture. The Afghani cops, like relatives in rural Kenya, still have to convert electronic money on the phone into cash in hand so that they can then buy goods from local vendors who don't accept electronic payment. But if more of their customers start asking about this method of payment, it won't take long for vendors to get on board. Remember, this technology is in its infancy. The idea for an ATM first emerged in the 1930s, but the machines weren't really a regular part of our lives until the 1980s. Likewise, credit cards took more than a generation before they went mainstream. Anyone who doubts that the overlapping worlds of telecom, apps mania, and

---

*The anthropologists had received permission from people in advance to track how they used M-Pesa and then interview them later.

finance aren't going to become even more creative and integrated in the coming decade is probably snorting a little too much cocaine from tightly rolled banknotes.

And counterintuitive as it may sound, Mas says the persisting role for cash in the shorter term will actually help catalyze its downfall. "Cash is a centuries-old army that you can't fight with a frontal assault. You need to infiltrate. Make everyone think what you're doing is distributing it, because that *is* what you're doing, pushing it out to those villages." That's what mobile money can do, by way of so many thousands, even millions, of stores throughout the world providing the conversion service to people in the countryside, who receive payments from relatives or customers in cities, where wealth is disproportionately concentrated. That in turn brings business and prosperity into rural areas that badly need it.

What that also does, however, is further marginalize cash. Before long, the baker where the Afghani cops buy bread, the store where the Kenyan farmer buys seed, and the pay-as-you-go medical clinic in the mountains of Mexico will all accept payment via mobile money. They will prefer it, for the same boatload of reasons about cash's costs and risks that so infuriate Dave Birch. When that day comes, says Mas, our wallets may become as obsolete as pay phones.

Already the race is on to imagine what that will look like, or at least to predict what country will be the first to completely quit banknotes and coins. Top seeds, perhaps not surprisingly, are Japan and South Korea, where technophiles willingly adopt the latest innovations faster than you can say "new model."[14] Government officials in the dispersed-islands nation of the Maldives are also taking a hard look at killing cash. The 2004 Indian Ocean tsunami literally washed many residents' life savings out to sea, and Maldivian people sometimes have to take day-long trips by boat to obtain cash to buy basic provisions. Since the 2010 earthquake in Haiti, development and technology groups have been hurrying to implement mobile banking there, and Thailand's central bank has made public proclamations in favor of cashlessness.[15] Kenya has a strong head start with M-Pesa, and of course in Sweden there's the bankers-led campaign against cash, backed by the full faith and trust of Abba.*[16]

No one is predicting that India could be first. It's too massive, too variable, and, despite ballistic economic growth, too poor. Yet if mobile money systems really are going to help curb poverty and marginalize cash the way evangelists predict, they must become as diffuse and pervasive as physical money. "The whole premise is to make it really, really big," says Mas. *Big* means "widely accepted," because new forms of money have to be if they're truly going to challenge cash. It also means big business.

Without operating on huge scales, there's little incentive for banks or telecom companies to invest in these systems, because the users themselves have little money. Collecting tiny fees from 10,000 customers and ten million are markedly different business propositions. "Because it's so massive, and the need so pronounced, India is the ultimate proof of principle for mobile money," says Mas. If it can work there, the impact and long-term viability of this technology will be undeniable. That is where Abhishek Sinha comes in.

◆

"I AM THE ASSASSIN OF CASH," Sinha tells me in his office in a quiet suburb of Delhi. He sits opposite a framed photo of his spiritual guru, a swami by the name of Niranjanananda Saraswati. The bookshelf next to me is full of back issues of *Fortune* and books about the ascent of Google, leadership lessons from Jack Welch, and marketing strategy.

---

*Even the pseudo-country of Somaliland is in the running. At the moment, $1 there is currently worth a toaster-size pile of 17,000 Somaliland shillings. That absurdity is why local entrepreneurs launched a mobile money service to facilitate incoming remittances (denominated in dollars) that attracted 80,000 customers in the first six months.

For a guy who not long ago had all of his credit cards rejected at a Pizza Hut—while on a date with the woman of his dreams, no less— Sinha is doing pretty well. In 2009, Bill Gates paid a visit to the offices of his startup company, Eko India Financial Services. In 2010 U.S. Treasury Secretary Timothy Geithner and *New York Times* columnist Thomas Friedman visited. That fall, during President Obama's visit to India, Sinha was a guest at a reception for the president and a small group of Indian entrepreneurs.

A mustachioed Delhi native, Sinha, thirty-four, wears glasses and a bland button-down shirt tucked into jeans. He speaks in the calm tones of an academic, and on his right wrist he wears a rosary from a famed Indian yoga school. His daily dealings relate to software, financial regulations, and antipoverty lingo; not exactly the stuff of high-stakes intrigue. Yet behind the business jargon and staid executive speak is some serious brashness.

The first computer in Sinha's home didn't show up until 1998: his father's bulky work-issue laptop. The family's Internet connection at the time was a lumbering dial-up modem, but Sinha was instantly captivated by the Web. He opened a Yahoo mail account and was online for hours at a time, taken especially, he confesses, by the endless variety of adult content. "This is something, as you know, really sought-after by a twenty-one-year-old guy."

The Internet may have been stimulating, but it didn't cross Sinha's mind that he could have a tech career. After graduating from college, he landed a job with a reputable manufacturing firm, but he felt like taking the job was more like checking predetermined boxes than living his life. So he bailed on orientation and, in 2000, moved to the high-tech boomtown of Bangalore.

He slept on the couch in a friend's apartment, took recruitment tests given on the weekends by huge technology companies, and hoped to land work before regret and shame kicked in. In 2001 he was hired to work at Satyam, a top Bangalore firm. Yet it wasn't long before he got the itch to exit. "I suppose something about the corporate world didn't fit with my personality."

Around this time, Sinha was noticing that cellphones could do more than just connect voices and send quick text messages. He guessed correctly, and relatively early, that whoever found a way to make useful apps for phones was going to make a killing. "I would bounce ideas off of my friends and we would joke about developing one and then selling it," says Sinha. Then he decided to do it, or try, even though he didn't have anything to sell. This was Sinha's second insight: you don't need to have a product to be valued. You only need to create the perception of value—faith, as it were. Later, you can scramble to come up with the goods.

Before quitting Satyam, Sinha took out a bank loan and as many credit cards as he could. Together with his younger brother, he began scheduling meetings with tech-sector executives, pitching nonexistent products. One firm eventually said yes. Suddenly Sinha was the co-founder and CEO of a company that now had to design and deliver software.

What kind of product, exactly? "One was a solution for pumping out huge numbers of SMS messages." SMS, short for Short Message Service, is what most people use when they text one another. An estimated 75 percent of all people who subscribe to a mobile voice service also use the phone to punch out short messages, usually with this technology. Behind these simple communiqués lie the minutiae of networks and programming, geeky details like *digital cellular standards* and *SS7 protocol*.

It took little time for the Sinha brothers and their freelance hires to burn through the bank loan and max out their credit cards. The humiliation at Pizza Hut was a low point. Worse were the groveling letters he wrote to loan officers and only being able to afford a one-day visit to an amusement park for his honeymoon. Then he had to ask his father-in-law for help to cover the rent. In India, says Sinha, people do not ask their in-laws for money. Full stop. "But I had no choice. That experience really gave me a purer understanding of the *ego*," he says, which I'm pretty sure means, *I felt like a complete failure*. Still, Sinha thinks anyone would have done the same. "If you were in a corner, wouldn't you go to any extent?" he asks. I tell him I don't know. I've never tried to sell non-existent software while dodging a swarm of creditors.

Finally, in 2005, their company, 6D Technologies, was delivering a real product to a few customers. They turned a profit, and Sinha settled up with lenders and paid employees who had gone months without a paycheck. But soon, in that insane yet admirable way entrepreneurs do, he again got the urge to abandon comfort for the frontier. First, though, he needed a fresh idea.

The seed was planted by a customer in Oman who asked if Sinha could come up with a program for topping up cellphone minutes at places like ATMs or supermarket checkout counters. It was a logical proposition: if you need to buy airtime minutes, why should you have to convert electronic money into cash via a bank withdrawal, only to hand it to someone who turns it right back into a different kind of electronic value, in this case airtime minutes?

One night in early 2006, Sinha awoke around 2:00 in the morning and called his brother. He had it. If buying minutes was something you could do via cellular infrastructure, why couldn't that same system be used for other, more everyday, financial transactions? He'd read about cellphones sending and receiving funds. But what if they could be programmed to do more than that—to work like a virtual bank teller?

His new company, Eko, is essentially a conduit between people and their bank accounts. The software enables mobile customers to open savings accounts with the State Bank of India, the largest and one of the country's most recognized banks. Eko makes the transactions possible with its transfer and security codes, ensuring that you are you before relaying the transaction data. Earnings come from small fees, which Eko shares with the telecom companies on whose networks the information travels between phones, Eko, and the bank. When I visited the pharmacy in West Delhi and met Kumar the electronics repairman, he said the fees don't bother him. He was looking at his phone while answering most of my questions. Compared to stashing his money or trying to get to a bank, "this is just much better," he said.

Money, as you know, depends on trust, and Sinha knew from the start that people, not only in India but anywhere, probably wouldn't entrust their money to an unknown startup. But most everyone in this country of 1.2 billion people knows of, and is more or less inclined to trust, the State Bank of India. This reputation stuff is key because it means Eko doesn't have to pretend to be a bank. It just makes the connection between the accounts and, Sinha hopes, millions and millions of people. The money, meanwhile, rests with the bank, and is insured just like an old-school deposit.

Caveat time. Many companies and nonprofits are trying to get financial services to the poor, and they don't all rely on cellphones. People like the Gates Foundation's Mas, digital-money man Dave Birch, and hundreds of experts believe that the phone *is* the answer, but that hardly makes it so. Other models use smartcards, for example, which you can think of as a hybrid driver's license and bankcard equipped with a chip for storing data. All you need to do to conduct your banking at the local corner store is bring your smartcard, which allows you to do the same basic suite of transactions as Eko. The rub is that the storeowner has to be equipped with a relatively expensive reader, which looks a lot like a credit card terminal. On the other hand, this sort of system might prove to be more secure, or more reliable in extremely remote corners of the world where cellphone coverage remains spotty.

But the advantages of phones are compelling. They don't require any additional investment in gizmos. They have also already become such an everyday part of our lives: people know what it means to trade in electronic value through the phone, because they know about buying, using, and transferring airtime minutes. As of October 2011, Eko had opened more than 200,000 bank accounts, and had another 800,000 people using the service to send money. That may sound like a lot, but the heat is on for Sinha to ramp the operation up another notch if he's going to prove the company's worth.

As big-hearted as this model may be for encouraging savings and all the rest of it, Eko and other mobile banking initiatives are still businesses. One pinstriped-suit wearing Indian telecom executive put it this way: "This is not about corporate social responsibility or public relations. We want to get paid." In the same breath, however, he painted an idealistic picture of branchless banking, and of what this technology could mean for his country and for the hundreds of millions of people in India struggling against abject poverty. "The backward classes and all that shit has gone on too long," he says. "Every man should be socially included. To do that, you need financial inclusion." To do *that*, you need a way out of the cash trap.

◆

IT'S·DUSK DURING my last drive with Sinha through the choked streets of Delhi. I watch an old man with no shoes weave a bicycle with a flat tire through the snarl of automobiles. Sinha keeps pointing to kiosks with signs for Vodafone, Airtel, Aircel, and other network operators, as if silently marveling at their presence over and over. Whereas I'm seeing countless dilapidated buildings, overcrowding, and borderline chaos, Sinha observes a cascade of transactions. It's almost like he can see the movement of electronic money. "At all of these shops, people are topping up airtime minutes." Others are paying for goods with airtime minutes, bypassing use of government-issued currency altogether.

The mobile money revolution underway in developing countries is something that technologists refer to as a *leapfrog scenario*. Two of them, actually. Less-developed economies never had good landline telephone service, if at all, which meant there were minimal obstacles preventing the implementation and adoption of a superior system. Now cellphones are everywhere.

That same thing is happening with mobile money and mobile banking. As one expert I spoke with likes to put it: the leading edge of this technology isn't in Silicon Valley; it's the African Rift Valley, West Delhi, and rural villages in Brazil. In the West, we have our (relatively) convenient online banking and our plentiful supply of ATMs. Our financial lives don't *feel* tremendously burdensome, and although it's cool that banks are rolling out apps for our iPhones and reducing our need for cash, alternatives to physical money aren't life-changing for us in the ways they can be for the poor. In the developing world, most people have no experience when it comes to financial services. That means there are no entrenched behaviors or mediocre precedents. The slate is clean. Poorer countries could hurry ahead of all this silliness with ATMs, expensive cash management, bank robberies, and easy tax evasion, and jump right to it with options that are better than cash.

The gridlock brings the car to a stop. Sinha nods toward one street-corner store beneath a faded awning. It's filled with magazines, drinks, newspapers, cookies, pens, tobacco, and a kaleidoscope of other merchandise. "The individual accounts for our customers are very low balance," he says. "That is the point. Banks will never want to serve these customers with a traditional branch. But look at how the economy works at the shops everywhere. In India, they sell single pieces of candy and cigarettes by the stick." Businesses find ways to succeed at a scale and price that works for the people. Sinha wants to do the same with banking and money transfer, and to do so where it works best for the population: on their phones.

"Why do you call yourself 'the assassin of cash'?" I ask.

"Think about the people and how they live," says Sinha. "They spend small amounts of cash, maybe three or five times a day, commuting to work, buying a lunch, getting groceries—things like this. Eko is not about assassinating the transactions that have already been replaced by credit cards. We want to go after all of these small cash transactions."

He's talking about the "final mile." Digital money nerds use this expression a lot, to indicate that while cash has largely been displaced, it seems to have an immovable position as the world's favorite method of payment for small-value transactions. Finding an equally trusted, fast, and universally accepted medium of exchange to unseat cash's place within this niche constitutes the final mile before arriving at a fully cash-less society. The task sounds so daunting that many people just assume it can't be done, or at least not for a long time to come.

But as Sinha sees it, mobile changes everything. Why would people bother with paper money when they can just use their phones to flash a few dollars or rupees from a bank account to a vendor's bank account? "You have to look beyond this infancy period for mobile money. Everyone is still figuring out the models. But we are already seeing cash getting pushed aside."

Earlier in the week, I had visited a few other shops around the city. At one of them I met Ravi Chandan, the owner of a stationery store. He had recently begun selling Eko accounts and depositing electronic money for customers in exchange for their cash. Three of the city's 500,000 rickshaw drivers were drinking tea just outside the store where Chandan, thirty-six, sells notebooks, pens, highlighters, badminton rackets, and Vicks-brand suckers. He told me that he knew a couple of twelve- and thirteen-year-olds in the area who are using their parents' accounts. The deposit amounts are small, just 200 or 300 rupees here and there. But already the kids have saved more than 2,000 rupees (about $40). "They're learning to save now," says Chandan. "I'm proud of them."

Before I left his shop, Chandan told me that he sees a point at which the cash in all of this would be irrelevant. A few of his regular customers have already started using money on their phones to buy goods in his store, without ever having to involve physical currency in the transactions. "This is the future," Chandan told me. "It is working."

◆

BACK HOME, when I mention to people that we'll soon just be texting money, they immediately worry. *Is the money really safe? Won't this be a boon for aspiring money launderers and terrorists? Are my transactions private?* Part of the allure of cash in hand is that it usually doesn't vaporize. It may get spent, stolen, and suffer from devaluation, but it doesn't go *poof.* When money is converted into and traded in electronic form, what assurances do we have of its continued existence?

The challenge of convincing people that a technology is trustworthy is nothing new. In Japan, consumers have long been comfortable making cash deposits into ATMs, whereas in the United States, many people are still reluctant to do so, perhaps because of a cultural mistrust of machines, and in spite of data indicating that most banking mistakes are made by tellers of the human variety.[17] Luckily, humanity has a solid track record of warming to innovations, including money-related ones. Online payments provider PayPal once sounded precarious. Making a check deposit via ATM initially struck people as chancy, and, a century ago, holding a deposit certificate instead of a satchel full of coins was seen as wildly risky.

The latest technologies will always be a tough sell for the risk-averse; even car radios once had their fifteen minutes in the antitechnology spotlight. On the other hand, when the pluses afforded by a new technology outweigh the perceived risks, people dive in. Look at the thirteen million M-Pesa users in Kenya who've welcomed mobile money into their lives, or the nearly one hundred million people who use PayPal accounts.[18]

Still, there are nontrivial concerns about mobile phones and money that need sorting out. One understandable reason for skepticism is the wireless network itself. Anyone who has ever had a call fail can imagine why. A dropped call is one thing, but you had better not drop my money. These systems must be engineered with enough redundancy to ensure that money moving through networks is treated distinctly from a voice connection. Any hiccup or true screw-up—in your phone, at a cellular tower, on Eko's servers, or at the bank—can't result in lost money or interrupted transactions. If there is even the slightest hint that mobile money might be less safe than cash in a tea canister, people will reject it. The risks are too severe, especially for people already on the margins.

But keep in mind that these are matters of perceived risk weighed against benefits, not absolute security. Credit and debit cards make for an interesting comparison. Although modern-day plastic is hardly impervious to hackers or identity thieves, the security failures are infrequent enough that customers keep coming back. Mobile money, given enough time, should be able to achieve at least that level of robustness.

Another concern, though, is protecting peoples' funds in the event that the mobile operator itself goes under or decides to quit the mobile money business. Part of what makes a bank a bank is rules. However imperfect they may be, these rules exist to keep the bank behaving responsibly, so that depositors' wealth is protected. By and large, regulations give us confidence that no one will walk away with our savings, even if the bank fails. Federal deposit insurance, at least in the United States, boosts that confidence even more. If M-Pesa, Eko, or similar initiatives fail, will customer savings go down too?*

When he's not trying to explain why cash is the enemy of the poor, Ignacio Mas's other job is to get financial regulators rethinking what constitutes banking. "The tradition is that the central bank gives you a license to open a branch. It has to have a vault to meet such-and-such specifications, glass this thick, a kitchen for employees—that sort of thing." But those rules are anachronistic now that mobile technology is enabling "branchless banking" accounts, allowing people to convert cash into electronic money almost anywhere and send it to a savings account. "That pharmacy you visited in Delhi—that is not a bank branch," says Mas. "The stores are essentially selling electronic money (for cash), just like they would sell rice. They don't hold anything."

Nor do the conduit companies. For M-Pesa users, Vodafone's subsidiary in Kenya doesn't hold the money. M-Pesa customer funds are pooled and held in trust in a regular old bank, depositor insurance and all. Should Vodafone go bankrupt tomorrow, or if executives suddenly

---

*Savings denominated in sovereign currency are guaranteed. Savings denominated in alternative currencies—if banks were to offer them—may not have that level of protection. That's another edge that government-issued currencies have, at least for now, over Ven, Ithaca HOURS, Bitcoin, and the like.

decide they want to ditch the mobile money business and buy the Chicago Cubs, peoples' money would, or should, be safe at the bank. The same goes for people using Eko: the money is with the State Bank of India and insured like the funds of other bank customers, whether or not Eko thrives or dies in the years to come.

OK, but what if hackers decide to worm their way into these new electronic money systems? Anyone who runs a software company will insist the system is hack-proof, and any highly trained computer scientist will tell you that is a lie, or at least a fib. No one can say with certainty that a software program is absolutely unbreakable.

To understand why, you need to delve into enigmas like the P versus NP problem. In simplest terms, it's a speed question. Most of the digital security in our lives is based on the premise that computers can't solve all problems in the same amount of time: 2 + 2 versus some insanely difficult equation—of course they don't take the same amount of time to solve. Don't be ridiculous. Most mathematicians are confident that this is the case, but they haven't proven it. A proof to the contrary could unlock a bazillion secrets, and dollars, hidden behind what were once the most unbreakable blockades in cyberspace. (That proof will also win you $1 million from the Clay Mathematics Institute, for solving one of its seven Millennium Prize Problems.)

If our lives were dictated by purely theoretical understanding of computer security, we wouldn't have bank accounts or feel safe conducting wire transfers, let alone shop online or allow machines to fly airplanes. The digital technologies we've incorporated into our lives have to be secure enough to satisfy our risk calculations. Mobile money still needs to earn its security stripes, but it shouldn't be expected to do the impossible just because people worry about their money and tend to be tentative about the latest technology.

The thornier aspects of the mobile money revolution actually have to do with money laundering, terrorism funding, and privacy. Today's banks are required to verify that potential customers are who they say they are, by gathering information like an applicant's address, proper identification, references, and sometimes employer information. When people sign up for a money transfer service like M-Pesa, or a branchless banking program like Eko, how can banks, and by extension the authorities, be sure that the people opening those accounts aren't criminals trying to hide money, or extremists who can't wait to start distributing funds to their terrorist buddies?

Sinha, Mas, and other mobile-money enthusiasts aren't nonchalant about these concerns, but they warn against creating unwarranted paranoia and against thinking too narrowly about what constitutes security. For example, limiting transfer amounts is an easy first step for deterring widespread abuse of these systems. Remember, target customers are people like Kumar, the electronics repairman, not millionaires who already have plenty of access to financial services, tax havens, and sophisticated methods of laundering their money.

Enterprising terrorists could easily end-run this transfer maximum, though, by having many people direct funds to a single operative. To prevent that from happening, the system could also have a maximum amount that can be received into a single account in a given time. The software could also have tripwires that alert authorities about suspicious activity, just like when your credit card company contacts you to be sure you really did buy that $20,000 necklace yesterday in Macau.

These are only a few low-level controls to keep the system kosher. As far as chasing the bad guys, Mas reminded me that the traceability component of mobile money should be attractive to law enforcement. "They *want* money in electronic form." Digital-money lover Birch is more adamant: "If cash were proposed now, governments would never endorse it," because it's by far the most convenient way to conduct crime and remain anonymous. Besides, "it's not like the war on terror and corruption is going to be helped by encouraging people to keep using cash."

Let's hover on this point for a moment, with the help of Acting Assistant Secretary of the U.S. Army Peter E. Kunkel. Writing in *Military Review* in 2008, Kunkel detailed "the unrealized strategic effects of a cashless battlefield." It's not the first thing that comes to mind when you think about the battlefield, but troops need readily accepted money. In Iraq and Afghanistan, U.S. Army units used (and to a lesser extent still use) cash to buy construction materials, flooring, tents, and bottled water. Greenbacks are used to pay tipsters, and even to compensate locals for damage to private property.

Every year between 2003 and 2008, the army used cargo aircraft to transport $1.5 billion in cash into Iraq, and used that cash for at least a million payments. "This heavy logistical burden endangers Soldiers [sic], both in the air and on the ground, transporting required cash to commanders at forward operating bases and combat outposts." But that is only the start of it. With some $19 billion in greenbacks now circulating in Iraq—and who knows how many more in Afghanistan—insurgents, terrorists, and smugglers have a ready supply of the most readily accepted and untraceable payment mechanism in the world. Whatever your opinion about U.S. military operations abroad, you can't be too thrilled that while there, U.S. troops have little choice but to hand out paper money that could indirectly come back to haunt them. The Pentagon, concludes Kunkel, should take a keen interest in promoting mobile money programs as a way to mitigate these dangers and bring more local commerce into the formal and, yes, traceable economy.*[19]

There, I said it. *Traceable.* That word inevitably leads to questions about the creepiness line. And they are fair questions. As Pastor Guest reminded me that cold day in Georgia, the anonymity of cash transactions is something we hold sacred. Despite cash's ever-declining relevance, this association between tactile money and the freedom to pursue happiness without being monitored seems unshakable. It is a God-given right, many people believe, protecting us from intrusive marketing companies and government snoops.[20] For Americans, the idea that we have a right not to be interfered with, even though no such right is detailed in the Bill of Rights, is a part of who we are.

---

*The billions in U.S. cash floating about Iraq equals about 20 percent of that country's GDP.

Speaking with an executive from VISA at the Digital Money Forum in London, I raised some of these concerns about compromised privacy in a cashless world. She kept reminding me that a lost or stolen wallet means an economic loss equal to whatever cash is inside it at the time, whereas cards can be canceled and reissued, and consumers aren't liable for fraudulent charges. Cash users who keep significant savings at home are also vulnerable to theft, and to potentially disastrous loss due to fire, rot, or the next Hurricane Katrina.[21] Zeros and ones on computers may be the more abstract form of money, but they're longer-lasting than decay-prone bills, which, in the case of U.S. dollars, only circulate an average of sixteen to twenty-four months before being committed to a shredder. She was making a decent argument that cash isn't exactly safe, but she was also dodging my question. Security and privacy are not the same.*[22]

Dave Birch isn't the most neutral source on the topic, given his work with credit card companies. But his technical expertise with secure networks, transactions, and cryptography gives him insight that is informative and, I think, pretty fair. When I bugged him about the Big Brother question, he took his Oyster card out of his wallet as a visual aid. Oyster is a stored-value card providing "tap and go" convenience to London transit passengers on area trains, buses, and subways. There's money "on" the card, and when you use it to pass through the turnstiles or tap a reader as you step onto a bus, your Oyster account is debited the corresponding fare.

"If you just say to people, 'Do you want to be registered, tracked, and traced,' they'll of course say, 'No!' But the first time they lose a card and want their money back, they'll see the risks of anonymity, and the next time they get one, they will register. People say *anonymity* is an advantage of cash, but what they really want is *privacy*." In the case of the Oyster card, data about you is stored for eight weeks, or so says the issuer,

---

*Fifty- and 100-dollar bills last longer, between fifty-five and eighty-nine months, because—wait for it—people stash them!

Transport for London. If you lose a card and a couple of days later call to have it replaced, you can get a new one because your payment information is on file.

More significantly, if a serious crime is committed at a Tube station, police will want to know who was in the station at the time. Within that eight-week period, they can do so. By Birch's reckoning, this is a reasonable sacrifice of privacy for the sake of crime prevention, provided it's set up to minimize the abuse of power and requires a warrant from the court. After eight weeks the information is gone. "By anonymizing the data, no one can go back through and troll years of data about people. That, I think, would be wrong and intrusive." A Columbia University law professor named Ronald Mann put it similarly in a 2011 radio interview. Ordinary consumers don't care about absolute anonymity. "The main people who are excited about a wholly anonymous payment system are people who are violating the law." He was talking about Bitcoin, the virtual currency project, and how regulators might step in to take action against it if they determine that it's used primarily for nefarious purposes. Yet he very well could have been speaking about cash.[23]

Mobile money and banking apps should not keep customer information on the phone—all the data should vanish once the transaction is concluded.[24] Yet if you're unemployed and suddenly start receiving a ton of incoming money from Yemen, or if the software detects that your transaction patterns shift from small transfers now and then to merchants in Raleigh-Durham, to a sudden and huge outflow of money to the Cayman Islands or the border regions of Pakistan, maybe it would be appropriate for the authorities to have some way to be sure everything is copacetic.

Not to suggest that we should blithely relinquish our civil liberties, but don't we want the cops to be able to break the glass, so to speak, to access the records necessary to trace a Tucson gunman's Glock, at least back to the point of purchase? This compromise between the rights of the individual and the state is echoed, of all places, on those crazy Georgia Guidestones: "Balance personal rights with social duties." There is no perfect equilibrium between the individual need for privacy and government interest in information. The best we can do is try to engineer systems that are as fair as possible and chockablock with checks and balances.

Another issue to keep in mind with the privacy puzzle is the distinction between what we say we value and are concerned about, versus how much we actually act on those concerns. Many millions of consumers don't seem to mind that Amazon recommends book titles based on their previous purchases, or that Facebook lines up ads that its algorithms determine might be of interest, based on users' profiles and online activities.[25] Much of this is semantics. Ask the people of Kenya (or anywhere) in a survey if they want a giant telecom company to store data about them and track who they send money to or receive it from, and they'd surely say no. But ask them if it would be OK to shut off their M-Pesa service and they'll say hell no. In one recent study 84 percent of M-Pesa users said that the loss of this service would have a "large negative" effect on their lives.[26]

Some skeptics may still want to know what would happen in the cashless future if the whole Internet or electrical grid were to fail. Won't we need something to transact with? "Ah, yes," Birch told me back in London. "There is this idea out there that a hacker is going to knock the Internet down for days, or that if we start to do a lot of transacting over telecom networks, those networks become targets for economic terrorism. If I were to pick a fight with me, that is the point I would raise," he says, in a modest concession to technophobes and ardent defenders of cash. My disaster preparedness guide from the American Red Cross even instructs families to keep some cash in their emergency kit, alongside flashlights, canned food, and bandages.

But Birch's rebuttal to his hypothetical self is swift. "Look at what happened in Ireland in the 1960s. The banks went on strike, but pretty soon I.O.U.s began circulating like currency. Today, it would be the same." Just a few years ago, none other than the state of California was handing out I.O.U.s, and they worked, insofar as people believed in their value. Should sovereign currencies ever fail, instead of paper I.O.U.s denominated in the national currencies we're so accustomed to, we could ramp up digital trading in Facebook Credits, airline miles, cellphone minutes, virtual currencies, coupons for merchandise at Walmart, Ven, carbon emissions credits, Kilowatt Cards, or future currencies that we can't even yet imagine.

As for a complete blackout of the power grid, rendering electronic money inaccessible, or maybe even nuking it entirely, Birch's view is that were that day to ever come, we'll have more substantial things to worry about than the fate of our digital money accounts. Hiding from rabid dogs and roving bandits, say, or securing stocks of food and water. Should that apocryphal day come, not even all the gold in Fort Knox will buy you anything of value.

◆

FOR THOSE OF US UNWILLING to cast our lot with the Cormac-McCarthy-meets-Book-of-Revelation scenario, we're left to wonder what will happen to cash in the decades ahead. My money is on cellphones, or something of a different name but that is a futuristic version of today's smartphones: completely networked computers in our pockets, embedded in wristwatches, or maybe even tiny chips worn behind our ears (sorry, Pastor Guest!), that will also serve as a wallet, bank branch, currency converter, and seamless payment tool, propelling commerce forward, eliminating the monstrous costs of cash, and providing a critical leg up to billions of people.

I could be wrong, of course, and in some ways I hope I am, because that will mean incredible innovations are coming. If the weatherman can be so off the mark forecasting rainfall a few days from now, how could anyone reasonably predict the course of technology over the next ten or forty years? What we do know is that these alternatives must beat cash at its own game—ease of use, fungibility, universal acceptability—while succeeding where it currently fails. Cash is dying a death by a thousand cuts. We just can't know if it's 109 or 9 more cuts until it's dead.

I'll leave you with one last idea, courtesy of the Gates Foundation's Mas. His concern about cash, remember, isn't necessarily the objects themselves, their peripheral costs, or the fact that cash is a tax-free loan from the people to the government—none of that. Mas's beef with cash is all about inconvertibility, and the punitive price the poor pay because of it.

In a recent paper, Mas describes a sentiment that I don't share, but that is probably more true than not: "People don't want to entirely let go of the physicality of cash." If cash is going to coexist alongside electronic money for a long time to come, how could we rebuild it to satisfy the human desire for tactile money while eliminating its constellation of inefficiencies and hazards?

A couple of years ago, Mas had a brainstorm. In a way, he had been building to this concept for years, ever since he started thinking about barriers to savings. He calls it the "smart banknote," and the best way to think of it is to imagine that an iPad had sex with a $20 bill.

The offspring would be a banknote-shaped piece of paper that isn't paper at all. It's an electronic display, but as thin, crumple-able, and durable as a typical $20 bill. The smart banknote has two modes: When it's deactivated, it looks like the screen of a computer monitor or an e-book reader that's turned off. It's blank and has no value. In its activated form, it appears like a banknote—whatever the issuer wants, be it political propaganda, corporate logos, tone-deaf design, or other elements signifying that it's a trustworthy medium of exchange.

With your phone, you could transfer money onto the note, via the tiny antenna nestled in its fibers. The note would "become" of value by displaying the amount of money you've transferred from your bank account. Let's say $20. That note is tradable as is, as if you'd gone to the ATM to withdraw it like an ordinary banknote. Holding it might even boost your tolerance for pain, just like today's paper money.

You hand your activated note to a merchant in exchange for goods. She now has two choices: hold it as a $20, or use a phone (or something like it) to deposit $20 into a bank account, thus removing the value from the object and rendering it deactivated. The image broadcasting the idea of that value is now gone. Result: instant convertibility between the physical and the electronic world, as well as instant access to the wider financial system, anywhere, anytime. Merchants could maintain a supply of deactivated notes, without the need for security or fear of robbery, because who's going to rob a store full of worthless e-paper? On the other hand, customers could receive cash back during transactions, like people do today when paying with a debit card.

My preference is still to go digital all the way. Counterfeiting and hacking would eventually cause problems for smart banknotes, just like all banknotes throughout history. But what I like about Mas's idea is that it could be the perfect bridge: a bridge between physical and electronic money, and a bridge between the cash-dependent present and the cashless future. I also like that it caters to the quirks of human taste and behavior. Smart banknotes could satisfy both those who feel they must have some tactile form of money and those who have no such requirement.

Two years ago, Mas's team at the Gates Foundation funded a preliminary study of this "blue sky" concept of the smart banknotes, reasoning that it merited at least an initial assessment. They tasked some consultants to investigate technologies with names like *magnetochromatic microspheres* and *active-matrix organic light-emitting diodes*, and to report back with an appraisal of the smart banknote's feasibility.

Their conclusion: not anytime soon. In their closing comments, the researchers wrote that they don't think the necessary materials and technologies will be available for another ten to fifteen years. When I read that, I thought: ten or fifteen years? In the history of the technology known as money, that's almost no time at all.

CHAPTER 8

The Emissary

Warmed against and worn between
Hearts uncleansed and hands unclean,—
What is there I have not seen?

—RUDYARD KIPLING, *THE COIN SPEAKS*, 1907

T he Clackamas Banquet Center, just east of Portland, Oregon, is attached to a Denny's at an intersection shared by two gas stations and a McDonalds. On a September morning that can't decide if its fate is sunny or drizzly, I pull into a parking space next to an old Pontiac sedan. An elderly man is lifting a plastic bin full of coins from the trunk.

The Coin and Currency Show is underway in a teal-carpeted room lined with rows of rectangular tables, each with a desk lamp angled downward over the merchandise. The window shades are drawn to minimize the glare bouncing off the display cases. The carefully aligned collections of coins remind me of flying over port terminals and looking down on lineups of hundreds of shiny new cars, soon to be dispatched to the interior of the country, or shipped overseas.

This regional coin show is tiny compared with national events that easily draw thousands, sometimes tens of thousands, of visitors and collectors. But the woman at the entrance tells me many people here will still do $10,000 in business today. I'm not in that league, but I *am* here to transact. The year of living cashlessly is over, and inside my briefcase is a thin gray metal box, once used for storing slides, as well as five old yellow Kodak film canisters and two Zip-lock sandwich bags filled with a motley assortment of coins.

A few months ago, my father sent me his childhood coin collection. The coins were bought with earnings from his days running a paper route in Columbus, Ohio, when he was eleven and twelve. They aren't a collection in the connoisseur's sense; more like a relic of youth, resting somewhere between pocketknives and photography on the continuum of boyhood hobbies of the 1950s.

Knowing that I was neck deep in information and meditation about the role and fate of physical money, my father had dug the coins out of storage and put them in the mail. What he doesn't know is that I'm look-ing to sell some of them. I want to see what it'll feel like to part with physical money that has a different kind of value.

Shunning cash for the year turned out to be troublesome only now and then. I never got a shoeshine. I was disappointed the few times when I couldn't give anything to street performers, and more than a few times when ignoring panhandlers, although we all know that's a no-win no matter what. I also skipped on visiting a few farmers markets and street fairs, where most of the vendors only accept cash, and I became some-thing of a Grinch to kids at neighborhood lemonade stands, frequently passing them on my jog and always delivering the same excuse.

But most of the parking meters where I live take plastic, I don't use Laundromats, and I'm lucky enough not to have to patron the payday lenders on nearby Martin Luther King Boulevard. With the exception of my week in India, the time I had to buy that ticket on the New Jersey Transit train, and one evening in Iceland that I'll explain in a moment, coins and banknotes just kind of fell out of my life; or at least out of my day-to-day dealings. (Inside my head, it was just the opposite.) I don't have any cash in my wallet, although I do have a few Kilowatt Cards that

I'm hoping to transact with, and the sample gift card the Japanese printing experts gave me during our conversation about counterfeits. Looking back on my year, I now see that it would have been exponentially harder for me to *only* use cash.

◆

IT TAKES ALL OF FOUR MINUTES of chat with a dealer at the Clackamas show to learn that my father's collection isn't impressive: "junk," to use the numismatics term of art. It's mostly coins that are utterly plentiful, and none of them have famous production errors that would pump up market value. They are in half-decent condition, if that, and all the coins lack the kind of stellar back-story that might turn a dud into a jewel. I suppose I could make one up. *This is the same Belgian coin Teddy Roosevelt and his guide flipped while on safari in Africa, to see who would get to pose next to the rhino.* But without credible paperwork backing my claim, no one would buy it. Numismatists have a nose for authenticity.

Up to now, I've avoided coin geeks and notaphilists; they constitute a snag in the case against cash because their stake in keeping physical money around feels more valid than others. The doomsayers, counterfeiters, drug dealers, central bankers, scalpers, technophobes, zinc industry lobbyists—no one makes a very convincing defense. In the short term, fine, we still need cash to facilitate certain kinds of commerce, and I don't want to stick a fork in it until we have a proven alternative—or more likely, alternatives—that meet the needs of working people who currently depend on cash. But as its relevance declines and its costs keep skyrocketing, we should think about funeral arrangements.

Yet there is something about the collectors' specialized knowledge of, and affection for, coins that gives me pause. When they talk about physical money, they're talking about sculpture, civics, markets, industry, and history all in one. What will happen to the entire subculture of numismatics and notaphilia when my cashless paradise is finally here? Have I become so averse to physical money, so single-minded in the pursuit of friction-free transactions and more currency options, that I no longer appreciate the romanticism of a hobby anchored to the physical world and fueled by a little national pride?

◆

ONE NIGHT DURING my trip to Iceland, I joined Anton Holt, the mustachioed curator of the country's national coin collection, and his wife, Gillian, for dinner at their home. Over boiled potatoes, salmon with chutney, and coleslaw, I asked about Holt's personal coin collection, separate from his work for the central bank. "Did you hear that, love?" he said to his wife, rubbing his hands together like a scheming villain. "Let it be noted that I didn't force anyone's arm." Gillian rolled her eyes.

We carried our tumblers of scotch into the cozy sitting room, where Holt opened one of two elegantly crafted wooden boxes resting on a bookshelf next to thick maroon volumes about the coins of the Indian subcontinent, and opposite the desktop computer where Gillian does her daily Facebook browsing and posting. Inside the box were maybe twenty delicate wooden trays, each filled with rare coins lying on a bed of green felt. Holt delighted in starting my tour from no place in particular. "I have a fairly comprehensive collection of coins from the Maldives for the 200-year period between 1700 and 1900."

Using the extra-long fingernail of his fifth finger, he lifted a coin off the felt mat to place in my hand. "And you thought the fingernail was for snorting cocaine!" Every few minutes, we would take a look at another coin, and Holt would serve up a breezy synopsis of its place in history. One coin he showed me is a ten-pence piece from Ireland, dated 1969. Too recent, I presumed, to be of much interest. "Look closely. See where it says 'UVF'? The unionists defaced coinage of the [Irish] republic to protest Republicanism. It stands for Ulster Voluntary Force."

Holt is a numismatist's numismatist, a descriptor that is easier to write than to say. He has been collecting since the age of five. "I started with a bag of twenty or thirty coins that my father gave me. In it, there was this one coin, a five *mils* piece, from Palestine. It had three different languages on it. Mind you, I was only five, but I found that fascinating.

I wanted to know more about where it came from. Why it looked that way. The people who used it." As banknote designer Kristin Thorkels-dottir had put it, material money is like heritage you can hold in your hand.

To Holt, that physical connection is key. He can't stand to see coins entombed in plastic cases to protect them from damage or contamination that might bring down their market price. (Hence the expression, "mint condition"). "The whole point is handling," he said, passing me a bronze 1,000-year-old coin from the Kushan Empire. "If you're going to appreciate coins, David, you don't collect pieces you can't touch. Either they're your babies, or forget it." Tactility is what transforms coins and paper into talismans.

From the Yuan banknotes that so stunned Marco Polo centuries ago, to the five *mils* coin that dazzled Holt as a little boy, physical money has, and probably always will have, this unusual power. I turned a small silver coin a few times in my fingertips. The whiskey was dulling my memory of the day's chilly rain and conversations about Iceland's economic tribulations. "That coin you're holding—it was drawn, designed, and made by Leonardo da Vinci. Leonardo held that very same coin!" Holt declared with exaggerated certainty. "Now, you may not be able to prove that, but you can't prove otherwise. In any case, it's the idea that he might have—that's the wonderful thing."

The *idea*. Like money itself. Only in its material form can money connect this coin collector in Reykjavik to Leonardo da Vinci, and now to me. If cash is a representation of an abstraction, of a social construct, then digital money is an abstraction of an abstraction, inevitably diluting that sense of connection even further. The truth is that I can't be sure something won't be irretrievably lost with an end to the production of physical money. Yet I'm not convinced that its end would be a betrayal of heritage, either. "Evolution is natural," said Holt. "If change means no more coins, then no more coins. Besides, I collect backwards in history. Not forward."

◆

ALONG WITH THE COINS I've brought with me to the Coin and Currency Show are my father's accompanying series of blue and green coin folders published in the 1940s by the Whitman Publishing Company in Racine, Wisconsin. With titles like "Indian Head Cent: Collection including Flying Eagle Cents 1856 to 1909" and "Barber, Liberty Head or 'Morgan' Quarter: Collection 1906 to 1916," the books provided an easy way for young enthusiasts to organize their possessions and begin collecting in series. As a boy, my father would ride the bus to the coin shop in downtown Columbus to see what new pieces might be available.

I open the folders gingerly, so as not to damage their fragile spines, and am greeted by rows of worn coins resting within cutouts in the cardboard. A label below each spot marks the year and sometimes the location where that coin was minted, and the total number that were issued. The 1884 bronze Indian Head cent, which had 23.3 million coins in that run—my father has that one, and it's set in the right place.

Upon inspection, however, other coins are in the wrong place, and the placeholders for the more valuable coins are either empty or plugged with more commonplace ones from a different year. I can almost picture my father, sixty years ago, with his dimples, buzz cut, and that vintage striped T-shirt I've seen in a few of his childhood photographs. He's pressing coins into place, pleased with the ones that match up, but unfazed by the ones that don't.

After a few conversations with dealers, I find out that a 1931 Lincoln penny from my dad's collection might be worth as much as $90. The coin lists for significantly more than that if it's in great condition, but this one's grade is "fair." I sit across from a dealer who has appraised my Lincoln cent and confess that I'm in a bit of a pecuniary pickle, stuck between disliking physical money, the undeniable allure of an easy $90, and not feeling too hot about mortgaging these pieces of family history.

"You love your wife. You like your coins," the dealer tells me.

While not exactly emotional handholding, this input strikes me as reasonable. After double-checking the "red book" price to assuage last-minute concerns that I might be getting ripped off, I gently pluck the

THE EMISSARY | 201

coin from its placeholder in the green folder, and close the deal for $87 in cash. There's no turning back now.

And I must say: it feels pretty good. I suddenly have $87 that I didn't have a minute ago, and per the dealer's suggestion I may just have to earmark it for a fun dinner out with my wife. Either that, or perhaps something a little less enjoyable, like my cellphone bill. But cash is fungible! As long as I go to dinner *someday*, this $87 will contribute to that outing, right?

Minutes later I find myself in a round of friendly banter with Rick Hennessey, a gun enthusiast, climate change denier, and coin dealer who generously helps me part with what eventually amounts to $300 worth of coins. I sell him quarters and half dollars mostly, all of them between fifty and 150 years old. All are in rather poor condition and appraise in the range of $5 and $18 apiece. Their value stems almost exclusively from their silver content. Hennessey pays out in $20 and $10 bills, none of which look counterfeit to my un-expert, but now obsessively curious, eye.

Two pimply teenage boys inspect Hennessey's plastic-encased 2006 gold American Eagle $1 coin at the other end of the table, but it's apparent that they're only browsing. I'm his only customer for the time being.

"You got any more of those Barber or Morgan quarters?" Hennessey asks.

I tell him I do have some more, but that I'm feeling reluctant to relinquish them.

"Do you love 'em?" he asks.

"That's the million-dollar question," I say.

"Is there something you could do with the money that you love more? That is the *two*-million-dollar question," Hennessey replies.

The profit margins of Hennessey's business are slim, at least for the merchandise he's getting from me, and lately things have been especially tough. I had assumed that in gloomy economic times, people liquidate more assets, like jewelry or coins, so that they have funds to meet everyday expenses. And many people do (*We Buy Gold!*). But in the years since the crash of 2007–2008, it feels like everyone—not just Americans, but people all over the world—are especially confounded by how money works, and worried about preserving value. When people get nervous, they often collect or hoard possessions like coins, for much the same reason that fears of inflation or shaken faith in national currencies send people running for gold. If your coins are gold, all the better.

Hennessey says he might be able to sell silver half-dollars for a buck or two more than what he's paying me, but the logistics of dealing with overflowing inventory and getting product to someone who can sell it for melt value eat at his profit. As he complains about how lackluster my dad's coins are—the ones he's buying—Hennessey almost makes it sound like he's doing me a favor.

Maybe he is. I now have almost $400! Without feeling anything that might be diagnosed as seller's remorse, I send my wife a quick text message. *$400!* A pragmatist as well, she writes back: *"Way to go!"* She also doesn't send any warning to slow down a little, so that I don't do anything I might come to regret. The absence of this message, of course, gets me worrying about exactly that. Am I pawning these heirlooms for a few bags of groceries, a dinner out, and a day on the slopes? Maybe money really is a soul-devouring demon.

I don't think so, though, and here's why. Coins, especially in the context of a coin show, have all different kinds of value. There's the monetary value, set by the state and legitimized by our belief in it. There's the intrinsic value: the silver content of pre-1965 coins that Bernard von NotHaus cherishes, or the market value of the zinc, alloys, and tiny bits of copper in today's U.S. coinage. There's also the market or collectors' value, what someone will pay for that 1931 Lincoln penny because it completes his collection, or that rare Roman coin that a dealer aspires to acquire, only to turn around and sell it at a premium to a Roman-era coinage fanatic in Houston.

As a noncollector, I don't find a measurable distinction between two very physically similar coins, like my dad's 1887 versus 1889 Liberty Head nickels, or his many 1864 two-cent pieces. Provided none of them have an astronomical red-book price tag that would throw this experiment in valuation and incentives off track, none of them convey any special comparative value. The 1931 Lincoln penny is worth more than the others in the collection folder, but its worth to me is only on paper. I can't *feel* it.

But there's another type of value, one that's even more elusive: the personal kind. What do the objects in your life mean to you? What makes one thing an heirloom and another a tchotchke? Only you can say. Only you can determine what you're willing to pay for it, and that's true even if it happens to be a kind of money.

While negotiating with Hennessey, I notice an odd thing happening. Without even planning it this way, I'm not selling anything in the collection that is one of a kind or the last of its type. I even transfer these coins into a separate compartment of my briefcase, so as not to sell them by accident. They are off limits.

I'll probably keep a couple of them on my desk at home, but the rest of these keepsakes will end up in a closet, and probably not see daylight again for another ten, perhaps forty years. It's really up to my son. If he's ever curious about them, we'll take a look. Maybe we'll check their value in a 2050 price guide. If he decides to sell them, he'll get to choose what to do with the earnings flashed into his bank account in the wireless cloud, or beamed into the holographic wallet floating above his hand.

Me? I've decided to use that $400 windfall to take my son to visit his grandparents. Money well spent, I think.

ACKNOWLEDGMENTS

Many, many people helped make this book happen. To everyone who is mentioned within these pages: thank you for time, patience, and insights. I would also like to thank the following people for providing assistance with resources, added explanation, logistical support, research guidance, editing, encouragement, and invaluable criticism: Aaron Ernst, Adam Rogers, Aiichiro Kurata, Aimee Geissler, Allen Kupetz, Andrew Steckl, Andy Jordan, Anil Kakani, Anne Marie DiStefano, Anthony Effinger, Astrid Mitchell, Carlson Chambliss, Carol B., Charlotte Webb, Coert Voorhees, Daniel Lowther, David Abrams, David Tidmarsh, Diane Coyle, Einar Baldvin Stefánsson, Erik Jensen, Erik Steiner, Frederick Reimers, Glenn Wood, Greg Lastowka, Hannes van Rensburg, Heather Wax, Heidar Gudjonsson, James Grant, Jan S., Jason Jarrell, Jim Bruene, Jim Rosenberg, Jonathan Carver, Jonathan Lipow, Joshua Davis, Julian Smith, Kabir Kumar, Kakha Bendukidze, Kathleen Vohs, Kiera Butler, Lee Voo van der, Lewis Iadarola, Liana McCabe, Lisa Rutherford, Mark Pickens, Mark Robinson, Marta Peiret, Matt Dill, Matteo Chiampo, Michael Linton, Michael Salmony, Mugdha Bhargava, Neha Mehra, Nick Hughes, Nick McKenzie, Oakley Brooks, Ólafur Ísleifsson, Pallab Mitra, Paul Collins, Paul Makin, Peter Fishman, R. S., Rawls Moore, Rebecca Clarren, Richard Heeks, Rick S., Roy Vella, Ruud van Renesse, Shayan Bardhan, Shelle Santana, Shravya Reddy, Shrayana

Bhattacharya, Tamar Mayer, Tim Murdoch, Tim Verstynen, Tom Ferguson, Tom Zeffiro, Varun Bangia, Verity W., and Yuki Maeda.

Thank you Giles Anderson, my agent, and Lissa Warren, my tireless editor and ally at Da Capo. Thank you to my friends near and far, and, of course, to my family.

Finally, thank you Spencer, for being such a magnificent kid. And Nicola—for everything. I love you.

NOTES

Introduction

1. http://www.nydailynews.com/news/national/2010/01/03/2010-01-03_plane_questions _dont_fly_right_warning_signs_were_evident_yet_bomb_suspect_still.html.

1: The Missionary

1. Gene Hessler and Carlson Chambliss, *The Comprehensive Catalog of U.S. Paper Money*, 7th ed. (Port Clinton, Ohio: BNR Press, 2006), p. 8.

2. http://www.theatlantic.com/technology/archive/2010/10/googles-ceo-the-laws-are -written-by-lobbyists/63908/.

3. http://www.neuroeconomics.net/article.php/471.html.

4. Jack Weatherford, *The History of Money* (New York: Three Rivers Press, 1998), pp. 22– 25; David Smith, *Free Lunch: Easily Digestible Economics* (London: Profile Books, 2009), pp. 172–173.

5. Georg Simmel, *The Philosophy of Money* (London: Routledge, 2004), p. 129.

6. As quoted in "Market Man," *The New Yorker*, October 18, 2010. (Book review of Nicholas Phillipson's *Adam Smith: An Enlightened Life*.)

7. Weatherford, *History of Money*, p. 30.

8. *National Geographic*, January 2009, p. 43.

9. http://www.nytimes.com/2010/12/18/opinion/18lipow.html.

10. Klaus Bender, *Moneymakers: The Secret World of Banknote Printing* (Hoboken, N.J.: John Wiley, 2006), p. 20.

11. Stephen Mihm, *A Nation of Counterfeiters: Capitalists, Con Men, and the Making of the United States* (Cambridge, Mass.: Harvard University Press, 2007), pp. 26–27.

12. Jason Goodwin, *Greenback: The Almighty Dollar and the Invention of America* (New York: Henry Holt, 2003), p. 99.

13. Ibid., p. 256.

14. Craig Karmin, *Biography of the Dollar: How the Mighty Buck Conquered the World and Why It's Under Siege* (New York: Crown, 2008), p. 101.

15. http://www.theonion.com/articles/us-economy-grinds-to-halt-as-nation-realizes-money,2912/.

2: The Messenger

1. Frank Herbert, *The White Plague* (New York: G.P. Putnam's Sons, 1982), p. 125.

2. http://www.canada.com/montrealgazette/news/story.html?id=07c0a52f-2c9b-469a-ba85-ae0fa1d27396&k=76062.

3. From Michael Salmony's presentation to Digital Money Forum, London, 2010, "You're All Crazy—Cash Is King."

4. http://www.ncbi.nlm.nih.gov/pubmed/18359825.

5. Klaus W. Bender, *The Moneymakers: The Secret World of Banknote Printing* (Hoboken, N.J.: John Wiley, 2006), p. 27; http://www.abc.net.au/science/news/health/HealthRepublish_1684553.htm.

6. http://www.npr.org/templates/story/story.php?storyId=111944477; http://news.bbc.co.uk/2/hi/uk_news/464200.stm; and http://news.bbc.co.uk/2/hi/8204857.stm.

7. Lawrence Weschler, *Boggs: A Comedy of Values* (Chicago: University of Chicago Press, 1999), p. 121.

8. http://www.finextra.com/finextra-downloads/newsdocs/TheWayWePay2010.pdf.

9. "Technology and Its Future Role in the Mining Industry," April 2007 presentation by BHP vice president of technology, Megan Clark, at the World Conference of Science Journalists.

10. "For One Business, Polluted Clouds Have Silvery Lining," *New York Times*, July 12, 2007, A4.

11. As quoted by Paul Wachter in "Why Tip?" *New York Times Magazine*, October 12, 2008.

12. http://news.bbc.co.uk/2/hi/uk_news/7628137.stm.

13. "Penny Dreadful," *The New Yorker*, March 31, 2008.

14. Ibid.

15. *Numismatic News*, February 16, 2010.

16. http://financialservices.house.gov/Media/file/hearings/111/Moy%20Testimony%207%2020%2010.pdf.

17. Francois Velde, "What's a Penny (or a Nickel) Really Worth?" Federal Reserve Bank of Chicago, February 2007.

18. "In Praise of Inflation," *The New Yorker*, September 27, 2010.

19. "Why the US Keeps Minting Coins People Hate and Won't Use." http://www.bbc.co.uk/news/world-us-canada-10783019.

20. Jack Weatherford, *The History of Money* (New York: Three Rivers Press, 1998), pp. 156–159; also, Bender, *The Moneymakers*, p. 20.

21. http://www.youtube.com/watch?v=VemU6EZtnwc.

22. Digital Money Blog, May 10, 2010; and Dave Birch, personal correspondence, November 2010.

23. William Greider, *Secrets of the Temple: How the Federal Reserve Runs the Country* (New York: Touchstone, 1987), p. 53.

24. Michael Salmony, Digital Money Forum address, London, March 10, 2010.

25. http://www.federalreserve.gov/boarddocs/rptcongress/annual09/sec5/c1t11.htm; and "As Plastic Reigns, the Treasury Slows Its Printing Presses," *New York Times*, July 6, 2011.

26. John McCormick, "Loomis Fargo & Co.: Making Money Move, Efficiently," http://www.baselinemag.com/c/a/Projects-Processes/Loomis-Fargo-Co-Making-Money -Move-Efficiently/, November 8, 2005; also Steven Levy, "E-Money (That's What I Want)," *Wired*, December 1994.

27. Ronald Mann, *Charging Ahead: The Growth and Regulation of Payment Card Markets* (Cambridge, UK: Cambridge University Press, 2006), p. 39, quoting Swartz.

28. Daniel D. Garcia Swartz, Robert W. Hahn, and Anne Layne-Farrar, "The Economics of a Cashless Society: An Analysis of the Costs and Benefits of Payment Instruments," Washington, D.C.: AEI-Brookings Joint Center for Regulatory Studies, 2004), p. 25, citing Humphrey et al.

29. *Currency News*, July 2009, pp. 6–7.

30. Digital Money Blog, May 11, 2009, "Viking Expedition," citing "China sees change scarcity," chna.org.cn, November 20, 2007.

31. David Birch, *The Digital Money Reader* (Guildford, UK: Mastodon Press, 2010), pp. 54–55, citing "Police Escort for Elderly ATM Users," *Daily Telegraph*, May 6, 2009, and "DIY Students Tackle Japanese ATM Fraud," Finextra.com, November 8, 2008.

32. http://online.wsj.com/article/SB10001424052748704482704576072231420350872.html ?mod=ITP_pageone_3.

33. http://www.finextra.com/news/fullstory.aspx?newsitemid=21762.

34. BEP press release and personal interview with media relations office. For the 2008 part, see *Biography of the Dollar*; also see http://www.slate.com/id/2277404/.

35. "The Government's $110 Billion Currency Goof," *The Week*, December 8, 2010.

36. http://www.bos.frb.org/economic/ppdp/2009/ppdp0910.pdf.

37. http://digitaldebateblogs.typepad.com/digital_money/2010/08/by-cash-we-mean -cash-and-not-cash.html.

38. From *Review of Network Economics*, 2003, as cited in "The Future of Money," *Wired*, March 2010.

39. "A Penny Saved . . . " *Time*, August 9, 1999.

40. Swartz, Hahn, and Layne-Farrar, "The Economics of a Cashless Society," p. 24.

41. "New York Restaurant Loses Its Appetite for Cash," *Wall Street Journal*, September 11, 2009.

42. http://www.paymentscouncil.org.uk/media_centre/press_releases_new/-/page/855/.

43. Swartz, Hahn, and Layne-Farrar, "The Economics of a Cashless Society," p. 6; and http://www.telegraph.co.uk/finance/newsbysector/banksandfinance/6968143/Is-a-cashless -society-on-the-cards.html.

44. "Who Will Speak up for Cash?" *Currency News*, October 2009, p. 2.

45. http://www.bis.org/review/r060427a.pdf.

46. *Currency News*, August 2009, p. 3.

47. http://digitaldebateblogs.typepad.com/digital_money/2009/10/the-swedish-exper iment.html.

48. "Sweden Weighs Benefits of Ditching Cash," BBC News, July 17, 2010.

49. http://www.washingtontimes.com/news/2009/dec/09/new-underground-economy/; and "As Plastic Reigns, the Treasury Slows Its Printing Presses," *New York Times*, July 6, 2011.

50. *Currency News*, December 2009, p. 16.

51. http://www.americanbanker.com/bulletins/consumers-turn-on-cards-1015107-1 .html.

52. Digital Money Forum Blog, "Anti-Anti Money Laundering," July 6, 2009.

53. Bender, *The Moneymakers*, p. 261.

54. http://www.moneyfactory.gov/uscurrency/smalldenominations.html; and "Turning Paper Into Cash," *Bloomberg BusinessWeek*, December 20, 2010 (citing U.S. Treasury statistics).

55. http://www.slate.com/id/2277404/.

56. http://www.irs.gov/pub/irs-utl/tax_gap_facts-figures.pdf.

57. http://www.irs.gov/pub/newsroom/tax_gap_report_-final_version.pdf.

58. http://digitaldebateblogs.typepad.com/digital_money/2010/07/morals-guvnor.html.

59. http://www.chron.com/disp/story.mpl/world/6966561.html; and Salmony, Digital Money Forum address; also *Bloomberg Business Week*, January 3, 2011, and "Dodger Mania," *The New Yorker*, July 11 and 18, 2011, p. 38.

60. http://www.time.com/time/world/article/0,8599,2033515,00.html.

61. "Turn in Your Bin Ladens," *New York Times*, December 17, 2010; also http://www .nytimes.com/2010/12/03/world/asia/03wikileaks-corruption.html, and Peter E. Kunkel "How Jesse James, the Telegraph, and the Federal Reserve Act of 1913 Can Help the Army Win the War on Terrorism: The Unrealized Strategic Effects of a Cashless Battlefield," *Military Review*, November–December 2008, p. 88.

62. http://www.youtube.com/watch?v=zwvxK0YY0zI.

63. http://online.wsj.com/article/NA_WSJ_PUB:SB10001424052748704532204575397543634034112.html.

64. http://www.economicpolicyjournal.com/2010/02/greece-bans-cash-transactions -over-1500.html.

65. Digital Money Blog, "War on Cash: A Report from the European Front," July 6, 2010.

66. http://www.reuters.com/article/idUSTRE64C1KF20100513.

67. http://articles.latimes.com/2010/jun/03/world/la-fg-mexico-cash-20100603.

68. "The Case Against Cash," *The Futurist*, July–August 2011.

69. http://www.fbi.gov/stats-services/publications/bank-crime-statistics-2010/bank-crime -statistics-2010.

70. http://www.msnbc.msn.com/id/32305195/ns/politics-more_politics.

71. "Afghanistan Money Probe Hits Close to the President," *Wall Street Journal*, August 12, 2010.

72. David Gorman "Demonetize the $100 Bill," op-ed printed in the *Providence* (Rhode Island) *Journal*, March 6, 2008; and Digital Money Blog, "Viking Expedition," May 11, 2009.

73. http://digitaldebateblogs.typepad.com/digital_money/2011/01/benjamin-3d.html.

3: The Counterfeiters

1. "North Korea's Dollar Store," *Vanity Fair*, September 2009.

2. http://www.justice.gov/usao/can/press/2009/2009_01_30_chen.sentenced.press.html.

3. "The Inkjet Counterfeiter," *Details*, September 2009.

4. http://www.justice.gov/usao/can/press/2009/2009_01_30_chen.sentenced.press.html.

5. "No Ordinary Counterfeit," *New York Times Magazine*, July 23, 2006.

6. http://libweb.uoregon.edu/ec/e-asia/read/dopekor.pdf.

7. "No Ordinary Counterfeit," *New York Times Magazine*, July 23, 2006.

8. http://currency_den.tripod.com/War_Counterfeits/2009.html; and R. L. van Renesse, "What's 'Funny' About Funny Money?" *Keesing Journal of Documents & Identity* 20 (2006), pp. 3–9.

9. "North Korea Revalues Currency, Destroying Personal Savings," *Washington Post*, December 2, 2010.

10. Statement of Michael Merritt, deputy assistant director of the office of investigations at the U.S. Secret Service, testimony before the Subcommittee on Federal Financial Management, Government Information, and International Security, April 25, 2006.

11. "No Ordinary Counterfeit."

12. Klaus Bender, *Moneymakers: The Secret World of Banknote Printing* (Hoboken, N.J.: John Wiley, 2006).

13. "No Ordinary Counterfeit."

14. Ibid.; also Statement of Michael Merritt.

15. "North Korea's Dollar Store."

16. "No Ordinary Counterfeit."

17. Ibid.

18. "North Korea's Dollar Store."

19. *New-Yorker*, August 5, 1837, p. 315. As cited in Stephen Mihm, *A Nation of Counterfeiters: Capitalists, Con Men, and the Making of the United States* (Cambridge, Mass.: Harvard University Press, 2009), p. 9.

20. John Cooley, *Currency Wars: How Forged Money Is the New Weapon of Mass Destruction* (New York: Skyhorse Publishing, 2008), p. 39.

21. http://financialservices.house.gov/Media/file/hearings/111/Jenkins%20Testimony%207_20_10.pdf.

22. John F. Chant, "The Canadian Experience with Counterfeiting," *Bank of Canada Review*, September 2004.

23. Statement of Michael Merritt; and http://financialservices.house.gov/Media/file/hearings/111/Jenkins%20Testimony%207_20_10.pdf.

24. http://www.fas.org/sgp/crs/row/RL33324.pdf.

25. Statement of David L. Asher, Ph.D., Before the Subcommittee on Federal Financial Management, Government Information, and International Security, Senate Homeland Security and Government Affairs Committee, April 25, 2006.

26. http://financialservices.house.gov/Media/file/hearings/111/Jenkins%20Testimony%207_20_10.pdf.

27. Ibid.

28. "North Korea's Dollar Store."

29. http://www.rcmp-grc.gc.ca/pubs/ci-rc/cf/weber-eng.htm.

30. Chant, "The Canadian Experience with Counterfeiting"; also, RCMP account of the Weber affair.

31. Chant, "The Canadian Experience with Counterfeiting."

32. U.S. Secret Service contact—personal interview.

33. http://www.pbs.org/newshour/art/blog/2010/04/new-100-bill-gets-a-design-facelift.html.

34. Van Renesse, "What's 'Funny' About Funny Money?"

35. "Ben Franklin Will Get a Security Makeover," National Public Radio (npr.org), August 29, 2007.

36. http://www.pbs.org/newshour/art/blog/2010/04/new-100-bill-gets-a-design-facelift.html.

37. Statement of David L. Asher, Ph.D.

38. "Counterfeiting and the Public," *Currency News*, August 2009, p. 2.

39. http://ja.wikipedia.org/wiki/%E5%81%BD%E6%9C%AD.

40. David Tidmarsh, personal interview, 2010.

41. In addition to Dai Nippon's expert, Suzuki as well as Reconnaissance International's Glenn Wood also echoed this opinion about the new $100 bill's mediocre security.

42. "Currency Detector Easy to Defeat," Wired.com, January 14, 2004 (citing BEP statistics).

43. http://financialservices.house.gov/Media/file/hearings/111/Jenkins%20Testimony%207_20_10.pdf.

44. The name combines the word *Orion* with the EUR code that represents the euro.

45. http://www.adobe.com/products/photoshop/cds.html.

46. "Intricate Insect Patterns on Bank Note Could Combat Forgers," *Top News Singapore*, May 31, 2010, available at http://www.topnews.com.sg/content/21917-intricate-insect-patterns-bank-note-could-combat-forgers.

47. *Currency News*, July 2009, p. 2.

48. "Losing Our Touch," *Currency News*, November 2009, p. 2.

49. Klaus Bender, *Moneymakers*, p. 45.

50. http://www.rbi.org.in/scripts/BS_ViewBulletin.aspx?Id=11107.

51. http://www.guardian.co.uk/business/2010/sep/07/de-la-rue-serious-fraud-office.

52. http://www.smh.com.au/national/exsecurency-boss-charged-20110916-1kdwk.html.

4: The Loyalists

1. $220 ticket from "Lead Us Not Into Debt," *Atlantic Monthly*, December 2009, p. 32.

2. "An ATM That Dispenses Gold," *Wall Street Journal*, May 14, 2010.

3. http://www.telegraph.co.uk/news/worldnews/middleeast/unitedarabemirates/7720491/The-ATM-that-dispenses-gold-bars.html; and http://www.gold-to-go.com/en/.

4. http://www.creditcards.com/credit-card-news/credit-card-industry-facts-personal-debt-statistics-1276.php#ixzz1A6FJAWr8.

5. http://youtube.com/watch?v=-1OVqKZymdg&feature=related.

6. Elizabeth Warren, promotion blurb for Robert D. Manning, *Credit Card Nation: The Consequences to America's Addiction to Credit* (New York: Basic, 2001).

7. Ronald Mann, *Charging Ahead: The Growth and Regulation of Payment Card Markets* (New York: Cambridge University Press, 2006), p. 1.

8. Priya Raghubir, personal interview, September 2009.

9. Federal Reserve Bank of Boston, "The 2008 Survey of Consumer Payment Choice," Kevin Foster, Erik Meijer, Scott Schuh, and Michael A. Zabek.

10. Manning, *Credit Card Nation*, p. 112.

11. Ibid.

12. Feinberg, cited in ibid., p. 47.

13. Drazen Prelec and Duncan Simester, "Always Leave Home Without It: A Further Investigation of the Credit-Card Effect on Willingness to Pay," *Marketing Letters* 12, no. 1 (2001): 5–12, citing Feinberg (1986).

14. Ibid.

15. Ibid.

16. Ibid.

17. Irving Fisher, *The Money Illusion* (New York: Adelphi, 1928), pp. 17–18.

18. Dan Ariely, *Predictably Irrational: The Hidden Forces That Shape Our Decisions* (New York: Harper Perennial, 2008), pp. 233–234.

19. Priya Raghubir, "Psychology Meets Economics: Why Consumers Can't Count Their Money Correctly," from http://www.mycbtextbook.com/Consumer_Behavior_2010_Psychology_Meets_Economy.pdf.

20. http://www.npr.org/templates/story/story.php?storyId=104063298.

21. Priya Raghubir, Vicki Morwitz, and Shelle Santana, "Europoly Money: The Impact of Currency Framing on Tourists' Spending Decisions," in Darren Dahl, Gita Johar, and Stijn van Osselaer, eds., *Advances in Consumer Research*, vol. 38 (Duluth, Minn.: Association for Consumer Research, 2010).

22. Kathleen Vohs, et al., "The Psychological Consequences of Money," *Science* 314 (November 17, 2006): 1154–1165; and "Handling Money Minimizes Pain," National Public Radio April 14, 2010.

23. "Google's Search for a Digital Wallet," *BusinessWeek*, January 10–16, 2011, p. 33.

5: The Patriot

1. "Coming in from the Cold," *The Economist*, December 18, 2010, p. 141.

2. http://www.therightperspective.org/2009/02/04/norway-to-buy-iceland/; and http://www.icenews.is/index.php/2010/01/19/%E2%80%9Cnorway-should-be-iceland%E2%80%99s-aid%E2%80%9D/.

3. Interview with Astrid Mitchell of *Currency News*.

4. "Designs on Policy," *Atlantic Monthly*, July 19, 2009.

5. "New $100 Bill: Too Sci-fi?" *The Week*, April 21, 2010.

6. *Currency News*, August 2009, p. 4.

7. "Currency Exchange," *Atlantic Monthly*, June 12, 2009.

8. Daniel D. Garcia Swartz, Robert W. Hahn, and Anne Layne-Farrar, *The Economics of a Cashless Society: An Analysis of the Costs and Benefits of Payment Instruments* (Washington, D.C.: AEI-Brookings Joint Center for Regulatory Studies, 2004), p. 24.

9. Associated Press, October 27, 2009 (clipped from the Portland *Oregonian*).

10. Ignacio Mas, "Things Governments Do to Money: A Recent History of Currency Reform Schemes and Scams," *Kyklos* 48, no. 4 (May 1995), p. 2.

11. "Beware of Greeks Bearing Bonds," *Vanity Fair*, October 2010.

12. "A Long Odyssey," *The Economist*, November 10, 2010, p. 59.

13. http://www.nytimes.com/2010/02/06/world/europe/06europe.html?hp.

14. "The Making of a Euromess," Paul Krugman, *New York Times*, February 15, 2010.

15. "Joining the Euro: What's the Hurry?" *Bloomberg BusinessWeek*, January 10, 2010, p. 14.

16. "Love in a Cold Climate," *The Economist*, November 4, 2010.

17. "Global Currency Could Save World Economy," *Telegraph*, March 26, 2009.

18. Craig Karmin, *Biography of the Dollar: How the Mighty Buck Conquered the World and Why It's Under Siege* (New York: Crown, 2008), p. 104.

19. "Beyond Bretton Woods 2," *The Economist*, November 6, 2010.

20. From *Exorbitant Privilege*, as quoted in ibid.

6: The Traitor

1. "A Mug's Game," *Newsweek*, October 8, 1973; David Ganz personal interview, December 2010.

2. http://www.libraryofmu.org/display-resource.php?id=389.

3. http://online.wsj.com/public/article/SB117519670114653518-FR_svDHxRtxkvNm Gwwpouq_hl2g_20080329.html.

4. http://english.mofcom.gov.cn/aarticle/newsrelease/commonnews/200906/200906063 64208.html.

5. "Bitcoin, Ven, and the End of Currency," TechCrunch.com, May 20, 2011.

6. http://online.wsj.com/video/the-coming-currency-revolution/25225F5A-B979-4609 -A55D-1BAE9A1BA158.html.

7. http://www.economist.com/node/18836780.

8. "In Gold We Trust," *Wired*, January 2002.

9. "Workers Spurn Cash for Virtual Coin to Fund Online-Game Habits," *Bloomberg News*, June 17, 2010.

10. From Liberty Dollar advertising leaflet.

11. http://www.kidscreen.com/articles/magazine/20100923/virtual.html.

12. http://www.bloomberg.com/apps/news?pid=newsarchive&sid=aSmAKY4Wzk7g& pos=10.

13. http://www.nytimes.com/2011/05/30/us/30gold.html?pagewanted=all.

14. http://canopycanopycanopy.com/4/bullion_with_a_mission.

15. Eric Jackson, *PayPal Wars* (Los Angeles: World Ahead Publishing, 2004), p. 26.

16. http://www.youtube.com/watch?v=1VaBX7A9FqA&feature=related.

17. http://www.youtube.com/watch?v=XhWRDP8v9ss&feature=related.

18. Lawrence Weschler, *Boggs: A Comedy of Values* (Chicago: University of Chicago Press, 1999), pp. 142–143.

19. Georg Simmel, *The Philosophy of Money*, as quoted in Weschler, *Boggs: A Comedy of Values*, p. 23.

20. *Wall Street Journal* headlines from October 6, 2010.

21. http://canopycanopycanopy.com/4/bullion_with_a_mission.

7: The Revolutionaries

1. http://seattletimes.nwsource.com/html/thebusinessofgiving/2013447052__as_a_part_of.html.

2. Daryl Collins, Jonathan Morduch, Stuart Rutherford, and Orlanda Ruthven, *Portfolios for the Poor: How the World's Poor Live on $2 a Day* (Princeton, N.J.: Princeton University Press, 2009); also "Banking on Technology to Bridge Financial Inclusion Gap," citing Wharton study, http://www.livemint.com/2010/12/15212742/Banking-on-technology-to-bridg.html.

3. See video from CGAP (Consultative Group to Assist the Poor), "Scenarios for Branchless Banking in 2020," presentation on December 1, 2009, Washington, D.C. Approximately 6.5 minutes into the video, CGAP CEO Littlefield mentions these numbers and the studies that produced them.

4. Ibid; http://www.pymnts.com/with-4-6-billion-mobile-phones-worldwide-will-financial-services-spread/?nl.

5. Bharti Airtel's Pallab Mitra, from interview notes; *The Economist*, September 26, 2009, special report on mobile money, p. 4; and Associated Press, "More Cell Phones than Loos in India," (Portland) *Oregonian*, October 31, 2010.

6. Andrew Steckl, Cincinnati University nanotechnology researcher, personal interview, December 2010.

7. "The Apparatgeist Calls," *The Economist*, January 2, 2010.

8. "Calling Freedom," *The Economist*, December 19, 2009.

9. GSMA, "Mobile Money for the Unbanked," annual report (pdf sent by D. Lowther of GSMA); and http://mmublog.org/global/gsma-publish-2010-mobile-money-for-the-unbanked-annual-report-2/.

10. http://www.npr.org/2011/01/05/132679772/mobile-money-revolution-aids-kenyas-poor-economy.

11. Ignacio Mas, personal interview.

12. http://dailycaller.com/2010/04/10/kenya-owes-monetary-advances-to-imf-world-bank/; and http://allafrica.com/stories/201010240045.html.

13. http://technology.cgap.org/technologyblog/wp-content/uploads/2009/10/fsd_june2009_caroline_pulver.pdf (p. 27).

14. "South Korea Ready to Hang up Cash," BBC News, February 13, 2009.

15. "Mercy Corps Mobile Wallet Innovation Brings Purchasing Power to Haitians' Cell Phones," (Portland) *Oregonian*, December 27, 2010.

16. "Sweden Weighs Benefits of Ditching Cash," BBC News, July 17, 2010; also "Central Bank Wants Cashless Society," nationmultimedia.com, October 27, 2009.

17. Hitachi group, personal interview, June 2010.

18. https://www.paypal-media.com/documentdisplay.cfm?DocumentID=2260.

19. Peter E. Kunkel, "How Jesse James, the Telegraph, and the Federal Reserve Act of 1913 Can Help the Army Win the War on Terrorism: The Unrealized Strategic Effects of a Cashless Battlefield," *Military Review*, November–December 2008, pp. 88–96.

20. Glenn Guest, *Steps Toward the Mark of the Beast* (Belleville, Ontario: Essence Publishing, 2007), p. 82.

21. "New Underground Economy," *Washington Times*, December 9, 2009.

22. http://www.federalreserve.gov/generalinfo/faq/faqcur.htm#13.

23. NPR's "Planet Money" podcast, posted July 12, 2011, http://www.npr.org/blogs/money/2011/07/12/137795648/the-tuesday-podcast-bitcoin?sc=tw&cc=share.

24. http://www.npr.org/2011/01/04/132657646/Smart-Phone-Banking-On-The-Rise-But-Is-It-Safe.

25. Farhad Manjoo on Marketplace (NPR), regarding Facebook and privacy: "They're concerned with it. In surveys and other things people say they're concerned about privacy online, but they're not really doing anything about it. They're not really acting out on those fears."

26. http://technology.cgap.org/technologyblog/wp-content/uploads/2009/10/fsd_june2009_caroline_pulver.pdf (p. 27).

BIBLIOGRAPHY

Albrecht, Katherine, and Liz McIntyre. *Spychips: How Major Corporations and Government Plan to Track Your Every Purchase and Watch Your Every Move*. New York: Plume, 2006.

Ariely, Dan. *Predictably Irrational: The Hidden Forces That Shape Our Decisions*. New York: Harper Perennial, 2008.

Bender, Klaus. *Moneymakers: The Secret World of Banknote Printing*. Hoboken, N.J.: Wiley-VCH, 2006.

Birch, David. *The Digital Money Reader 2010*. Guildford, UK: Mastodon Press, 2010.

Boyle, David, ed. *The Money Changers: Currency Reform from Aristotle to E-Cash*. London: Routledge, 2003.

Collins, Daryl, Jonathan Morduch, Stuart Rutherford, and Orlanda Ruthven. *Portfolios of the Poor: How the World's Poor Live on $2 a Day*. Princeton, N.J.: Princeton University Press, 2010.

Cooley, John. *Currency Wars: How Forged Money Is the New Weapon of Mass Destruction*. New York: Skyhorse Publishing, 2008.

Coyle, Diane. *The Soulful Science: What Economists Really Do and Why It Matters*. Princeton, N.J.: Princeton University Press, 2009.

Dibbell, Julian. *Play Money: Or, How I Quit My Day Job and Made Millions Trading Virtual Loot*. New York: Basic Books, 2006.

Eichengreen, Barry. *Globalizing Capital: A History of the International Monetary System*. Princeton, N.J.: Princeton University Press, 2008.

Evans, David S., and Richard Schmalensee. *Paying with Plastic: The Digital Revolution in Buying and Borrowing*. Cambridge, Mass.: MIT Press, 1999.

Ferguson, Niall. *The Ascent of Money: A Financial History of the World*. New York: Penguin, 2009.

Friedman, Milton. *Money Mischief: Episodes in Monetary History*. New York: Mariner Books, 1994.

Galbraith, John Kenneth. *The Affluent Society*. New York: Mariner Books, 1998.

Goodwin, Jason. *Greenback: The Almighty Dollar and the Invention of America*. New York: Henry Holt, 2003.

Greider, William. *Secrets of the Temple: How the Federal Reserve Runs the Country*. New York: Touchstone, 1987.

Guest, Glen. *Steps Toward the Mark of the Beast*. Ontario: Essence Publishing, 2007.

Hanke, Steve H., and Kurt Schuler. *Currency Boards for Developing Countries: A Handbook*. Richmond, Calif.: ICS Press, 1994.

Herbert, Frank. *The White Plague*. New York: G.P. Putnam's Sons, 1982.

Hessler, Gene, and Carlson Chambliss. *The Comprehensive Catalog of U.S. Paper Money*, 7th ed. Port Clinton, Ohio: BNR Press, 2006.

Jackson, Eric M. *The PayPal Wars: Battles with eBay, the Media, the Mafia, and the Rest of Planet Earth*. Los Angeles: World Ahead Publishing, 2004.

Jackson, Kevin, ed. *The Oxford Book of Money*. New York: Oxford University Press, 1995.

Karmin, Craig. *Biography of the Dollar: How the Mighty Buck Conquered the World and Why It's Under Siege*. New York: Crown Business, 2008.

Kersten, Jason. *The Art of Making Money: The Story of a Master Counterfeiter*. New York: Gotham, 2010.

Kupetz, Allen H. *The Future of Less*. Austin, Tex.: Emerald Book Co., 2008.

Levenson, Thomas. *Newton and the Counterfeiter: The Unknown Detective Career of the World's Greatest Scientist*. New York: Mariner Books, 2010.

Luce, Edward. *In Spite of the Gods: The Rise of Modern India*. New York: Anchor, 2008.

Mann, Ronald J. *Charging Ahead: The Growth and Regulation of Payment Card Markets Around the World*. Cambridge, UK: Cambridge University Press, 2007.

Manning, Robert D. *Credit Card Nation: The Consequences of America's Addiction to Credit*. New York: Basic Books, 2000.

Marsh, David. *The Euro: The Politics of the New Global Currency*. New Haven, Conn.: Yale University Press, 2009.

Mihm, Stephen. *A Nation of Counterfeiters: Capitalists, Con Men, and the Making of the United States*. Cambridge, Mass.: Harvard University Press, 2009.

Naim, Moses. *Illicit: How Smugglers, Traffickers, and Copycats Are Hijacking the Global Economy*. New York: Anchor, 2006.

Sargent, Thomas J., and Francois R. Velde. *The Big Problem of Small Change*. Princeton, N.J.: Princeton University Press, 2002.

Simmel, Georg. *The Philosophy of Money*. London: Routledge, 2004.

Smith, David. *Free Lunch: Easily Digestible Economics*. London: Profile Books, 2009.

Steil, Benn, and Manuel Hinds. *Money, Markets, and Sovereignty*. New Haven, Conn.: Yale University Press, 2010.

Weatherford, Jack. *The History of Money*. New York: Three Rivers Press, 1998.

Weschler, Lawrence. *Boggs: A Comedy of Values*. Chicago: University of Chicago Press, 2000.

Zelizer, Viviana A. *The Social Meaning of Money: Pin Money, Paychecks, Poor Relief, and Other Currencies*. Princeton, N.J.: Princeton University Press, 1997.

INDEX